1980's

Prologue

Sara started to wake up, she tried to open her eyes and as she struggled, she had no sense of anything real or imagined. She felt as if she was emerging from a bath of treacle, her senses all blurred around the edges. For a few brief minutes she thought all was well, and as the light filtered through her sticky lashes, all too soon she knew what was next. Her head started to ache, her stomach started to do cartwheels and she felt the familiar need start to gnaw.

'God can't I have just a few minutes more, a few minutes of nothing?' she muttered but knew it was futile. She'd been back on the gear or heroin, for around 12 months and the only sure thing she felt at that moment was she needed to get out of where she was and score as soon as possible, it was the same every day. Once that was done she could concentrate on sorting out her beloved little brothers, they were all that mattered to her in her shitty life. The love she felt for them was somehow pure and clean.

Sara sat up, looked around the room and tried to remember where she was, focusing on the sleeping people who looked as bad as she felt, lying round on every available bit of furniture. There was a grotty blue couch filthy and rancid, with five unconscious bodies on it, the stale smells of body odour reaching her nostrils the same time the smell of the rest of the room did, and she felt herself start to retch. Putting her hand over her mouth she scrabbled up as best she could and ran out into the hall, taking in the peeling paper, the graffiti and the dirty floorboards. Desperately now trying to reach somewhere to be sick she spotted the kitchen. There was a disgusting over flowing sink full of greasy water and cigarette butts, and it was this that finished her off. As she retched, her stomach strained, burning her throat and making her feel as if she was going to die on the spot from an embolism.

Eventually, after she had thrown up every last bit of moisture in her body, she managed to sit down on a tiny bit of clean lino to get her breath avoiding the rest as it was filthy. Cupping her hands she got a little cold water in her mouth from the taps, swallowed gratefully and shut her eyes to avoid looking at the contents of the sink.

Now fully awake Sara started to remember where she was and what had happened. She was in a squat on the housing estate, and before she even dared to remember the night before her thoughts went to the little wrap of heroin in her purse. There was just enough to straighten her out so she could get her head together enough to sort out her serious score for later. Panic gripped her as she realised she'd left her bag in the room where she'd slept. Terrified now in case she had woken anyone up with the noise of her retching she took a deep breath trying not to scream. She knew her bag might be gone or her purse and gear removed. Sara went to run and slipped on her vomit, smacking her face on the way down. Even with her cheek throbbing she scrabbled on her hands and knees and any dignity she may have had gone. She reached the room and looked in panting and sweating, and saw it was where she'd left it. Stepping over as quietly and quickly as she could she retrieved her bag and left just as fast. On wobbly legs she reached the stairs and sat down to open it. Relief flooded through her bones as she saw her tin, her blade, foil and her wrap untouched.

Feeling a little better she reached in and noticed how heavy her bag was, her fingers wrapping around a roll of paper, puzzled, she pulled it out and when she saw the roll was a bundle of 50 pound notes, she nearly screamed out loud. She stuffed it back in as fast as she could, she felt more of the rolls and her heartbeat increased. She ran her fingers through her long dyed black hair and spitting on her fingers tried to wipe off the mascara that must be under her eyes. She had hardly any spit in her mouth, but tried anyway. Acting as calmly as she could she focused on getting to the front door and out of this hellhole. Nothing had come back to her yet about where the money was from, her mind refused to focus on anything but her fix, and where to do it. She knew vaguely that she'd been to a casino, with a punter but the details were just too hazy. Apart from that she had more pressing things on her mind as her body started its withdrawal, the familiar aches and cramps starting to nag. Feeling antsy about the money and not knowing what else she may find in her bag she decided to get away as fast as possible. She didn't want to have her fix in the squat. Her instincts were screaming to get out anyway. The squat was full of the lads and girls off the estate. She remembered that some would slit their own mothers' throats for a tenner, never mind a roll of fifty quid notes. Sara focused on the front door and went through it as quietly as possible. As she went out into the gloomy wet morning, no one seemed to have stirred in the house. Thanking the Virgin Mary she did the sign of the cross and allowed herself to relax a little.

For the first time in over a year she felt a glimmer of cautious hope. A little spark that all was going to be okay for a change. Her family and the guilt she felt were on her mind constantly. She'd left her baby brothers asleep with their neighbour Kay looking in on them. Kay was great with the boys and as long as mother didn't turn up was no need for all this worry. However she felt she was neglecting them if she went out to earn money without putting them to bed or being there if they woke up. She

3

brightened up within a minute when she thought of how much she must have in her bag. The last of the guilt was pushed out as she focused on how she'd treat them to whatever they wanted, sweets , comics some toys and maybe a day out. God she could get off the gear now, she could buy methadone so she didn't have to score. She could register with a private doctor known as Dr. Feelgood who was infamous in Rodney Street. He'd give you six months scripts for five hundred quid. She could have got meth from the clinic free, but she didn't want them snooping round and finding she was the boys only carer. Images started to come back in little pieces, the casino, a hotel room, a man, sex. She knew she'd looked good, last night, she was aiming for a big hit to give her a break from it all. Most importantly spend time with the boys. She didn't inject herself, like other users. Most of the time her beauty was enough to make men and the odd women over look her little failings. She prided herself on being clean, in all ways and her regulars knew it. If you were male and wouldn't wear a condom you didn't have sex with Sara it was as simple as that. Female punters had to use a dental dam if they wanted that type thing. She got all that for free from the street workers. She came back to the present. Her mind was racing with the excitement of having enough money to escape. With the boys of course. Even having a fifty quid a day habit didn't seem that bad at the moment, and as she often told herself reassuringly she only smoked it. As she went down the road trying her best not to look suspicious Sara took a final look back at the derelict house and there was still no movement. She thought of going to another empty house, there were plenty in this street, but she would feel trapped. She remembered that there was an old red phone box at the end of the street, the windows hadn't been kicked out yet as far as she could tell. As all these thoughts swirled in her head, the need for her fix growing with every step, she didn't see a man step out of a parked car on the other side. When the stranger came into her line of vision, he barely registered in her mind as he approached. As he got closer her only thought was he looked way too smartly dressed to be around here, so he was no danger to her. She decided to smile, as she went to pass him she noticed the light glinting off something in his hand. She felt a sharp pain in her stomach and her smile turned into a rictus grin of agony; she instinctively probed the small patch of her injured flesh, and there was strange warmth on her hand. She pulled her hand away and held it in front of her face, and watched as blood trickled down from her fingers to her arm, but that didn't make sense.

Just before her brain could process what was happening, her legs gave way and the stranger smiled. He caught her in his arms as she slid to the floor. He held her gently as a lover would. He smiled down at her with

4

what almost looked like adoration, but she looked deep into his green eyes and shivered at what she saw there. Then as the horror of her situation finally registered, she realised that she had never seen any eyes so cold, so reptilian and so totally devoid of humanity in her short time on earth. He stabbed Sara again and again but she didn't feel it as her life ran out of her. Even before her blood had even started to congeal on the pavement she felt anxiety consume her as she took her last breath. Her last emotions were fear mixed with worry for her beautiful baby brothers, and how would they survive in this shitty world without her? Left unguarded and alone with their evil twisted mother. Her last words were "please God protect them always. I beg of you."

1990s
Chapter 1

Michael was putting his trainers on, only the best for him. The one thing he and his brother Carl made sure of was that no matter how broke they'd been, they had always got the latest trainers, the latest sports clothes, even going as far to have a shell suit, but he preferred Armani. It was part of the chain of command in Liverpool, especially among the young men. Personally Michael thought they made you look like a bit of a dick, but as they were the latest fashion and it seemed the only way to look on the streets of Liverpool, he went along with it for now. He wasn't getting a bloody perm though, that was for friggin' sure. Even if his beloved L.F.C and his football heroes Robbie Fowler and Jan Molby had them he still wouldn't. He knew the skit about where he came from, and how famous they were for the perm. Kevin Keegan wasn't even from bloody Liverpool. How come they got lumbered with it? He almost laughed out loud then he remembered, all over again, what day it was.
'Are you ready yet? Carl shouted 'Come on let's get this over with.'
Michael felt a rare surge of anger towards his brother. How dare he say that about their Sara? He was fuming as he walked down the stairs, feeling his steps resound through their council flat, as the cheap wood creaked worryingly under each stomping footfall. 'Keep your hair on Mickey lad, I was only saying 'cos I hate this bit, it makes me mad even after all these years.'
Michael understood and was pacified almost immediately, his quick temper just as quickly gone, and a small smile broke out on his face as he

looked at Carl's hair. It was naturally curly, he was mixed race with caramel skin and ringlets, and was a good looking lad, by all accounts. 'Ooh look at your perm, how much did that cost?' Carl mock punched him in his massive bicep and grinned.

'You cheeky Scouse git as they say to us, just look at the state of your girly hair!' Michael shouted, he had straight blonde hair, a ruddy complexion and green eyes, they couldn't look any more different, but they were plenty alike in other ways. Both of them were around six foot four, and practiced weights, running and Kung Fu, they were very lucky as they had found a teacher in China Town, and he had known Bruce Lee, even attended his classes in America. It cost a lot for his sessions but he taught just the two of them privately, so it was worth it and they could afford it. He was their Sifu, about sixty and all of five foot four, but couldn't be beat, so the respect they had for him was tenfold.

Grabbing Michael in a head lock he ran him down the hall towards the door when their neighbour Kay stepped in. 'Watch what you're doing you pair of idiots, you nearly knocked me on my arse' she shouted.

'Well it's big enough to withstand the fall, and you'll bounce right back up, no worries Kay.' Michael laughed knowing full well he was going to get a clout across the ear even if she had to stand on a chair. 'You're dead you, you're not too big for a good slap' Kay laughed smacking him none to gently, but even on tip toe she couldn't' reach his ear. Michael laughing now, picked her up as if she weighed nothing and swung her round, much too Kay's' delight.

As Michael was spinning her round she was reminded of a pair of young wolves or lions at play, and not for the first time was amazed at how the two little boys she used to babysit could turn into such big handsome men, with a raw power that was frightening, even to her, and she trusted them implicitly.

They were both in their twenties and there were none closer than these two, both with different dads, and the same useless slag of a mother but they had survived and Kay was sure they were going places, and she knew she'd done herself no harm endearing herself to them, not that it mattered, she loved them both anyway, and she had loved Sara fiercely after losing her little girl in a fire. Good God she thought, her and Sara had practically brought them up. She felt sad for Sara with her drug problem, and she had deserved so much better than what had happened to her.

'I just popped in to say I've been down already and left some flowers okay boys?' Putting her gently down Michael said a quiet thanks as did Carl.

Walking past they left Kay on their doorstep; 'Lock up for us will yer? You know how unsafe it is here!' Carl shouted with a sly grin. Kay laughed to herself, thinking if anyone did steal off these boys they most definitely weren't from around here. No-one she knew would be stupid enough to do it.

Carl and Michael walked down the road and away from the council flat they'd been brought up in and out into the day. Both of them were now silent, both lost in their own thoughts of Sara, and their journey. They went to the local florist on the way and picked up a bunch of flowers they'd ordered the day before, Brian the florist gushing and complimenting them both, thinking that their one bunch of flowers had cost more than he usually took in a couple of days. He was so relieved when they paid. He fussed and fawned until they left.

Then they took 30 minutes to walk to the street where she'd been stabbed to death all those years ago. They both had decent motors now, but the walk was part of their ritual on this horrible day as it had been the first time they'd done it, not having any money left for their bus fare after spending their meagre pennies on a bunch of flowers from the all night garage. As they approached the area where she was killed they were pleased to see some flowers and cards already there. Michael bent down to put down their flowers and to read some of the cards that were there already, the usual platitudes you see where someone has lost their lives in the most wasteful of ways, either knocked down or stabbed or beaten, most often murdered.

Michael was almost amused by some of the cards; he knew that they were there not in tribute to Sara, but for his and Carls benefit. He knew in his heart before she'd died Sara had been back on the gear, she'd tried really hard to kick it. Even at this young age although he didn't understand what drugs did, he knew that they hurt Sara, so him and Carl grew up despising smack and who ever gave it to her. He was thinking of how Sara was a despised junkie even by other drug takers. It didn't matter if you drank, took coke, ecstasy, smoked weed, snorted speed, uppers downers and all the things that most of the people they knew did, if you were a junkie on heroin you were the bottom of the pile. Despised by most and hated with a vengeance. People had long memories, and everyone who was burgled or mugged in the eighties, remembered, because they'd had so little to take at the time. But Sara had never stolen from her own, and she had sold her body as it was all she had, and she may have been a smack head but she never hurt anyone except herself.

As they grew up in the 80s both Michael and Carl talked of how they'd seen Merseyside nearly brought to its knees by heroin, it had boomed, and families had been ripped apart. Destroyed not by the recession, they'd survived worse but by the smack that flooded the streets, especially in their world. It was rife, the Moffats owned a few drug businesses but they wouldn't touch smack with a bargepole. It had eventually died down with many more of the generations to come preferring other drugs. The hypocrisy of the drug world was one of those peculiar things that made no logical sense. Many of the people now stole for their addictions whether substance abuse or gambling, but the need that heroin produced was far greater and made its addicts do far more for their fix of choice. The only one was that came close was crack, but even then in the madness that came with a crack withdrawal it still didn't match the cold turkey that came with heroin. The only good thing now it was cut so much, that its purity was far less deadly than in the 80s. Also there was methadone that helped some. It was a fact of life now, no longer new or shocking. Michael remembered Sara telling them if they so much inhaled a fag while someone was using smack by them and she found out she would lock them up in their bedrooms for a week, he smiled at the memory. They were in charge of some of the drugs in Merseyside and although a lot of money to be made was through heroin and crack they didn't touch either and made sure none of their network dealt in it. It was double standards but no one cared, Pete Jones who had been Michaels best mate from school had tried to talk him into dealing smack and crack, but he wouldn't hear of it, and Carl told him to stop it or he'd be out, they didn't mind the weed, tabs, speed, moonshine and even straight coke but they would have no part in the drugs that had taken their sister. Leave them for TJ and his bunch of dickheads, even more reason to hate him.

But Sara was their sister, and for that alone she was remembered and no one would dare talk about her being a smack head, or prostitute or whatever else she had been. Growing up both Michael and Carl had made sure of that. Amongst the cards and flowers their colours pastels and white, Carl noticed a red rose, with a black card and silver writing, he wasn't sure if it was the blood red colour or the simplicity that made it stand out. Then as Michael noticed it he almost laughed. 'God that's a bit over the top talk about tacky that belongs to the nineteen seventies, especially if it's off a bloke, only a right ponce would have sent this, I mean look at the writing it's like a birds!'
Totally serious now and feeling a little flutter in his stomach Carl reached out and read it. 'It says to Sara my first, never forgotten but never missed.' Michael felt his jaw tighten up, his anger rising. 'What the fuck does that mean? Cheeky bastard! Is there a name? I will kill him or her, I'll make them eat it and I'll stick the rose up their arse.'

In any other circumstances they'd have laughed at his description but this just wasn't funny.
Someone had the cheek and balls to take the piss out of Sara, the sister who through exaggeration and selective memory had become almost a saint to them. They knew she had problems but that's what made her

even more special, the fact that she was so young and handled all that and still cared for them as best she could. No one but them was allowed to talk about her in anything other than positive terms, no matter who it was and now someone here, in their special place where Sara had died, had the gall to put a card there taking the piss.

In his rage Carl went to crush the rose and tear the card, Michael stopped him, sometimes the more rational of them both, 'Stop mate, we can use this to maybe find out who it is. We can find out who sells them at least, and maybe get some info from it. We're here to remember our Sara so come on let's do that.'

Carl nodded and stood silently, head bowed by the site of their sister's death.

Michael bowed his head too. He needed quiet to think. They both knew it was a blatant taunt aimed at them about who had killed Sara. Both men felt a quiet and vicious anger at whoever had done this, and it went without saying when they found out, as they knew they would, they would find out if the rumours were true about Tommy Jonas Murphy. Otherwise known as T.J. Liverpool's current self proclaimed Mr. Big.   Most of Liverpool's serious crime started and ended with him and his nasty little firm. Carl and Michael Moffat both knew then, that if he really was responsible for Sara's murder like people had whispered all this time, that he and the waster who'd actually done the murder were about to find out that they were no longer too young to be ignored. They had waited patiently until they'd built up their businesses and money, so they no longer felt powerless and naive. They had planned and plotted for years and both felt that they were born to run the city. To only to kill when it was righteous, that was true power. They both wanted this, and could taste it now it was so close. They'd known forever that this was their destiny. Carl said 'What's that saying bro, a life for a life?' Michael answered with a sinister smile 'Nah ours isn't, ours is five lives to one, so we can take out TJ and his head men plus the one who did that to our Sara.'

Chapter 2

Shelagh Moffat teetered drunkenly on her heels the light too bright as she walked out into the sunshine. She had just left a flat in the Liverpool water front, one of the poshest bits by the Albert Dock. She'd met some old yuppie, and gone back to his flat last night. Mainly because the stupid balding, fat ugly sod was flashing cocaine around as if there was no tomorrow. He was taking a chance because the bouncers were not

9

amused. If he hadn't been so rich they'd have took it off him and kicked him out. But he had money and knew the management so he was tolerated for the time being. They knew no police had been in undercover and as it was recorded on the clubs security cameras, it may come in handy in the future, so he was left alone. The coke was all it took for Shelagh to home in on him as she had built in radar that picked up drugs at five hundred feet. That and some free drinks had sealed the deal. The fact he really thought she was younger than she was in the dim lights of the club only added to the illusion created by the coke. He thought he'd landed on his feet, with a fit younger woman, but to Shelagh it was nothing to lie her head off to get a free night out and somewhere to sleep. They'd gone back to the huge flat, and snorted so much coke, drank so much vodka and smoked so much weed they'd both passed out on the bed. He was still snoring like a baboon when she'd finally came to, so she'd helped herself to a fair bit of the coke and the 20 pound note they'd used to snort it. She was well aware he knew someone like TJ Murphy, because of the way he'd been ignored his sins by the bouncers. She thought it best not to push her luck. She was tempted to heft his wallet too, but her instincts told her it was more trouble than it was worth. You little shit she thought as she spotted his hair plugs, it reminded her of a cheap dolls head, you are way older than you said, he was lucky he knew TJ or his credit cards would have been winging their way around Merseyside and Manchester every penny on them spent by tonight.

She knew it was a special day, maybe one of the kids' birthdays, or something. She just couldn't remember what it was at the moment. She ignored her children except when she wanted something, and when she wasn't able to use them anymore she left. She couldn't talk to the boys about Sara they got too angry, what could she tell them to soften them up? She had a thought; at least she had shared something with her one daughter Sara. She had seemed to also like drugs and prostitution, hadn't she? However for God's sake she couldn't say that. She was so often out of it she couldn't remember her name until she'd had a drink and a smoke. When she'd done that she'd remember what day it was. There was no similarity between them at all. Sara didn't like drugs and prostitution she had been forced into selling herself by her mother, and the monsters she sometimes brought home. Shelagh had picked this life, loving the power over men using her looks and body, and the highs from any drug she could get her hands on. Sara had been forced into it, but still managed to love despite the evil she lived with, and she had loved her brothers with a vengeance. She had done her best to protect, feed and care for them, from when she was still a little girl to the day she died.

Even then Shelagh hadn't much cared about her babies, but had always cared about herself. Once a stunning woman, who relied on her looks to get her what she wanted, she now looked hard and haggard. Although still boasting a good figure and a thick head of blonde hair, her nastiness and the savage abuse of her body were finally catching up. She had never believed beauty was skin deep, and now her rotten soul was showing through, her ego still thought she looked as good as she had in her twenties. Her vanity knew no boundaries. She looked on the floor at what she thought was a pound coin in the light, bending down, nearly falling over head first, she realised it was a gob of spit, and withdrew her hand in disgust. A group of school boys going past laughed out loud at her drunken antics.

'Oi you old slapper!' one of them shouted 'Give us a nosh for 50p.' She wasn't in the mood so she turned around and growled at them 'Go and screw yourselves you little bastards, you couldn't friggin' afford me.' One of the boys went to say something back then recognised who she was. His face went ashen and he whispered something to the others. They took off faking laughter because after it sank in just who's mother this was it was out of bravado that they pretended to mess around. They didn't say a word while they were within earshot. She was filled with self righteous indignation, and decided there and then it was about time she went to see her sons. How dare some little arsehole say something to her! She'd tell the boys. Her boys, she now thought, because as their reputation spreading around the area, She would be treated really well by some because of it. It hit home then, she could get so much out of it, and some respect too at long last. Most of the women on the Estate wouldn't give her the time of day for the way she had treated her kids. Many a time she'd been ignored or spat at or worse still, a good hard slap across her face. She was more worried they would damage her face than what was causing such hostility.

She told herself self righteously that she had never been a conventional mother, and if she had, she wouldn't be reaping the benefits now. If she'd have been at home for them cooking and cleaning, they'd be soft and probably signing on or working in a dead end job. What was all the fuss about? What Shelagh Moffat failed to realise was that's how it worked in the world, and there were plenty of good people out there who worked hard and worked every day just to get by, and she'd taken advantage of a fair few of them. She really thought she was something special and apart from being an escort hadn't worked since her teens. She thought it was beneath her, something only mugs did. She reached into her bag for her cigarettes, and noticed a white envelope with no name on it. She just looked at it and feeling something inside, hoped it was some drugs or money, excitedly she ripped it open. All that was in there was a cheap tarnished necklace, in the shape of a dolphin, and a black card with silver writing. On the card she could barely make it out but it said *'To Sara, it felt so good, why did it have to end so quickly?'* She couldn't make sense of it, barely registering her daughter's name, only feeling disappointment that there wasn't' anything of value in it. It obviously wasn't gold, maybe silver but so what she couldn't get anything for it. Must be a mix up, she thought, or a sick joke? Stuffing it back in her bag and lighting up a fag, it then occurred to her what day it was, the anniversary of Sara's death. Maybe one of the bitches off the Estate had put it in last night at the club, to remind her of her daughter, the cheeky cow. After a few minutes she made the decision to maybe keep away from Carl and Michael today. God knows why, after all she was Sara's mother, she'd lost a child all said and done, they'd only lost a sister. She should be the one who had all the fuss made of her. She'd milked it when it happened, and why the boys should take it so to heart was beyond her. All this nonsense laying out flowers and candles where Sara had been stabbed, it was bloody creepy, if you asked her. She remembered from past years, that the boys weren't particularly nice to her on this date, sometimes blaming her for what had happened. Best not let them see her after all.

Shelagh quickly changed her train of thought, and as it was second nature to her, she pushed her children out of her mind. Instead she concentrated on who she could stay with and where she could get more money, pills or booze. Perhaps all three. She could go to any number of older men she knew who'd be glad to put her up, and treat her like a queen, just for a blow or a hand job. Fuck! Today she just wasn't in the mood for any type of sex, her head still aching from the night before. Annoyed now at having to find an alternative place to go she stomped off up the road, her face like thunder as she went past the estate, she remembered a randy old pensioner called Eric. He was so near to death he probably would be glad just to have company. He'd probably have a heart attack if she flashed her tits at him. He had a home help who came in twice a week so the place was nice and clean. Better than some of the shitholes she stayed in. After all she thought, her face brightening, wasn't it pension day? She could play on it being the date of Sara's death. The sympathy alone could pay for her to get smashed tonight. God if she was really lucky he'd have his prescription as well. That was the best part of being old to her, the amount of drugs the O.A.Ps round here got off the NHS. Anything from aspirin to Temazepam, even morphine. Ooh all sorts of goodies! She drooled. Some sold them to help with their miserable pensions, but Eric didn't. He liked to give them away, well at least to her. And she was nearly there, by his house, she'd not even realised she must have done it automatically. It was starting to spit, the rain fine but cold so she speeded up. Almost sober now with a little spring in her step she walked into the alley, ignoring the smell of piss and the festering bin bags. She bounded up Eric's path all her concentration on just how much she could take him for. She was happy again.

Chapter 3

Thomas Jonas Murphy clipped the end off his cigar, and smiled at the man in front of him who had brought them back for him from duty free. 'So how goes it my old mate? How are you after so long?'There was a little sarcasm in his question but not too much. He knew what he was dealing with and as long as this man was on his payroll he was okay. The man in front of him was called Stephen Bentley, assassin and genuine grade A psychopath.

'Not too bad Mr. Murphy thanks for asking' Stephen replied. Lighting his Cuban cigar, he blew out a plume of blue smoke, and said. 'You know you can call me TJ, I insist.' But secretly TJ was thrilled that someone as feared and reviled as the man who stood before him showed this much respect. Little did he know that Stephen Bentley didn't much care what this idiot thought of him. He knew to flatter this man and his ego, knowing then the prices he always asked for would be met, with little or no negotiation. Everything was good as long as he played the game with this plastic gangster.

'Where have you been Stephen?' TJ asked with what he thought was an understanding smile on his face, 'We've missed you round here, had a few near misses with the coppers due to some of the amateurs I've been forced to use. It's a bloody good job I've got a judge and a few of the blue bastards on my side' he almost shouted. 'You know me Mr. Murphy, I work best when rested and I needed to go on a little tour around the Far East, enjoy the local culture.' Stephen smiled remembering one exquisite Thai girl, her name was Lawan, who had been so beautiful in death that he had stayed with the corpse for days until it really was too hot to tolerate. The once beautiful body had started to become bloated and ugly, the wounds from his torture seeping and foul, even the ice in the bath no longer helped.

TJ reacted with what he thought was none threatening body language and went to fix them a couple of new drinks leaving him to his thoughts.

13

TJ grimaced inwardly at the expression on Stephens face, it was so unsettling just seeing a little of this man's soul; he had a good idea what Stephen enjoyed, but didn't like to dwell on it. TJ knew deep down he was a monster too, but his god was money and he knew that he hadn't had an active role in hardly any violence that he had ordered since he was a young stud around town. Even then he'd relied on others to do all the dirty work. He really thought he was the best, the hardest and virtually untouchable. Although small and squat, his bulk had made him almost intimidating. When he also had youth on his side he wasn't unattractive to the opposite sex, and of course being a player, women had wanted to be seen on his arm. The fact that he was now middle aged, his muscle gone to fat and he had hair pieces and wigs that wouldn't have looked out of place on a scarecrow had nothing to do with it. He was used to paying for the best escorts and although they too catered to his ego, they were paid a hell of a lot to do so. He still thought he had what it took, and looked good for his age. His dress was pure Miami Vice, pastel jackets with the sleeves rolled up and a white or cream trouser, as he was stuck in the 1980's, and he refused to accept it was the 1990s. When he looked in the mirror he was impressed. It's a pity no one else was. To him all of it was fair game, the fact that he had ordered and paid for plenty of violent acts, sometimes on innocent people, didn't matter. If he wanted it he got it, it was that simple. Enjoying the myth that his money and status would always protect him, he smugly thought he was the better man, his stupidity guarding him from the fact that he and Stephen shared a lust for power, but he didn't get his hands dirty anymore. No that's why he paid people like this psycho so much money, to do it for him. He was pleased he had Stephen on his payroll.

Rumour had it that Mad Maisie from Kirkdale had wanted him to work for her. Maisie Malone was called a big bull dyke by most of the men who were frightened of her, and had once ruled her firm with a rod of iron, however lately she had got lazy preferring hedonism to hard work, but as her reputation was still sound everyone thought she was still the same. People took the piss out of her name too, it sounded like a thirties gangsters moll but no one would say it to her face. It wasn't her real name but it was how she was now known. Although she had gotten lazy she was still as tough as any man and twice as feared as most, she was one of the only serious contenders for TJ's throne. She worked out of a club in Bootle, and had a voracious appetite for young attractive women, she had her long term partner Linda but rumour had it, they had an agreement and Linda knew what she was dealing with. What Maisie wanted she got, and although she played around she was very jealous if anyone came near Linda. Especially men, as Linda had experimented with her sexuality and

14

had decided she was heterosexual until Maisie come along. Linda was also a big part of the business. They seemed to have the perfect partnership, she oversaw all the money and staff, and Maisie enjoyed hunting new prey and doling out her own special punishments for people who pissed her off. TJ liked to think Stephen was loyal to him and it was the male camaraderie that made him so, that and the huge wages of course. Stephen had no problems working for anyone if they paid enough; gay, straight, black, white green with spots, he had turned Maisie down because she was much smarter and harder than TJ so when he decided to take it all from him it would be so much easier. He may even join forces with her one day who knew? Let TJ think he was untouchable he was already sloppy and bone idle, it was going to be easy when he decided to make his move.

While he was thinking about it all, TJ had walked twice round his huge desk and stood by Stephen at the window Stephen had also been lost in this own thoughts. 'Well good to hear Stephen well I hope you enjoyed your little jaunt and you're ready to do a few things for me?'

'Of course Mr. Murphy what do you want me to do? Is it anything to do with the big dyke I hear she's taken over some of your girls' Stephen replied.

'Don't get your hopes up yet,' TJ chuckled. 'I don't need your specialist skills just yet, just a little information gathering for me. Go see a few of your contacts and find out about the Moffat brothers for me. I thought it was Maisie who'd muscled in on the toms in Kirkby and Knowsley. But as I'm not supposed to be involved I've had to swallow it. I've not got any tame coppers there, so I've always kept it very low key. I mean Kirkby for Christ's sake! My home town of all places! They're getting a bit too big for their boots. Just like their bitch of a sister who tried to have me off all those years ago.' 'Oh don't worry Mr. Murphy I've sent them a little reminder already about that. What a happy co-incidence, seeing what day it is.' Stephen said. Again TJ was reminded just how mad but useful this man was. 'Nothing to worry about is it?' He asked. 'No body parts involved?' 'No of course not, Mr. Murphy just a couple of cards to remind them of how she died. It's been so many years since you gave the order, she was my first and I had to do something a bit special. Nothing like your first proper kill, well of a human being anyhow' His eyes almost rolled back in his head such was his ecstasy at remembering how it felt when he'd slipped the knife into such a beautiful but flawed creature.

TJ not quite knowing how to cope with such a show of emotion from this usually sombre man, tried desperately to joke. 'Oh Stephen go get a room or something!' he said weakly, truly unnerved. Stephen snapped back into the present and for a fleeting second glowered at TJ for ruining his delicious memory. He struggled but knew he had a role to play. He couldn't afford to let anyone see his true self. Not even this loser with his vast amount of money, and stupid nickname. That would soon be his. He smiled then thinking of the nickname this idiot had around town. It was Kirkby Kirk, as in Captain Kirk. This was because the actor, who had played him called William Shatner, had also played TJ Hooker in a popular eighties cop show of the same name. It now had cult status, apparently. It was still on ITV late at night. Cunt status more like people joked when they referred to TJ Murphy. Apart from soothing his ego, he called him Mr. Murphy also because he couldn't quite get himself to say TJ out loud. He felt pretty sure that nobody would have taken the now feared TJ Murphy quite so seriously if it wasn't for him and some of his other employees. Gathering his thoughts he replied. 'I'm sorry Mr. Murphy I don't know what came over me. It's most unusual for me not to control my impulses in public. I apologise profusely. You will never see a repeat of this behaviour. I'll be on my way now, to go and do as you asked.' TJ just wanted him out of his office, still unnerved at how the balance of power had shifted so quickly He just nodded a curt goodbye to Stephen as he left the room, all pretence of their false camaraderie now gone.

Chapter 4

Stephen went hurriedly into the car park, he was annoyed at himself, and he couldn't believe how stupid he'd been. He must never show anyone his true self except his chosen ones, or those unlucky enough to be on one of TJs stupid lists. Then it didn't matter they weren't ever going to be around to tell anyone were they? The ones left alive were so frightened and traumatised by his lunacy they couldn't bring themselves to tell anyone normally. They knew he may come back. He pushed his victims out of his head and looked at his Jaguar XJS 2 seat convertible, but felt none of the usual joy at seeing it. It was a beautiful black car, and he enjoyed the jealous glances as he drove through Liverpool back to Neston on the Wirral. He was in the queue for the Queensway tunnel, when he started making his plan of action. He needed to go home and change cars for a start. No way on earth could he use his Jag for this assignment? He had to go around North Liverpool. If he parked in the wrong place his car would be gone in minutes. It would be then taken to a garage where every identifying mark on the car would be removed, including the chassis number. It would then be re-sprayed, the expensive sound system replaced with a pile of crap and then hidden until it was shipped abroad in a container on a big cargo ship. It was usually for the Far East ironically, his favourite place. It was the same in Manchester, Sheffield every big city come to think of it. He had a scruffy little Volkswagen golf, a couple of years old. It may have looked nothing but it had an excellent and reliable engine. He wasn't going to take a chance of it breaking down while he was working. It wasn't registered to him, but he had a full set of paperwork with it, in some ghost's name. He used it on jobs like this; changing the plates now and again just to be sure it wasn't remembered from a crime scene. It was hidden on the substantial bit of land that had come with his house, out of the way in the barn. He almost smiled when he thought of his house. Neston was as the locals in Liverpool and Birkenhead said 'dead posh'. It was a countryside residential area, boasting an old market town, but had many properties on decent sized bits of land, usually a couple of acres at least. He had acquired his from a bent but retired judge, Craig Joseph Bell somehow connected through one of TJ's coppers, Declan O'Grady. He told Stephen all about the nasty old bastard who had been caught out once too often with underage children, so they decided to join forces. Declan managed to get some photos thanks to a bit of private surveillance. It was agreed Stephen would have the house and O'Grady the money and any assets. So Stephen approached him with what he thought was a decent enough offer for the house but it still was only a fraction of its true worth even without the land. A cash sale, he gave the judge a month to sort out the paperwork and then he said he'd be back. The judge's wife Sally had taken one look at Stephen and virtually agreed on the spot. It was then that Stephen knew for sure that she'd known about what her husband was doing to young boys and girls on his boat.

He'd explained how it was only fair as they were getting old now and should move into a little bungalow away from here, and although the old pervert had put up a bit of resistance he knew he was beaten. He eventually gave in. In exchange for the house he'd given the judge and his wife the assurance that if Declan wasn't happy with the money the judge had given him he would sort it. Declan was more than happy with nearly a quarter of a million in cash and jewellery. He even let the judge keep the money Stephen gave him for the house. Apparently Sally had left Craig the posh judge after finding out for sure what he was capable of. Stephen had no sympathy for her, apart from being incapable of feeling anything good for anyone but himself, it was because he knew she'd only stayed for the money. She was no better than a prostitute with leprosy in his estimation. In fact she was lower because at least the whores were honest about what they wanted. The minute the real money had gone Sally had gone all noble and decided that she'd leave her perverted old husband, after seeing the pictures. Funny she'd not cared before. Stephen had picked this couple carefully, researching them for months. He found out that they had no

17

immediate family and certainly none alive that were close enough to leave the house and grounds to, so there would be no annoying offspring to deal with or to attract attention to him. To the locals he was just another rich businessman who'd bought a house and if he had that type of money he must be okay. It was easy enough to stay anonymous; there were no immediate neighbours he could talk to the nearest one just about in view. This suited him and gave him a feeling of freedom.

He'd originally come from a middle class home, going to a good grammar school and had never wanted for anything. He'd grown up in the South, near Essex. He'd been estranged from his parents for years, finding their love for him stifling and repulsive as he grew older. He said goodbye to them when he left home with a couple of thousand pounds in his bank account, plus all the money he could find in the house. The little Ford Fiesta they'd bought him for his eighteenth birthday, and evil in his heart. He'd headed up to Manchester, getting a job in a slaughter house, which he enjoyed. He had a little flat, where he liked to enjoy his fantasies, dreaming and staring into space for hours at a time. He even managed to find some videos to cater to his tastes, supposed snuff films, and he would look forward to them after a hard day at work. There was one with a girl who looked just like one of his neighbours and he almost asked her out, but decided it was too risky, feeling he was meant for greatness and if he did something to her and got caught, his real career would never begin. So he concentrated on butchering animals, and he learnt the trade from a Scouser called Jerry who taught him the best ways to kill the animals as humanely as possible. He got sacked on the spot after Jerry caught him torturing one of the beasts, even before he'd left the abattoir he decided he would get his revenge on Jerry, and followed him home the next day. He tracked him for weeks and he learnt Jerry was a predictable man. Every night he went home to his family, in Bebington on the Wirral. He'd have his tea, pacify his wife and play dad to the kids, and then straight off to his mistress in Liverpool, a skinny little blonde called Chantelle, the complete opposite of his big breasted dark skinned wife. Stephen almost admired him, how he got away with it. He almost wished he felt the pull of sex like other men. He'd had a few fumbles that had ended in embarrassment for all involved. It just didn't do it for him. The only time he didn't have to struggle to get an erection or reach orgasm was when he watched his snuff films. Or had a fixation on a certain woman if she was to be one of his victims. He knew he was attractive, he looked slim, but his clothes hid his wiry musculature. He had a gym and training equipment in his house, and he would spend hours training. He was incredibly strong. Thick sandy hair and green eyed. A killer smile by all accounts he was told. If only they knew.

He followed Jerry on and off, knowing his routine, while he was with his family in Bebington, Stephen would drive around the area getting to know it, that's how he found Neston following a route to Clatterbridge Hospital one night. Instead of turning round and back to Jerry's, he missed the turn off at the roundabout and went up a country lane. He was charmed by Thornton Hough as he passed the real and mock Tudor buildings, encouraged to keep exploring, he finally ended up in Neston. He knew then he was going to live there.

He had eventually got a job in Liverpool on the doors. Although there were new regulations being brought in, most clubs would look the other way if you were hard enough to handle it, anyone who looked the part could work as a bouncer or doorman in the pubs and clubs. They'd meet at an office in Toxteth and be allocated their place for the night by a haggard old redhead called Vera. She would always have a cigarette hanging out of a mouth smeared with a foul pink lipstick. She always dressed the same in a frilly white nylon blouse gone grey from being washed a thousand times, a navy blue skirt and 5 inch stilettos. The skirt was so thin you could see she wore stockings and apparently she had been a right looker when younger.

Stephen couldn't by any stretch imagine Vera being attractive to him now. He worked hard to control the involuntary shudders when she touched him. At first the bigger older men took the piss out of him, teasing him for being a southerner, and young, slim and good looking. He took it all in his stride, hiding his hate, looking forward to the blood. Jerry wasn't forgotten he just had other things on his mind. He would sort out Jerry when it was right for *him*. After all wasn't revenge a dish best served cold? He knew he was destined for much more than this, he knew he would get what he wanted no matter the cost. Again he buried his urges for a while knowing he couldn't risk getting noticed by the police.

He was good at the job and once he'd proved how strong he was by grabbing a drunken man with a bad reputation and twice his size one night, he had easily won the vicious fight that followed, the teasing stopped. The other bouncers always gossiped more than a bunch of Catholic mothers on speed when they met at the office, so his reputation spread quickly. He quite enjoyed his new reputation, as only a narcissist could. However it soon became apparent that a couple of the older bouncers, best mates Danny and Steno didn't like this at all and felt threatened, by the younger fitter man. They tried to intimidate him when they were working with him. Deliberately stirring up trouble with drunken women, and leaving it until the last minute to help him if someone attacked him. However this didn't last long as one night, one of the women's husbands decided to get revenge for his wife. Steno ever the bully, had pulled out a chunk of her hair and made her fall on the ground scraping her knees and hands badly. Furious the husband had gone for a few minutes, and then come back and put a Stanley knife in Steno's eye. He was aiming for the jugular but had missed a couple of times before he got lucky and the knife went into his eye. As Danny stood there in shock, not moving, Stephen watched the whole scene fascinated, not able to take his eyes off the blood and gore. Also the expression of terror on Steno's face as he lay screaming on the floor made it all the better. Danny still didn't move, he was frozen staring and gibbering about his best mate. Eventually Stephen thought slyly it was time to help, now the damage had been done. He grabbed the Stanley knife off Steno's attacker and kicked him swiftly but neatly in the balls, making it look simple. After he got him down, he knelt on his neck telling him to shut the fuck up. Danny had watched the whole thing, shame making him stutter more nonsense through his tears.

He also saw how Stephen had looked,   and he knew then what they had been dealing with an utter nut job. Danny knew Stephen had enjoyed it, really enjoyed the fight and the power and blood. As he got in the ambulance with Steno, quiet with humiliation, shame making his cheeks burn Danny decided there and then that he'd had enough, and wouldn't ever be able to work as a bouncer again. Word spread quickly Danny was finished anyhow; no one wanted to work with a doorman who wouldn't watch your back. Steno lost his eye, and his job. His wife left him soon after not being able to deal with himself half blinded and scarred so he made her suffer too. She waited until he went to the off license and she grabbed a bag she'd prepared and left quickly in a taxi. So now truly alone he killed himself, quietly with a bottle of vodka and a handful of painkillers. Danny found him as his guilt made him a regular visitor, calling at least twice a week. He hated seeing his oldest mate so down. He was used to the Steno who'd been cocky and cruel, scaring and bullying since his fifth birthday.   Steno's body had been there festering for three days, with the heating on high. Danny couldn't accept that the foul thing he'd found was once his friend. When the police arrived he had screamed and shouted so much they had called the local community health team who had him sectioned straight away. Stephen was pleased with the outcome, this just reinforced his belief that he was special, belonged to the dark and nothing or no one would or could stop him. See what happened to Danny and Steno when they'd crossed him? He truly was blessed by the Devil himself; it never occurred to him just how insane a notion that was.

He thrived, as his reputation spread he was introduced to various local gangsters and bosses, who used him to collect serious debts. He loved the thrill of the chase. If someone left the area and most of them couldn't or didn't want to, he then had the fun of finding them using his looks and charm to get information. That and access to a lot of money, and he could find anyone. He soon discovered he was disappointed when people paid up, and liked it far better when they didn't. Mainly because then he had permission to torture and abuse these losers and their wives. As his confidence and torture techniques grew, he went too far one night, and almost killed the young wife of a local car dealer. He had never been so turned on in his life, and as she begged him to stop he almost came. Feeling his first real erection, caused by a person not a film, was so powerful, that even though he would have found it distasteful if someone else had done it made him sloppy and stupid. He didn't lock the door or even care. It was only that the husband returned early that stopped him masturbating on her and then killing her. Walking in finding Stephen with his penis in his hand and his wife bleeding all over, and semi conscious on the floor, he had actually screamed. Some of the more sensible people who'd previously hired him, decided to stop using his services after hearing this story. However it was this very viciousness that made TJ want him exclusively on his team. It proved to be a match made in hell. He still thought of Jerry now and again, but if it wasn't for him he wouldn't have all that he had now. Maybe he'd give him a break and let it go, or maybe when he was bored and had no one to play with he'd go and see Jerry's wife or slut on the side. The little blonde mistress looked just ripe for the picking.

Snapping back to the present he realised he was pulling in his drive. He felt the usual pride in his home, wishing in a way he could show his stupid fucking parents, in their miserable semi how well he'd done. This was the price he paid as he didn't want anyone to know his true identity, so he couldn't. Anyhow let them worry. Who cared? Not him, his mind was now on the job in hand. He parked his car and went into his beautiful house, to have a bite to eat and get changed before he took the Volkswagen out and went back to Liverpool. He sat at the pine table in his huge kitchen eating a cheese sandwich deciding whether or not to take his torture kit with him. No it was too early, he decided so he put his cup and plate in the sink and went out to the barn.

Chapter 5

At the same time Stephen and TJ had their meeting, Carl and Michael walked back to the flat; it was their nest, their place of safety. 'Hey bro, 'Carl said. 'The old slapper may come round today on the scav she'll want her share of sympathy and money knowing what day it is.' Michael smiled

21

grimly 'God I hope not, I'm not in the mood for the stupid cow. Especially since we have to find out who's taking the piss with that fucking rose and card.'

'We will don't worry about that, we'll find out and then we'll kick ten tons of crap out of them, or torture them, maybe both.' Carl replied.

'Tell you what we'll go home and have a rethink see if the old whore's been around, and then we'll take it from there.'

Michael feigned a look of horror. 'Oh my, wash your mouth out with soap, calling Mama a whore. It's awful' he said putting on a posh voice.

'One knows she is a respectable and caring mother, only wanting what's best for her offspring.'

Carl for all his sadness laughed. 'You're a head case mate.' Punching Michael gently on the arm said 'Come on then let's go back to the homestead get our heads together and we'll take it from there. If she is about then we'll bung her a few bob and get her out. I saw her landlord the other day, she never goes back to her flat except to sleep and eat, and apparently there's now a rodent problem because she leaves the food and it rots. He was shaking as he told me expecting me to smack his head in, but I thanked him and called in the exterminator.' Michael smiled then said 'I know you're thinking it's lame but I'm going to say it anyway,' and both men in perfect unison said 'how much extra to kill the big rat?' They high fived each other and laughed.

Once back in their front room, doors shut, familiar noises coming from the surrounding flats through their paper thin walls, and safe in the knowledge it was probably too late now for Shelagh to come round, they busied themselves making a coffee and putting their feet up on the coffee table, the big television was on, and Michael flicked through all the channels. They needed time to lose themselves in their normalcy and think their next moves through. They'd done most of their growing up within these four walls. They also owned a big town house on the edge of Toxteth where they did their business dealings. They had numerous bedrooms, their mates stayed there when they wanted or needed to, sometimes to chill out or if they were in trouble. It was by Faulkner Square on the way to Toxteth, which was an area still full of beautiful old Victorian buildings. They'd paid for it to be decorated by a local interior designer, tasteful and understated, black and white, plump couches and lots of leather, both real and faux. All transactions were in cash and on paper they didn't own any of it. Half their properties were registered to Sara; it was another way to show their sister their peculiar love and loyalty. A dodgy solicitor had done all the paperwork and had managed to write in a clause to cover all eventualities, and if either the taxman or the law came after them it could never be proved that they were theirs. The eighties hadn't been kind, so they had got a lot of bricks for their money, but the area was now getting revamped and would eventually shine again. The millennium was on its way and would be here before you could blink, Liverpool was a city brought to its knees in the dark days of Thatcherism. Art and music had grown and they'd survived with style, and to the brothers it still had a magic like nowhere else on earth. They owned quite a few places now, cash sales, of course but easily acquired. They'd worked hard, they'd been doing the cigarette and booze run for a couple of years, and it had proved very lucrative. They ran all the pirate videos on the estates now, and had a fair few pubs and clubs who bought their wares, and now they'd taken over a gang of working girls. The girls had had it rough, a few dickhead pimps but a lot of them working on their own. Carl and Michael had gone to see a feisty old girl called Fiona Clegg, or Fat Fi as she was known, they'd known her years and she had a soft spot for them because of Sara.

She had always worked there, one way or another, and you had to admire how old she was and still went with the odd punter by all accounts. She ran the local wine bar now and allowed the girls to use her toilets and so on as long as they got the punters in for the odd drink, and sorted her out with a few quid if they didn't. The ones who didn't have a bedsit to take them to, or didn't do it in the punters car she let use the alley round the back of the bar. However recently there'd been a spate of prosi bashing as it was locally known. The worst case when a couple of lads had roughed up some of the older girls badly over a dispute about money, of course. These little scallies had decided to use the services of two of the older girls called Tracey and Julie. They'd agreed on 30 quid each, and after their fun had handed over their bundle of cash in the dark alley. The lads thinking it would be funny had gotten two fivers and put them either side of newspaper cut in the same shape as the notes, so it looked like 60 quid. It was one of the oldest cons in the book but of course these young chancers thought they were the first to do it. When Tracey had seen what they'd done she and Julie gave chase. The lads had turned on the older women, giving them both a good kicking. The girls had put up a good fight but the lads had youth and a baseball bat on their side. Of course the police weren't involved so they thought they'd get away with it. The little shits had then gone boasting and laughing about it, to all who'd listen to their cruel tale, inevitably other chancers followed.

Fiona had known the Moffats for a long time and she knew the lads were doing well, building a reputation and would probably end up owning half of Liverpool. She also knew they were good kids at heart, and as she'd cared for Sara, they would always go and see her if she asked. Fiona explained what had happened and how some of the scallies thought it was okay to rip off the working girls and resort to violence if they didn't cooperate and it was getting worse. When she'd tried to tell TJ's cronies she was ignored, and told the Moffats how much she and the girls paid a month and how they were supposed to be protected by him and his men.

Carl had realised that there was yet more money to be made, and it was a way to get on TJ's tits so he and Michael gathered a couple of their crew together, and they'd gone and seen the scallies who weren't so hard when faced with men. The people they used were friends they'd known since the cradle, and the Moffats were well liked. They also had something that TJ would never know, respect and a sincere loyalty from most of the people they'd grown up with in and around the flats. A shared hardship had brought them much closer than just money ever could. They were the leaders of their crew and some of their men would die for them or each other.

They'd given the little gobshites a really good beating, and an even worse scare, and told them to put the word out that they owned the business now and if anyone hurt any of the girls they'd have them to answer to. The lads' tails were then put firmly between their legs, once they knew they weren't going to get bones broken, well they had been so grateful to survive they'd gone around telling all who'd listen that the Moffats were hard but fair. They carried their bruises and wounds as if they were medals of honour. They also knew that if TJ had been bothered to deal with them they wouldn't be walking round now, especially if that weirdo with the green eyes had anything to do with it. They'd apologised to Tracey and Julie and given them as much money as they could beg, borrow and steal. Carl and Michael discussed the prices with some of the girls and most of them agreed to work from and around Fiona's and pay for their protection. Their natural charm did a lot of the work for them but the working girls knew now they had someone to look after them, and somewhere to run, they watched out for each other and now took the registrations of cars that any of them went off in. Any so called pimps hanging around were swiftly dealt with and everyone was happier. Well except for TJ who had been taking protection money for a long while from Fiona, the working girls and even some of the pimps. It wasn't much to him and he wasn't really interested until it had stopped. Fiona knew there was a storm coming, she'd seen so much in her years on the game, but one thing she knew for sure is that she nearly always backed the winner. That was the secret of her long survival in a world most people wouldn't last a week in, and choose to pretend doesn't exist. When she told one of TJ's thugs there was no money that week and to take it up with the Moffats she prayed that she was right this time too. Still she really enjoyed telling his thugs to fuck off and die, no matter how dangerous it could turn out to be. Like everyone round here, she hated TJ and knew he'd had something to do with Sara's death. She'd liked Sara, pretty little thing with a good heart. A good earner by all accounts, it was a waste that was for sure, and not for the first time she wished it had been her fucking useless mother Shelagh who'd been stabbed. The world wouldn't miss that excuse for a human being.

Michael walked over to the window, earlier they'd been doing their accounts in the flat, and were in good spirits. He heard the local kids running round down below, playing football in the near dark. 'Come on then bollocks,' he said throwing a shoe at Carl who was asleep on the couch. He raised his voice to make sure Carl heard, 'let's go and see Fat Fi and if she knows anything about this card nonsense. If she doesn't she can ask round for us, you know what the girls are like for gossiping. If it was one of their punters we'll know soon enough.'

Carl woke up instantly he sat up and stretched his huge shoulders. 'Okay then shit for brains what car, the Beemer or the Range Rover? It'll do them and us good to be seen up there. Plus I'm wondering why Kirkby Kirk hasn't responded yet. There's bound to be trouble.'

Barely 20 minutes later, dressed in smart Armani suits, with crisp white shirts, they ran down the steps and round the back to their lock up. Michael jogged over to their black BMW and said 'I'm driving.'

Carl grateful for the chance to wake up properly, threw him the keys and replied 'Fine but don't go too fast we don't need a pull off the bizzies tonight. I took the liberty of stocking the boot with a sawn off and assorted tools.'

Grinning in the dark Michael said. 'It must be our lucky night, our excuse for a mother didn't turn up *and* we're going hunting!'

Michael carefully backed the car out of the garages then after making sure to secure the doors of their lock up, he turned out into the now dark night heading for Kirkby. The Shaman's Ebenezer Goode blaring out from their top of the range stereo.

Chapter 6

Lying on Eric's couch Shelagh opened her eyes cautiously, she'd been pretending to be asleep, but wasn't in the slightest bit tired. In fact she was feeling pretty damned good. She was nicely smashed on some of Eric's painkillers and a quarter of bottle of malt he'd had. Plus a sly snort of the coke she'd had stashed in her handbag. She had a nice bit of cash off the old goat and plenty of his prescribed drugs now as well. What a good night, she was content to stay there listening to the television while Eric kept looking at her waiting for her to wake up. She had no intention of doing what he wanted tonight, she wasn't that off it. He'd asked for a blow job and there was no way on earth she was sticking that in her mouth. A hand job perhaps or a glance of her tits fine, but that wasn't going near her molars. Eww she thought I might bite it off. He wasn't dirty exactly but due to his age, she was pretty sure he didn't' bathe very often. No she thought with an inward shudder, he'd have to pay her at least fifteen times what he had and she'd have to finish a whole bottle before that was going to happen.

So she played the waiting game, Eric would pass out soon she was sure of that, apart from relying on his age, she'd crushed and put in a couple of his Temazepam on the chip butties she'd kindly made him. It was just a matter of time before the sleeping tablets would knock him unconscious. Almost on cue she heard his snores starting at first quiet then building to a phlegmy crescendo. Stretching deliciously like a cat she wondered whether to stay here after all. She had, in fact every intention of staying until now, but she felt too wired to just sleep it off on the couch, it would be a waste of a good hit. Cautiously sitting up and to make sure he was definitely out for the count she crept over and checked him. He was fast asleep, the noise was deafening. Seeing the semi toothless mouth open and the drool running down his stubbly, wrinkly chin made her decision for her. She was out of there. She'd find somewhere else to stay and if not she'd go back to her boys flat, they were bound to be out. She'd have to ask St. Kay next door to let her in, the only annoyance Kay would probably go in with her until the lads turned up. Hmm but they'd probably be out all night, so Kay would have to eventually give in and go back in her own boring little flat. She was too mean to go to a hotel now; she'd missed the check-ins by hours and wouldn't pay for a room after missing so much time. She had enough for now, the world was her oyster.

Realising it was only around 9 o'clock she grabbed her things, and in her bare feet crept silently out of Eric's house, shutting the door gently, and creeping up the path. As she reached the gate she put her shoes on and decided to go fat Fi's for a drink, or at least head that way. She nearly always had a lock in after hours. As long as you were paying the greedy cow could be as nice as pie, and for once Shelagh had some money of her own. She walked out of the Estate to the main road that ran into town and flagged a black cab, giving directions to the driver.

As she got out of the taxi, hand thrust rudely out while the driver counted out every penny of her change he knew he wouldn't get a tip off this one, she didn't notice Stephen's Volkswagen drive past her. As he spotted her he pulled past the taxi and parked further down outside the off license. 'Bingo!' he said out loud. He knew it would be an easy assignment but this easy? Wow there she was the dead whores' mother, getting out of a taxi. He had got Gez to put his card and Sara's cheap necklace in her bag without her even knowing. She was usually so out of it she was easy prey. But now it was dark and if he could get her on her own he may be able to get some information out of her. He'd had her so close but that was before he knew what TJ wanted. He got off on causing mental pain nearly as much as he loved inflicting physical pain. He had done that purposefully to piss off the Moffats, for nothing more than a bit of sport, and to remind them just how vulnerable they were. He still marvelled at the happy coincidence of it all, and how he was divinely protected. This proved he was going to take over the top spot in Liverpool. He hated them just because they reminded him of the doormen he used to work with, all muscle and limited brains, and their thick Scouse accents. He was unaware that he had picked it up and although he'd been taught how to speak with expensive elocution lessons his accent now had become more and more guttural. He watched Shelagh again, as she grabbed her change and tottered dangerously on her heels. Straightening herself up and fixing her clothes, she walked purposefully to the door of fat Fi's.

Stephen drummed his fingers on the steering wheel. He just had to wait now until the stupid bitch came back out again. He could be in for a long wait, just hanging around. Sitting still didn't bother Stephen. He could take himself off into his own little world very easily, and he had plenty of new scenarios to relive after his recent visit to the Far East. He didn't need just fantasies anymore; he had real material to refer to. He even recorded some of his more magnificent moments with his Polaroid camera. He loved them all, Dao and Kanya were two of his favourites, they had been strong and lasted the longest, the light in their eyes dimming after they lost the will to fight, the instant photographs were not the clearest in the world. He barely needed to glance at them sometimes because his memories were always there. Lawan was his ultimate favourite the last one he'd had, she was amazing. Her uncle had sold her to him for three hundred American dollars and he'd have paid a lot more, worth every cent. He made himself comfortable in his seat and settled down to wait. He had barely shut his eyes when he heard a car radio blaring, very near. Sitting up senses on alert, his adrenalin on standby he saw the black BMW pull up outside fat Fi's pub. He watched angrily as the Moffats got out and went into the pub. He was annoyed now, say they took the whore Shelagh with them, she was their mother, and if she got too pissed they'd probably be forced to look after her, it wouldn't look good if they didn't.

27

He always had a backup plan, and knew there were others he could get information out of, for the right price or threat, but he had looked forward to talking to Shelagh. What better than straight out of the horse's mouth? She was after all notoriously disloyal to her sons, and once bladdered sufficiently would talk about anything she wanted, thinking herself untouchable. He knew that they didn't tell her much, but the next door neighbour Kay, couldn't wait to tell Shelagh all about her sons, rubbing it in that they would tell her more than their own mother. Kay loved to tell anyone who would listen what the lads had been up to, how they'd got away with this and that, how cheeky they were. He got all this second hand off his little informer. He may have even been able to take Shelagh somewhere quiet and have a little fun, frighten her and make her cry. She wasn't his type he liked his victims mostly young and innocent looking, but she was still a woman and she wasn't bad for her age. It could be really exciting he realised as it was Sara's mother after all. He shook his head and brought himself out of his reverie, deciding after all to have a drive around and see if he could see any of the little scallies he usually got information off, it's always better to get both sides of the story after all.

Carl and Michael went into the pub, people immediately aware of who'd just walked in. A few glasses were raised as well as winks and a lot of hellos, and the boys both shouted out their respective greetings. Carl was walking over to get a drink when he saw Shelagh at the bar, turning around he quietly said to his brother. 'Oi! Michael what were you saying about it being our lucky day? Talk about cursing us, look it's the old witch, would you believe it?'

'Oh God! Me and my big mouth that's all we need isn't it? We can't even leave there's too many people about and we can't let them see us running away from her. Oh shit!' Michael grimacing replied. 'Come on then let's face the music, she's the worse for wear as usual, we could buy her a few drinks and after that she probably won't even recognise us anymore.'

Shelagh saw the boys approaching in the mirror. She was as usual up on a high stool at the bar, double vodka in front of her and her usual fag in her mouth, legs on show.

'Oh my boys' she shouted nearly falling off 'look everyone it's my pride and joy! MY lovely boys.' She finished emphasising the my for Fi's ears.

Michael and Carl both went to steady her, 'Oh come on ma don't make a twat of yourself, stay there we'll get you a drink of water. Have a break' Michael said quickly, winking at Carl, more in a move to pacify him than anything.

Fi watched this scene unfold and rolled her eyes, and then went over to the three of them. By God she hated this woman and the way she had and still did treat her kids. She knew what Sara had gone through with this bitch renting out her body just as she'd hit puberty to the highest bidder or biggest pervert. She sometimes wondered if the boys knew exactly what she'd done with Sara not understanding if they did how they could even talk to her. She knew blood was thicker than water, but some things you couldn't forgive.

'Hello boys can I get you anything? A beer, some crisps an axe?' Carl despite himself smiled, he had a soft spot for this old girl, and wished someone like her had been their mum.

'A pint of lager for me and a coke for him he's driving back.' Michael said, feeling relieved that something had broken the tension. 'Oh and whatever this one's having as well as long as it's water or fruit juice' he said pointing at Shelagh. Fi smiled and replied 'Okay coming right up, a pint, a diet coke and an arsenic and ice then?'

Shelagh realising what Fi meant said 'I heard that you old slapper, don't you dare put me down in front of my boys.' Fi just snorted in derision and went to get the drinks.

'Stop it ma you're making a show of yourself. You know what day it is so knock it off show a bit of respect.' Carl said gritting his teeth now, like Michael had before.

Shelagh was incensed that her very own flesh and blood would take the side of that old slapper instead of her stood up suddenly the stool fell over and it clattered noisily. 'What are you talking about? 'She cried 'I've been down to see our Sara's special place today, are you forgetting I'm her mother? I feel pain too you know.' She lied. It went really quiet in the bar, even the jukebox had stopped, and the only thing missing was some cowboys drawing their guns or a piece of tumbleweed blowing past.

Carl grimaced and he was grinding his teeth so much you could see the veins sticking out in his neck. He leant over to Shelagh and whispered so even Michael couldn't hear 'You're not fit to mention her fucking name so shut it now while you're ahead you fucking waste of space. Talk about her like that again in public and I'll get someone to sort you out. It wouldn't' be fair if I paid someone to give a good slapping to me own mother but I swear there's women on the Estate who would give you a fucking beating for free.'

Shelagh although completely off it knew he meant business. She knew she was playing a dangerous game, and knew every word he said was true. Deciding to quit while ahead she pulled herself up and smiled at Michael saying out loud 'Oh Carl you're right honey, it's only fitting I keep my opinions to myself, forgive me I've had a few too many.' Michael putting on a show for all the other people in the pub, and very conscious of how quiet it had gone, smiled and grabbed Carls arm.

'Come on our Carl let's have a drink with Ma and toast our Sara.'

Fi after setting the drinks out in front of them lifted her own glass and said to them all, as loudly as she could manage 'To Sara, one in a million, we miss you.' Shelagh knowing she'd nearly gone too far lifted her glass and joined in. 'To Sara.' Everyone said. Michael now knowing his brothers temper was under control, smiled and said to Fi, 'A round of drinks for all these good folks please. Come on Carl get your wallet out, you can pay unless the moths have eaten all your money!'

'Cheeky twat' Carl replied. There were a few laughs and shouts at this, and as the punters approached the bar for their drinks, and Fi set about serving them. She silently thanked God that Carl hadn't kicked off in her bar, knowing that he wouldn't have hit his mother but may have taken it out on some hapless drunk who happened to be standing in the wrong place at the wrong time.

After it calmed down, people sipping their free drinks happily, finally Fi had a minute to herself. She lit up a fag and retreated to the end of the bar, gratefully sitting on her stool and resting her sore feet. Carl saw his moment and approached her, and discreetly showed her the card and rose he'd taken from Sara's' memorial site. 'Have you ever seen anything like this before? He asked, 'Or any ideas where you'd get a card like this around here?' Fi had a bad feeling, and gingerly took it in her hands and after scrutinizing it for what seemed like an age replied. 'I've seen these somewhere before love, but I'm not sure where. Let me have a think it may come back to me.' Carl hiding his disappointment said 'Okay Fi if you think of anything, please do us a favour and give us a ring, or get one of the lads to tell us, we'd be ever so grateful' Fi smiled and nodded making a mental note to ask some of the girls if they knew anything, or if anyone had seen who'd left it

Carl walked back over to Michael putting the plastic bag inside his jacket as Shelagh looked on, with interest. 'What's that you put in your pocket? Here let's have a look.' Grabbing it from Carl she squinted at it, holding it up to the light.

'Oh I've got one of them too. Do you know who sent it? It was in me bag I've no idea who put it there.' Michaels first thought was that this was another ploy to get attention but his stomach turned a little at the thought she may be telling the truth. Carl just looked on frowning. 'Well let's see it then?' Michael asked his guts churning.

As Shelagh rummaged in her bag, Carl controlled the impulse to grab it off her and tip the contents all over the bar. 'Here it is!' She said triumphantly and held it up for both men to see. Carl grabbed it and looked at it. Exactly the same card that they had, but a different message, and there with it was the silver dolphin necklace, the one he and Michael had given to Sara when it was just the three of them, clinging to each other after Shelagh had gone on one of her three day benders. He remembered with a sudden flash of pain how grateful she'd been for the little trinket. She'd hugged them both and cried for hours. Carl instinctively knew what was going through Michaels mind, and as he looked into his brothers eyes. They both knew with a sudden startling clarity that these cards were both from Sara's killer for sure, and he was publicly taunting them. Both grim faced now and in no mood for the pretended jollity of before they settled the bar bill, slipped Shelagh a hundred quid and then left quietly and quickly.

Chapter 7

Stephen drove up and down the roads looking for some of his little scallywag informers. There were gangs of lads hanging round either with BMX style bikes, hoods up scarves across faces, either showing off their skills, or just being menacing to innocent passersby. He had spotted one already called Gez, a skinny little shit, who desperately wanted to be a gangster. Oh how he hated this one, with his pimply greasy face, and who Stephen would have tolerated easier if he didn't try to talk like a character from the Bill. Still he was cheap to use, and one of the Moffats cousins, and there was no love lost between them. Some of the time Gez told him all the gossip for free, constantly trying to get a job working for TJ, sometimes it cost him a few quid but never more than a hundred. He'd got him to put the note about Sara in his Aunty Shelagh's bag after all. Seeing he was with his little gang, Stephen drove past until Gez noticed him and went round the back of the boarded up shops where they always met on the sly. Although Gez made no secret of the contempt he felt for the Moffats, in Stephen's company, he didn't do it in public. He desperately wanted the second hand glory that being their cousin meant. Being two faced wasn't really second nature to him. He was just really angry at his cousins success, and wanted some of it too. Stephen sat in his car and looked round as his passenger door opened. After dramatically standing there looking left and right Gez got in and sat down. Stephen felt like slapping him, but stayed calm. Stephen smiled at him, thinking of the things he could do to him, but then grimaced. He wouldn't want to get his tools or indeed his hands dirty on this greasy little turd. No thanks, he just didn't do it for him, and he was too easy to kill. He most definitely wouldn't enjoy sticking the knife into this one, but perhaps that was the wrong attitude. He could at least practice on him.

Gez started to fidget getting uneasy in case anyone saw him in Stephens' car. 'Relax will you?' Stephen said mockingly. 'Just pretend you're selling me some weed or a bit of coke. It's not as if you don't do it all the time.' 'Aww Mr. Bentley don't say that to anyone will ya? I don't do nuffink but a little bit of grass and some white, and if me cousins found out I was doing a bit of freelance, they'd disown me like.' Gez replied further irritating Stephen with his whining voice. Stephen answered through his clenched teeth. 'Oh for fucks sake you little twat will you calm down, I'm only pulling your leg. You know having a joke, a laugh; you don't have a very good sense of fun do you?'

Gez looked at him and then replied 'I don't have a sense of humour when it comes to the fucking Moffats, we may be related by blood but that means nothing to that pair of fucks. If they'd put me on their payroll properly I wouldn't have to do it now would I? What do they expect when they treat their own cousin like a dickhead? Anyway Mr. B what do you want? Are you still working for TJ?' Stephen his blood boiling but doing his best to control himself replied in a steady voice, trying not to sound incredulous but failing. 'Well of course I'm working for TJ! You do not think for one fucking minute I'd be here just for the pleasure of speaking to you now would I? I mean we could discuss the latest developments in stem cell research if you like or debate on the anti abortion laws, but somehow I don't think that would be a very good idea do you?' Gez scowled at the sarcastic tone, not quite understanding what Stephen meant, just sat there then replied in a sulky voice
'There's no need to be nasty, I'm just making conversation.' Stephen laughed at this comment, then unable to sit for a moment longer than he needed next to this little maggot said 'You know I'm just pulling your leg Gez there's a few bits of information I'm after about your famous cousins, so wondered if you knew anything about where and what they're setting up next? It's worth a tonne if you find out for me.'

Gez looked from under his hood and thought how clever he was, he already knew what they were doing, but wouldn't let him know that yet. A hundred quid, maybe he could ask for a bit more, if he was flashing that type of money about.
'Okay then Mr. B not a problem, I've got a rough idea but let me ask round and find out what's happening with those two. I'll ask me mum she may know something she's good mates with that Kay who lives next door, and neither of them can stand my Auntie Shelagh. If I find out I may ask for a little bit more, you know inflation and all that.' He grinned sneakily to himself and whilst congratulating himself didn't even see Stephen pull the knife and put it to his throat.

'You little shit, don't try it on with me, if I don't do this well mate your fucking cousins will if I tell them what you really think of them. Do NOT fuck with me! Do you understand?' Stephen whispered in his ear.

Gez felt his knees go weak and he had a sudden urge to clear his bowels. He had never been as scared as he was looking into Stephens' eyes, and even though it was dark in the car, they looked almost luminous. Even stoned he could see behind them lay something unspeakable. 'Yeah okay, okay I'm really sorry. I'll find out what I can for you. A hundred quid's great. I was only having a joke like.'

Stephen relaxed after reminding Gez just who he was dealing with, so put the knife away. 'Well weasel that's good to know, you go back to your mates like a good boy.'

Gez almost strangled himself with the seatbelt in his attempts to open the door quickly, once he had his feet firmly on the pavement, he looked over his shoulder and said.

'Leave it with me Mr. B. you won't be disappointed, I promise. I'll txt you when I get the info you need.' he stood up and then was gone, leaving Stephen smiling to himself and thinking how he'd almost enjoyed that. He shook his head clear and knew it was time to go back to Fi's to see if he could collar the slapper Shelagh on her way out. Speaking out loud in the car he said to himself. 'Who knows maybe I won't need Gez's words of wisdom after all, let's see what she has to offer.'

Chapter 8

Tiffany shook out her handbag on the floor, looking for her painkillers, some nice strong ones off a private doctor from Rodney Street in the centre of town. She shook out two and shrugging her shoulders took out another one. She then dry swallowed the three of them together, grimacing as she tasted the bitterness on the back of her tongue. She was a typical Liverpool girl in looks, basically quite beautiful, but with her over curled hair and her heavy makeup she ruined her natural good looks. She had one style and that was short. The more flesh she showed the better. There was a trend now where girls started to walk round with as much belly on show as they could. It didn't matter if you were thin, pregnant or fat they let it all hang out. She thought it was refreshing to see the cheek of some of them, after all her midriff was flat and toned, and after seeing the evidence first hand, no way was a pregnancy going to ruin her body unless the payout was worth it. She supposed she could have plastic surgery if the worst happened; it was the 1990s after all. Tall and slim, with good legs, she knew how men lusted after her, and she was convinced she was good looking and classy enough to catch a Moffat. She didn't care which one, and she'd imagined flirting with both, she just wanted one of them. Only 23 she'd already had two abortions, one on the N.H.S which to be honest had been a nightmare, and one at the private clinic her latest beau had paid for. She had no intention of getting stuck with a brat at this age, too many of her mates had. It was a laugh to some of them, that's all they wanted, but no she was too smart for that. She thought back to her termination on the N.H.S. She'd gone to the local hospital and she'd had the nurse from hell. This horrible old cow was obviously a Catholic, and she let it show she'd disapproved.

She had actually asked Tiffany while she was getting her assessment 'Have you got any other kids? You know alive and kicking like? You little whore.' Tiffany couldn't quite believe the nasty bitch could speak to her like that. Then after meeting that bride of Dracula she went into see an Indian doctor who had berated her for not using contraceptives and called her stupid. When she'd objected and told her the condom had ripped, she's also said to her that she'd better watch her attitude or she wouldn't let her get the termination, the power crazy bitch. After all that when she finally went in to get the operation, she'd ended up nearly dying because of it. They'd only half done the operation, leaving dead tissue inside of her, so while she was out in Birkenhead clubbing a few days later, she'd passed out. When she'd come round in the ambulance one of her mates holding her hand, they thought she'd taken something and were giving her the third degree. Fortunately one of the ambulance drivers had recognised the rash she had, and after asking her to describe her symptoms, rushed her to Arrowe Park hospital with suspected meningitis and septicaemia. She often thought that that bitch of a doctor had either tried to kill her or hurt her. Christ she knew girls who'd gone to back street abortionists who'd fared better than her. If she ever saw the cows out and about she'd give them a hard slap or two. If she bagged one of the Moffat brothers she'd get him to sort it for her, bet they'd treat her with respect then. That was one of the reasons Tiffany wanted that power, no one would ever be that horrible to her again. She could just see herself being driven round in their BMW or being picked up in a limo.

The painkillers were starting to work, she sat at her flat window and looked out at the scrubby grass which poked out unhappily from the paving stones, and feeling a bit fuzzy headed decided to go and have a lie down. She grabbed her fags off the coffee table and headed to her bed. Hearing a tapping on her door, she carefully approached it, and looked through the spy hole. There in front of the door was Rodney, an aging gangster, strictly second rate but good for a few quid. He'd paid for her to go to the private clinic thinking the pregnancy was his, but Tiffany wasn't so sure, it could be anyone she'd been with over the last few months. She had bigger fish to fry than Rodney now, and he most definitely wasn't in the big pond. She'd decided he was a tiddler, and deserved being thrown back in a rock pool not the powerful Mersey.

Backing slowly down the hall so he wouldn't hear her she crept into her unmade double bed. Immediately comforted by the familiar smells and colours, amused by her thoughts about fish, and fell into a dreamy sleep made all the deeper by the opiates rushing round her system.

Rodney was not amused, he'd seen the way the spy hole in the door had the briefest of shadows across it and he knew then that she or worse still some other bloke was looking out. But as the main entrance had a wall of mail boxes, there wasn't a letter box on her door. 'Little bitch' he mumbled growing angry, she'd seen it was him and not answered. Did she have another man in there already? He knew she wouldn't stay faithful to him after all he was the married one, but he was used to having his cake and eating it. As one of TJ Murphy's right hand men he was respected and important round these parts. Lately he'd failed to notice how weak he'd become, fatter round the middle, a greasy comb over, he still thought he was quite a catch. Podgy and softened by too many good meals and bottles of expensive wine, he also had a permanent red nose, bulbous and full of open pores. This with his forty a day habit meant he looked fifteen years older than his forty eight years.   He'd also been hearing about these new up and coming lads the Moffats around town. If he'd been younger he'd have gone and pretended to offer his services and then give them a good beating and warn them off. At the moment though he had no real interest in the likes of them, he'd seen too many of them come and go, always swiftly dispatched by TJ. Who still had the most money and power, even if he was a dickhead sometimes. They had grown up together and gone on holidays to Talacre in Wales and on occasion got quite close, so he would always remain loyal to TJ.

A multiple murderer Rodney had been used to doing TJ's bidding, but he'd not had to kill or torture anyone for quite some time. Whenever he'd done time TJ got him the best Solicitor in the City. He'd done about 8 years if you added them all up including house arrest which wasn't so bad. He was sentenced to four years for the murder of a woman who'd spurned TJ and stolen a lot of money off him and he wanted her killed and made an example of. His solicitor got the sentence dropped to manslaughter and he got out in three, the family had objected but she was a young widow when she died and survived only by her mother, a young son and a couple of aunts and they couldn't afford any more solicitors fees. Eventually it went away. He'd done the time quite safe with plenty of money and house arrest was brilliant so had to put up with the odd tag on his leg, but TJ had made sure he'd been well recompensed for his trouble. He remembered when he'd screwed up setting light to a house with the family inside. But TJ had been ecstatic. The only survivor was a young lad, and Rodney had been trapped too but safely. He had to listen to their screams as they burnt. He still had nightmares yet he'd do it again if TJ asked him. Lately it really rattled him that he wasn't asked to do anything like that anymore, after all the real money was made that way.

Rumour had it he only used that weird fucker Stephen now for the real heavy stuff. TJ's little pet, he knew he wouldn't trust him or turn his back on that slimy bastard Bentley. Rodney hated that he was just a driver now for a couple of the younger lads, and TJ used him to collect off people he didn't want to upset too much. He missed the power he used to feel when someone begged for their life, but at least he didn't have the worry of getting caught anymore. It was getting harder now with all this forensics stuff people were talking about. It wasn't known that widely in the public yet, but those in the know said it was getting harder to dispose of a body. He still got a fair wage, much better than he would in a normal job, but he'd used most of his larger earnings on the women in his life, he'd provided a house, car and sundries for his wife and kids, not too flash as he didn't' want to attract attention, but he enjoyed his luxuries like eating out, and he enjoyed his women. It was nice having someone like Tiffany on his arm in the casino or fancy restaurant, she was a real looker, and young, but he always ended up back with his wife Allie at the end of the day. He always felt better after he'd been home and enjoyed his marital rights. It never crossed his mind to give a woman pleasure or to be kind and loving, the fact that he was there doing the deed should be enough as far as he was concerned. Rodney took what he wanted and didn't' care about the consequences unless it affected him, like now. He'd paid over five hundred quid for that operation for Tiffany, worth every penny as there was this new agency called the Child Support Agency, who were screwing absent dads for all they were worth.

The press was full of stories about dads who'd been unable to live on what was left of their wages after paying their maintenance. Desperate some had killed themselves full of despair. Not that he'd ever do that, as that was for the weak, they could go fuck themselves before they'd reduce him to that. Lately though he had felt a self righteous anger for his fellow men. No, no more kids for him he had enough already. He'd paid the cash to the private clinic so he knew she'd had the operation. He'd calmed down now, he would find out what the little bitch was up to. He would sort it out if he heard she'd been screwing someone behind his back, give them both a good beating if it were true. Then he'd save face. One less thing to worry about at least, no kid, so no hassle, maybe the quiet life wasn't so bad after all he thought. He got into his Ford Escort, revved the engine, put an old Dexy's Midnight Runners tape in the cassette, lit up a fag and drove noisily away. His only thoughts of what food was at home and whether or not to go and pick up an Indian takeaway or a Chinese for him and the missus, and some chips and pop for the kids.

Chapter 9

Stephen drove back to fat Fi's to wait for Shelagh to come out. He admired himself in the mirror and practiced his innocent look, and his most becoming smile. He just wanted to talk to her now; he was mildly interested about the woman who'd spawned Sara, and of course the two Neanderthals. He was curious only in the same way a scientist is, who can torture and hurt a small animal for his own research, and then be devoid of pity or feeling. He knew enough about her and how she had no loyalty to anyone but herself, a vacuous creature. The only thing they had in common was their selfishness. It was a good starting point. He would enjoy the chase and he would string her along for a while letting her think he was interested in her. Then he fantasised that when he could no longer stand her company no matter what TJ said he'd enjoy playing with her for a little while until he found a new project. He couldn't do that of course but it felt good to imagine it.

It was quiet outside the pub, a rare lull in the business that usually went on around here. He made sure to park far enough away so as not to be mistaken for a punter if the police did their token bust for the month. He'd never live it down if he got pulled in with a bunch of sad old bastards who'd been caught with their pants round their ankles. He walked over to the pub and glanced through the windows, no it was too dark to see or make out who was there. He'd have to go in. Opening the door and peering round he pretended to be looking for someone and took in the scene in a nanosecond. Ducking out quickly he'd noticed Shelagh propping up the bar, Michael and Carl were nowhere to be seen. Good they must have left, and there was the usual smattering of losers sitting around, absolutely no one to worry about. He'd make sure though and just wait until she came out. He didn't have to wait long, Shelagh with a renewed sense of purpose since the lads had given her money decided to get a taxi to town and treat herself to a room for the night after all, no matter how

many hours had passed. She had enough now to get a room for a few days and lots of nice food and a bottle of something and as it was a good hotel she intended on staying in, there would be guests to rip off. She'd always liked the Adelphi, it was a lovely old hotel but the staff were wise to her now so she was sort of banned, but there were few others she liked. As she stood on the pavement lighting up a fag Stephen approached her. He walked directly up to her and said 'Hello beautiful do you need help?' Shelagh looked up and taking in Stephens's age and good looks smiled seductively. 'That depends on what type of help you're offering?'
'Well when I see a beautiful lady in distress I can't help myself!' he then pulled his most innocent face at Shelagh and laughed at himself, 'Oh God look at me, can't even say things right. Sorry to have bothered you.' and the then pretended to walk away.

Shelagh thought straight away that not only had she found somewhere to stay for the night for free, her unknowing landlord was young and handsome into the bargain. 'No don't be daft! You're a lovely man, and I'm most flattered by your attention. Would you like to share a taxi somewhere?' she finished in her best throaty voice. Stephen took his cue seamlessly 'Well I have a car parked not far from here would you like a lift?' Shelagh thought this gets better and better a car too. 'Yes if you're sure and I won't take you out of your way that would be amazing, thanks.' Stephen asked her to wait while he fetched it, explaining he wouldn't be long and jogged off focused now on how best to achieve his goal for TJ by getting information without marking her too badly.

Maisie pulled on her leather boots, knee length, they were as black as soot with a blue shine and made from the very best calf's leather. She loved them, and when she thought of what Linda her partner had said, that they looked like very expensive Nazi boots, Maisie let out a little chuckle. She didn't care how much they had cost she loved spending money, especially on herself, besides a mixed race woman wearing Nazi boots was kind of fitting wasn't it? Maisie came from almost absolute poverty, her mum and dad had both been chronic alcoholics and were now dead. She'd become completely numb aged four as she'd been beaten from an even earlier age, ignored and starved, and by the time she started school there wasn't much that frightened her, even at five years old. Other kids cried about having to go to school, but she'd loved it. School to her was a warm place to be, the adults there were nice to you most of the time, the worst punishment a caning on your hand or back of the legs, which to Maisie was nothing after a spell with her dads belt or her mother's hands, made all the more vicious by the heavy, cheap and very sharp jewellery her mother always favoured. Even at five she'd known she had something other kids didn't have, and that was an ability to be unafraid, compared to what she'd already gone through this tough little soul found the rest easy. She loved lunchtime at school, the dinner ladies who all lived locally, and had a rough idea of what she went through at home, always made a fuss of her. They always gave her second helpings or extra large portions, it was generally the only hot meal she'd get all day, like quite a few of the kids in the school. They would have reported their suspicions but they were frightened of her mother. Apart from being a nasty drunk she used her background and access to their private information to make peoples' lives a misery should they cross her. She always threatened people with the police or the social services, which was ironic considering her apathy about her own daughters well being. As her dad was a retired Police Chief nobody stood much of a chance if they reported her, some had tried. Her father was abroad all the time on the lecture circuit and although he loved his granddaughter he despised his daughter more and avoided her at all costs. Weekends were the worst for Maisie unless she managed to get an invitation for a Saturday to play with a kid from her class, then it was easier. She would try to avoid being in the house with her mum and dad as much as she could, usually playing out even in deepest winter in the dark, far too young to be already used to the routine of living with two chain smoking addicts.

The weekends usually consisted of the same things every day like some crazy awful groundhog day. Maisie made coffee and tea as it was expected of her, then on to mid morning the coughing and retching in the bathroom, Maisie would try to become invisible and hide in her bedroom while her parents threw up. Then the good bit, when they'd had their first few drinks of the day. If she timed it right she'd get a few pennies and some food, as they were calm and friendly to her and each other, sometimes even cracking the odd joke. Usually it would stay like that for a few hours until the beers ran out then it was off to the pub or she'd be sent to the local off license for a bottle of whatever was on offer, and forty knock off fags. Usually some out of date vodka or nasty cheap spirit from abroad, kept under the counter for special customers. Her parents were certainly that, they were both functioning alcoholics, both keeping jobs in the local factory, her dad in accounting her mum the secretary, both had access to the personnel files that's where her mum got the information about some of her classmates parents. They made a decent amount of money but Maisie never got anything except the bare basics that was only to keep people from interfering and noticing what a neglected child she was, they far preferred to support the pub landlord and the owner of the off license than their only daughter.

Chapter 10

Maisie when sent to collect her parents fix carried that bottle as if her life depended on it, because even in her five year old head she knew it probably did. She would put it on the kitchen table and relief would course through her body, knowing she would be okay at least for a little longer. She liked it better when they went out, as she could play with the neighbour's kids, and sometimes even get fed at night and watch T.V. Then she could get into bed and be asleep before they came back in. She was a true survivor and as she grew older and realised that not every one's life was like hers, she started to use her considerable survival skills and lack of fear to get a reputation as someone not to be crossed. She was the tallest in her class by age thirteen, often fighting with the boys and winning, she gained their respect and some of those same boys worked for her now as men. She learnt to make money selling whatever she could steal, but mainly sold cigarettes at school. She was the person you went to if you wanted a cigarette or loosie as they were called. Some of the local shops did it, split up a pack, and then sold you one for a ridiculously inflated price if you couldn't afford ten or twenty. At school breaks Maisie cleaned up, her and her band of boys, when another young entrepreneur Marcus tried to take their business they put him in hospital by breaking one of his arms and giving him two black eyes. After Marcus's mum had finished at the school they were threatened with suspension but Marcus refused to confirm it was anything to do with them, so they got away scot free. Her reputation as someone to be scared of was sealed and as she went into her middle teens she started to wonder if she was gay, more comfortable as one of the lads, and able to appreciate sexually the lewd comments made about girls they teased. She also hung around the Magistrate Courts in Liverpool with all the alternative kids, who met there every weekend.

They all accepted who she was, a mixed race gay girl, how amazingly outrageous, they celebrated it almost, and she felt she'd finally come home. She carefully kept her two identities separate, one the tough girl who was part of a gang, and the alternative gay girl. It was through her friends at the Courts that she met Linda who was her first serious crush. Linda was also struggling with her identity and sexuality like a lot of their peer group, and she and Maisie formed a strong bond. Over the next few years they would meet at all the same social gatherings until one day Maisie asked Linda to be her partner, promising to love her like no one else could. She'd meant it at the time, with every fibre of her being, and still did but the money and power she craved sometimes took over and she'd realised a long time ago that sometimes she loved them even more. Deep down Maisie sometimes despised what she'd become but she would never share that with anyone, it would be a sign of weakness so to the outside world she celebrated her good fortune, sometimes with vulgar displays of her wealth. The pretty young things flocked to her, and she began to use them relentlessly. As she grew older her narcissism grew too, and any doubts about what she was were quashed under her love of herself and her hedonism.

She was always the same with the newest one, she'd obsess, pine for the object of her affection and then when she owned them and they began to rely on her she would cut them out of her life quickly and mercilessly. At the beginning of each affair she loved their enthusiasm, their willingness to please. Her real turn on was their innocence, she enjoyed their vulnerability and teaching them how to please her. In return she'd indulge them with jewellery, money, drugs and weekends away. Quickly bored of them she would then turn violent and aggressive in their love making and still most of them still wanted her and the lifestyle she represented. Eventually it would be back to Linda her guilt making her the attentive and perfect partner for a while. Linda tolerated it because she had truly loved Maisie once. Now it was a quiet love like one of the ones you had for your best friend and interwoven with years of loyalty, but she just didn't want sex with Maisie anymore. Linda was happy just to be the woman she was now, and who was taken seriously after years of hard work. One of their major concerns was if the other gangsters around town thought for one minute they'd gone soft, even some the men who worked for them might turn if the chance to take over their little empire presented itself. The truth was their partnership was failing behind closed doors for Linda, but to the world they always presented a united front no matter what the cost was. Sadly it was all about to change when Linda received news from the hospital that made her world start to collapse around her.

Chapter 11

Stephen was running through his mental lists, he remembered everything he had to do. He was still glowing with his own genius, thinking it was almost too easy. He'd snared Shelagh Moffat quickly and she'd willingly got into his car. Oh how he wished it wasn't just getting information, this was something to be maybe enjoyed for a night or two. The scummy Moffats wouldn't even know mummy dearest was missing for a while. His only concern was he must control his own needs and wants, and with an old pro like her it was a little easier. She wasn't that bad to look at, her face hard but he knew she had what was termed by other men a fit body and it was obvious that she had something even if it was good genetics. He imagined her as a pampered poodle with a foul mouth. She liked her drugs, it was a known fact, so if he did drug her he'd have to up the dose from what he'd used before. Still the thought of experimenting with her excited him, he was surprised too, as he didn't expect to feel anything about her. He reckoned if she didn't tell him what he wanted he'd drug her and then ask again, if that didn't work he'd maybe give her a shot of sodium pentothal, known as the truth drug as it made its victims speak the truth against their will. The Far East had its joys and bonuses, it really did, as he brought a fair bit of the drug home and had sold some to TJ for an inflated price, but kept the majority for himself. He was fascinated with the fact that in Liverpool you could buy almost anything if you knew the right people. It was down to the docks where most stuff came in. Weapons, drugs, whatever you needed especially if you worked on the doors like he had. He looked at Shelagh now in the passenger seat, she was oblivious to his sly looks as she was primping and pouting in the mirror in her compact. Shelagh knew darned well what she was doing, and it may have worked on OAPs but not on the young handsome psycho next to her. 'So how come a beautiful woman like you is on her own tonight then?' Stephen said, 'Especially in a pit like that.' Shelagh threw back her head and laughed in what she thought was a coquettish gesture but it just made her look deranged and ridiculous. The alcohol in her system making her exaggerate her behaviour while she thought she was acting totally normally. 'Keep up the flattery and you may just get lucky young man' she slurred and made an attempt to bat her eyelashes. She made a clumsy attempt to put her hand on his lap while he was driving and Stephen felt his skin crawl with revulsion. He just smiled and didn't move, thinking how he couldn't wait to get rid of TJ and then wouldn't have to do this type of shit anymore. It was the fact that she acted like she was in control sexually that bothered him most and had started to turn him right off.

He smiled at her as they approached the tunnel. 'Ooh do you live on the Wirral then love? The nice bit I hope, the posher bits at least.' Shelagh chuckled, impressed with her own wit. 'Of course honey my house is a veritable palace, I'm taking you there now if you don't' mind, of course I can run you home later or you can stay. It's up to you. ' Shelagh knew it couldn't get much better, some money, drugs and now somewhere to stay, maybe even a shag with someone young and fit for a change instead of someone who was alive in World War I. She smiled and said 'We'll have to wait and see now won't we?' knowing full well she would. Stephen grimaced then took a deep breath and got out his tunnel fare out of the virginal ashtray to pay the toll.

Stephen felt a flash of anger at her making him wait for an answer, and squashed it down. 'Oh come on don't be so bashful, so where does a beauty like you want to go? Home or to my humble abode for a bit?' he said. Shelagh of course delighted at the prospect of staying somewhere that was free and better than her shitty flat replied 'Oh yours of course, I mean if you don't' mind I'd like to have a drink with you, maybe a little snortie worty of something too? It's all good whatever you want.'

Stephen smiled at her and she looked up at him all hints of her refusing him forgotten. Her natural greed for drugs and drink taking over, she smiled and said 'come on then let's go to yours and have a little party.' Stephen smiled and followed the signs home.

Maisie kissed Linda on the lips as she left their club later on, she was meeting the Moffats in town. She knew that they had got a good reputation, and that they were vying for TJ's throne but that just pleased her more. Anyone who would take on that vile bastard and win would get nothing but praise from her and she was looking forward to seeing exactly what these two wanted from her. She also was wary enough to take Jojo Wilkins and Ginger Phil with her as well as four of the other men so they could meet the Moffats crew. Phil and Jojo were some of her oldest friends from before her teens, and both hard men in their own right. They never minded what they were asked to do by Maisie, they both had secretly harboured feelings for her, and Phil used to wish she wasn't gay. He had hoped against hope that if she had ever decided to take on a man it would have been him. To them her sexuality was something they didn't think about, because she was almost one of the boys, but most of them were loyal and hard working and very protective. She was fond of them both and trusted them more than any of the others. That she was a woman didn't mean she wasn't taken seriously these days, Maisie was a match for any man in many ways, and she could hold her ale, could shoot, appreciated a pretty woman and could throw a mean punch. She knew what she and Linda had was a fragile thing; they'd both worked hard enough to be something in their city, and Maisie would go to any lengths to keep it. She knew TJ hated her and thought it was only a matter of time until he tried to finish her and take her club. Maybe it would be one of his tame coppers to set them up, or he could get his men to sort out her men, or even have a go at just murdering one of them. Then try and blame her, she had a sixth sense and she knew something was coming, she always did.

It was one of the reasons she stayed on top of her game. She just hoped that she could get the Moffats on side before TJ tried to take them down too. Strength in numbers she liked that, and she was happy to help these boys as long as they helped her and left her business alone.

'Are you away with the fairies or what boss?' Jojo said 'You've been lost in thought for ages, don't suppose it's your latest fairy on the side on your mind' he finished with a snigger, emphasising the word fairy.

'Oi you cheeky twat, watch your gob. If Linda ever heard you there would be murder, she would make my life a nightmare, so zip it.' Maisie retorted but found herself smiling none the less. That was the level of trust and friendship she had with her men, born of years of watching out for each other in an often vicious world. Just like the Moffats and their crew. Some of the other men she employed she didn't trust so much, she knew if the right offer or major heist came along a few of them would disappear faster than shit off a shovel. But she was happy enough for now, her and Linda were okay they had plenty of money and plenty more to come. You never knew she was able to lend a hand in settling a score or two with that evil shit TJ Murphy. She sat back in the Land Rover she had bought for Ginger Phil and they drove into town to finally meet the Moffats, some of the others following behind in her BMW.

Chapter 12

Carl and Michael let themselves into their town house, and straight away started to put lights on, move paper work and tidy up in readiness for their meeting. Michael relaxed a little feeling a sense of safety now they were lost in familiar actions and tasks, in their other castle. Some of their crew were hanging about in the basement, where there was an assortment of games, a Nintendo 64, Sony Play station and Mega drive, a massive colour TV, a pool table, a CD player, a video and a collection of all the latest high tech toys to amuse themselves with. As they now manufactured a fair percentage of the pirated videos across Merseyside now, they were never short of a good film to watch. They kept their crew happy and if that didn't work there was always violence as an answer even if it was on Street fighter or Mortal Kombat.

They didn't really need to supply all the toys and treats. With all of the men around them, as they'd all grown up together and had the loyalty that comes from surviving the grinding poverty some of them endured together. At first the pirate videos that were sold regularly had the back of some wankers head in the corner of the screen, because the film had been filmed manually by someone in the cinema with an expensive video camera aimed at the screen. So it waved and wobbled then went in and out of focus, and there was always some idiot loser in the middle of the film who had to get up and walk right across the screen. As long as you didn't mind that type of interference, and the crap sound, you could see a film a year or two ahead of it going to video, you could see the latest cinema release in the comfort of your own front room. The pirate copies sold for a fiver each, but soon the novelty wore off, and people had had enough of the poor quality. The Moffats heard how the films were sometimes so bad they were unwatchable, and that once you'd bought it you couldn't change it. There was certainly no refund off the petty crooks nearly all TJ's minions who peddled them. When one of the men sick of taking flak from his customers dared to complain, TJ sent a few of his men round to see him, they took all his stock and beat him senseless in front of his four year old son. Everyone knew that TJ was responsible for many deaths. One nasty one was mother and her young had perished in a fire set by Rodney. The only survivor was a young boy Davie now an orphan with no living relatives nearby. They didn't think he'd go that far. But he had. So the people who were going to take his video business off him didn't.

At first Michael and Carl didn't want to be bothered by something they thought was a waste of time. All that hassle for what? Just to make and sell pirate videos, but when they found out how much TJs men made, they sat down with their mates, and a few beers and worked it out. After pulling in a few favours they found that they could get films ahead of release in U.K. straight from the United States. They found a man Nick, originally from Merseyside willing and able to steal the films from one of the main studios. Nick was a bitter man, who had boasted frequently to his family back home in Liverpool about his big job in the film industry. Never revealing he was just a junior editor with an expensive coke habit. It cost a hell of a lot more than someone with a video camera in the local cinema, but they soon sold out because apart from anything they were top quality and looked like the real thing. They invested in some top of the range video recorders, dot matrix printers and then paid people to copy them round the clock. The final touch was they stuck them in a box with a colour cover and people were far happier to fork out a fiver a piece. Not only did they look like the real thing, you could actually see and hear them. The worst thing was a subtitle that popped up now and again saying property of whatever studio but that was it. You could still buy TJ's videos at car boot sales, round the pubs and off the pop or ice cream man but as word spread how good the Moffats videos were, most of the locals stopped buying his. Better still there was far too many of them for TJ to punish so he had to let it go.

TJ was so angry when he found out, he couldn't think straight, his men waiting for his heart attack as he ranted, a few secretly pleased someone was standing up to the miserable little coward. Nearly all the people who sold the videos went over to the Moffats delighted to be seen as working for the up and coming hard men. They were also assured by the brothers that they would be fine and if TJ gave them any grief to get in touch and they'd sort it. TJ saw this for what it was, not just a threat, it was a direct attack on him. His head ached and he was so apoplectic with rage he kept having nose bleeds. If they'd have muscled in on his pubs and clubs, and his heroin and crack dealing he'd have to take them out now. He spoke to Stephen who reasoned that if he left it a little longer when they got complacent he'd be able to take over all their little investments. He liked the thought of that. Let them do all the work setting them up for him. He felt better already besides there was enough to go round for now, and when he did take over their shabby little empire it would be all the sweeter.

By the time Michael had talked to the lads and finally sat down to wait for Maisie and her men to come, both he and Carl were at least on the surface back to normal. The cards and flowers that mocked their sisters' death were soon to be analysed forensically. Then they may get some answers from that, but they'd learnt to push things to down or keep them in the back of their minds until they were ready to deal with it. A skill learnt by their horrible childhoods at the hands of Shelagh.

It was exhausting sometimes always having to watch your back, worry about if they had the right image and so on. They'd been so full of rage leaving Fi's that they'd almost come to blows with each other. The frustration and anger having nowhere else to go. It had needed to come out. Carl had calmed first and they'd talked it through. They apologised to each other and decided to put their efforts into concentrating on getting Maisie on side against TJ. Oh and maybe a few drinks and a good laugh.

Michael was still full of adrenalin from the ups and downs of the last 24 hours, and he found despite his nerves jangling he was looking forward to meeting the famous Maisie Malone properly. Even more importantly as an equal. That's what this meeting was about not just to plot against TJ but to prove how high up the ladder they were already. Just by getting her to come to them. It felt good it really did, and he knew that Carl felt the same.

Just as he got up to make a phone call he heard Jonna one of his men shout up to them, 'she's here lads! Do you want me to let her in?'

'Yeah bring Maisie up to us' Carl shouted back, 'you lot amuse her boys okay? Keep them busy if you can.' Maisie put her head round the corner of the stairs to where Carl and Michael were sitting, smiling at their surprise and said 'A bit late for that isn't it? I'm already here.'

Carl made a mental note to smack Jonna in the mouth for being such a moron and letting them in before he'd had chance to finish what he was saying, hence making him look a dick. Nonetheless he still grinned cheekily back 'Lovely to see you Maisie what would you like to drink?' Maisie weighed up the situation, she'd left her boys downstairs, as she knew she wasn't in danger. Her instincts reassured her, and right now she would prefer a cuppa, but she also knew even this small gesture was a test. So she took a deep breath and replied 'Okay honey a small JD no ice please.' A beat passed, and Carl smiled and went to make her drink, another gesture carefully thought out, reinforcing Maisie's importance. Normally one of the lads would do it, but he knew exactly what he was doing. She took a deep breath, a bemused look on her face and said

'So what do you say lads? Shall we get straight down to business?'

Chapter 13

Shelagh and Stephen pulled up to his house, and she was already so off it, she wasn't easy to control. He opened the door for her acting the perfect gentleman and ushered her inside, uneasy and wound up. His pride started to take over and even off her head she saw the grandeur and most importantly to her, the money it must have cost. Shelagh thought how stupid you were if you only understand the value of anything in cost of happiness or love. Only cold hard cash counted and what she could get out of a situation.

'Come on then cutie haven't got all day, just all night' Shelagh sniggered. Stephen smiled his best pretend smile at her, 'Just got to sort out a bit of business, go into the kitchen get a drink. When I've done that I'll take care of you.' He went into his big spacious front room as Shelagh smirked at what could be the double meaning of his last comment.

Oh if only she knew what he was capable of, he imagined tasting her terror, but then if she had an inkling of his true nature she wouldn't have

47

got in his car. He picked up his phone dialling TJ. He barely kept the glee out of his voice when he told TJ who he had in his clutches.

TJ was pleased he could tell, but seemed too tame when he told him to find out what he could but to be careful and not to freak her out, or make her suspicious by asking too many questions. Stephen felt a little confused and annoyed as TJ told him this, he wasn't stupid, and he was skilled at getting information. However as TJ was the boss (for the time being) he agreed. He was also angry now, disappointed as he had known it couldn't go too far, but he had been fantasizing and TJ forbidding him to do anything made him more confused. He kept changing his mind about hurting her, he knew that. If he couldn't do anything to her, then he would go looking elsewhere. He had been looking forward to playing with some flesh tonight, even if it was a bit on the old side. He was going to do things when she was unconscious. His spirits lifted when he thought this could be a test or a task. He would experiment and relished the thought of learning even better self control, perhaps as a treat a little cutting when she was asleep, and some psychological fear when she was awake. The real test was could he stop before it got too out of hand? He knew in the more rational part of his brain that it would be stupid to give the Moffats any warning or worry at this stage in the game. After all he'd worked really hard to hide and stay nearly anonymous behind TJ and that's how he wanted it. Most people called him the nutter with the green eyes. Which suited him fine. When he took over TJs little empire it would be glorious, no more pretending. Feeling proud of himself as he's finding it a little easier to control his urges, the anger of being denied his pleasures can be stored away for further use, and once he has that mastered completely there will be no stopping him.

TJ spoke and brought him back to the moment, 'Listen, just get what they're doing next if you can and who's hanging round them, the usual parasites etc. They don't tell their mother much but that gobby neighbour of theirs can't help boasting about them to Shelagh rubbing it in her face. Letting her know how much her own kids secretly hate her. I have heard that Shelagh will put up with that so she can make out they tell her everything, even if it is second hand. I don't want anyone knowing that I'm showing this much interest in them. Remember that would be seen as me being worried, and I want this to stay between me and you, is that clear?' Stephen smiled inwardly at TJ's desperation but made sure it stayed out of his voice. Then he felt a little annoyed he was telling him what he had worked out before about the neighbour Kay. So to get rid of him he replied 'of course Mr. Murphy whatever you say. I'll report to you tomorrow about tea time if that's okay?'

TJ puffs up arrogantly now, and feels good that he's back in control. It's the effect that Stephen wants, as he knows exactly how to pander to his ego. Firstly by calling him Mr. Murphy, and letting the stupid fat bastard think he thought of everything first. TJ's self belief in his power returned he grunts his approval and as he put the phone down. Stephen mutters out loud 'he's even mean with his words, the fucking imbecile.'

When Stephen went back into the kitchen Shelagh was sitting at his table with a drink in one hand and was using one of his beautiful Clarice Cliff plates as an ashtray. Anger sliced through his guts, and he thought this is the first part of his test to keep his feelings under control. Next to his antique plate was a round mirror from a compact, a razor blade, a rolled up note and a bag of white powder.

'Care to join me in a little snort? It's great for making you feel horny, or in our case hornier.' Shelagh simpered.

Stephen struggled to keep his temper, and through clenched teeth said 'Not right now, but you knock yourself out. I may have a little a bit later. I'll just have a scotch for now.'

He walked over to the drinks cabinet taking a lead crystal glass out and then poured himself a finger of scotch. He doesn't drink alcohol much as he doesn't like the way it makes him feel slow and stupid. He felt he had to pretend to be like her so that she didn't get suspicious of his real motives. He took a tiny sip and smiled at her.

He was aware of a tingle of excitement at the thought of using cocaine. He likes coke but since he's been testing his self control, he tries to limit it to his exclusive hobby. He can get it cheaply when he goes to play his perverted games in the Far East. It doesn't matter what urges he gets or what he does with them there. He is protected by money and disappears easily amongst the sex tourists, a lot of them vile paedophiles and creeps. They all hunt the innocent peddled by the people they trust most. Some sell them out of desperation for money just to eat, some out of pure evil. But even worse some out of indifference to their children's suffering as they were treated the same, so it's considered normal. Stephen doesn't really care he just hates their parents and guardians for being so fucking weak. Their flat dead eyes, only lighting up when he gets American dollars out. The only resistance when they barter for a few more dollars. He likes younger flesh but not children, they do nothing for him. He thinks that because he only maims and kills women in their early twenties to thirties that he is sometimes better than the rest of the perverts out there. There is nothing sacred to him.

Stephen has a computer now, it's how he learnt about the best places to go in Asia. The internet is still fairly young, not accessible to nearly all yet as it is so expensive. It has already becomes a place for the sex offenders to peddle their disgusting wares, the lists, observation and police international databases that will lead to their downfall are only just growing too. It takes hours to download an image so Stephen prefers to take his own, and document them on the computer. It doesn't cross his mind to share his work, not because of any morale reason or fear of being caught but because he's too selfish. He wants to keep his beautiful records of torture and death to himself. His madness tells him it's fine. He is jolted back into the room by an annoying nasally voice, hers of course. 'Do you want to get more comfortable?' Shelagh asked him.

'I'd love to see your bedroom, and the rest of your mansion, please Sir Steven.' She stands up and does a clumsy curtsey, nearly falling over. He automatically reaches over to steady her, grabbing her arm hard, but the coke is so strong she doesn't feel it.

Jesus Christ!' thinks Stephen something almost snapping inside him; could she be any more obvious about wanting sex? It's looking like it's going to be a long night. God how will he get through it without dying of boredom, knowing he's not supposed to hurt her too much? Based on this thought he makes a decision now that turns out to be the worst of his life, 'I will have a bit of your coke thanks. I'm up for a buzz like the next person. Let's line them up then go upstairs.' Shelagh feels better now, he's obviously up for a good time too, and he's loaded so she'll get the money back for the coke. Just as well it's really good stuff really strong, she's not used to such pure stuff. She's usually like a Hoover but only needs a little line of this to get the best buzz she's had for ages. However as she cut and chopped the coke up she put a huge line for Stephen on the mirror so he can catch up to her buzz. She feels a thrill thinking that she has turned him on to coke, and that this may last longer than one night after all. A three day bender here could just be what she needs. All that money, comfort and none stop drugs. Staying here would be definitely a few hundred steps up from the estate. Both of them have no idea that the latest batch of coke they've just taken apart from ketamin and icing sugar is half methamphetamine. It's used in the States and lasts for days. It is the most addictive form of speed, even more so than crack. It's already caused more violent crimes in the USA than all other drugs put together.

Chapter 14

The meeting at the Moffats town house was going well; Michael had done most of the talking. At first he'd been fairly cautious not wanting Maisie to know just how much they hated TJ and how they'd do anything to take him down. They all knew now it was no longer an option but a necessity, they were working on his tame coppers at the moment because without them and his creepy weirdo Bentley TJ would be much weaker. They couldn't be seen to give him too long or any mercy if they were going to be at the top. Maisie however knew how to mother her boys, and she did the same thing with Michael and Carl. They started to talk about Sara and Michael found he couldn't stop, the words pouring out, like poison from a ruptured abscess.

TJ had had Sara murdered when they were just little boys, it was common knowledge and it felt good to be vindicated by Maisie. Her saying it made it seem more real than ever. They knew now that their dream of revenge would finally come true, something that they had held on to and nurtured with hate. The police were less than useless too, one of the lead investigators they'd found out as adults was on TJs payroll. That certainly explained why not much was done to find her murderer. There were a couple of coppers who tried to help. They might be worth getting on board. He doubted they'd be bought, but then everyone has their price and not always money. That was something he and Carl were learning as they went further and further away from ordinary life. He realised for the first time he felt real hope at laying Sara's ghost to rest. Watch out TJ you slimy twat we're coming for you, and whoever actually killed her.
He remembered a daft quote from some show he used to watch. He, who laughs last, laughs longest……. or was it loudest? Either one would do he really didn't mind.

As was often lately he found himself transported back to the past, the weeks following Sara's murder. He remembered that there'd been two good men in the police who'd taken a stand and tried for them, even knowing the family's reputation. The errant mum on the game. The rumours that she was going to sell her little ones to the highest bidder. The oldest, the girl Sara had already been charged with prostitution, it was too late for her. Even with all that, Sara had done a good job caring and protecting the boys, and she deserved someone on her side. Bailey and Jessell the two junior detectives when they found out, just how much the kids had suffered cared about them. They were good men that was the pity, but corruption had been rife. They hadn't stood much of a chance in getting to the bottom of the investigation. It was the likes of Bailey and Jessell who had changed the force for good in the following years. He was grateful they'd tried and that's what counted to Michael. It was still an open case, to be reviewed again occasionally. It had been the 80s recession, heroin usage was rife. They were dealing with underfunding and no overtime and with a major crime wave. She was just another junkie who'd died over drugs and money, a prostitute. Perhaps a client had killed her or maybe one of the other girls had stabbed her over turf, they had been the theories flying around the squad room.

After asking round it was common knowledge who was behind it. Their boss, Jacobs did all he could to throw them off the scent. He'd been at school with TJ and was well in his pocket. They knew then if they were to prove anything they would have to play the long game. Jacobs ended up in prison where he was murdered in under three days. Nobody cared, his corruption had put more than one innocent man away. TJ was too well established by then to care. Jacobs had got rid of all the evidence between him and TJ so the bastard got away with it all again.

Michael snapped back to the present. As the drink flowed a little more, there was cannabis and coke if preferred, they became more and more comfortable. They seemed to form a bond that night that could last a life time. Maisie became their surrogate older sister and they all agreed to put business each other's way, and discussed a couple of group ventures. All drugs in her club would be supplied by the Moffats, and she agreed to keep heroin and crack off the menu. It was all ecstasy, speed and coke anyway, maybe a bit of weed when you were coming down. Oh and prescription drugs of course. Maisie felt that these lads had something, brains and brawn. She knew that if she played it right they'd help her when and if she needed it. It was a reassuring thought, but she also knew not to cross them or take them for fools. They pretty much knew that once she accepted them into her circle that many of the other big shots around the city would do the same. It was a good feeling. As it was getting late and Maisie needed to get back to the club before kicking out time, they called an end to their meeting. They decided to meet in the next few weeks to sort out the logistics of their plan.

The best part taking even more business and money off TJ of course. It was good knowing that now they'd joined forces he would now lose enough to get him to come out of his safe little world. She warned them about their cousin Gez, said he'd been seen talking to Stephen Bentley TJ's right hand man. She also let them know that he often slagged them off behind their backs. Then she finished by telling them he was doing a spot of dealing for himself, using their name to get credit off some really nasty people.

It was her parting gift to them, and a way of letting them know they'd passed all her tests, as she'd passed theirs. 'Well I'm off now lads, it's been a pleasure and I look forward to seeing you again.' Maisie said standing up feeling a little light headed. She'd been polite and had a few drags of a spliff and a snort of coke just to show willing. It was stronger than normal, and she nearly lost her balance. It was really good stuff.

'Careful there Maisie we don't want people thinking we've been leading you astray.' chuckled Michael. 'No that wouldn't do at all now would it Carl?' He agreed, smiling. They were both keen for her to go now as they wanted to discuss what they were going to do to Gez for daring to go behind their backs. Plus they were family no matter how they'd not bothered with him since they were kids, you just didn't do it.

Maisie smiled at them and said 'I'm not soft you pair, you know I may be off it but I know you want rid of me while you decide what you're going to do to Gez.'

Michael and Carl just looked at each other and burst out laughing. 'God she's psychic as well!' Carl said and Maisie just smiled benignly at them. 'Do us favour lads go and see what my supposed bodyguards are up to and ask them to get the car started. Please.' She said 'while I go to the little girl's room.' Michael showed her to their bathroom while Carl ran downstairs and shouted Jonna. He passed on Maisies message and stood by the door waiting for her to come down. As he watched her make her way down the stairs his head was still full of Gez's betrayal, he suddenly felt exhausted, he had been looking forward to his bed. That of course was screwed as he knew that he and Michael had to decide what to do with the little runt, their cousin. Then he could sleep and switch off all the thoughts running through his head. Maisie came down the stairs amazingly elegantly considering how off her head she now felt, and Michael watched her carefully in case she fell. She stopped at the door and kissed them both on the cheek, in view of their men who were standing around watching. It was a sign all was well. Although both of their crews had spent a pleasant few hours watching films and having a drink and chat in the basement, it was good to know they could all get on in public. They were mostly pleased with the turn of events, more money coming in meant more for them all as well. There was only one who objected and that was Pete. He'd gone to school with Michael and thought he had more influence over him than he actually did. He was furious that he'd been treated like the rest of the goons, put in the cellar to entertain Maisies men instead of being upstairs. He'd been pissed at Michael for a while now and had been talking to Stephen Bentley behind his back, hate and anger filling his head leaving no room for thoughts of loyalty.

As Maisie was driven off by Ginger Phil, Jojo in the back, Pete was standing behind Michael and he felt a nauseating wave of hatred for her. He hated strong women, and if possible he hated lesbians more. He knew all about her the perverted bitch and he hated that the Moffats supposed hard men and up and coming top dogs were even bothering with her. Why weren't they tooled up and round there smashing up her club and taking out her men? Then he'd be happy to be part of it all, by Michaels side just like at school. It never crossed his mind that they were doing the right thing as he only understood cruelty and violence. He was a cowardly bully at heart, and hid his true feelings as he knew which side his bread was buttered., He liked to think he was a master at stirring up trouble. He had had a serious crush growing up on Sara, and when he found out when he was older what she was and what she did, he felt almost abused. A fucking prostitute and the way they bloody went on as if she was a saint. He despised her too, and his hatred and jealousy was building daily. It was only a matter of time before he'd be in charge he was sure of it, and when his day come he'd get rid of them all. Even that twat Carl, so there would be just him and Michael left. He could replace Carl. He was holding Michael back. He'd be there to take his place. If that didn't work he had a backup plan and not for the first time wondered how much TJ would pay him to go over to his side. He had a long term girlfriend and a kid and he enjoyed being cruel to them both. He hid all this, and was careful not to go too far, as he knew that if Michael or Carl ever found out they'd bin him quicker than a used condom. He was like all bullies, cowardly and only concerned with not getting caught. They despised wife beaters, nonces and anyone who hurt kids or women in general. Pete thought this proved they were weak underneath; having no concept that this common decency was what made them all the more popular with everyone from their world. From the likes of Kay next door to Maisie and the other important faces around town.

Chapter 15

Stephen was in his kitchen drinking a cup of coffee, contemplating what to do. He had the shakes, and he wasn't sure what was causing it. The mistake he'd just made, the adrenalin or the pleasure he'd felt, he was sure of only one thing. He'd fucked up big time, royally and most definitely was he in the shit. He knew he'd really need his wits and luck to get out of this one. He sat there unsure of what to do next, and he just carried on sipping his coffee.

It was that stupid bitches fault if only he hadn't had those snorts of coke, and it was still racing around his system. He hadn't even needed it and had taken it thinking he was going with the moment, and look where it had got him. He walked into the basement where Shelagh lay on the table, her lifeless eyes staring up at the ceiling, and she looked more beautiful in death even with her injuries. He felt a twang of pleasure and berating himself did his utmost to stop these feelings. He had been fine and in control, even managing to get over her using one of his pottery investments as an ashtray. So calm in fact that he'd accepted the huge line of coke, he didn't think in a million years it would be so strong. It was a bit of blur to be honest but he still couldn't quite get his head around what he'd actually done. He'd killed two of the local mobsters' mother, and that meant big trouble. He had wanted to deal with the Moffats when he had inherited TJ's throne and not before. No matter how good he thought he was it was impractical to take on more than one until he was good and ready. He switched his attention back to Shelagh, or what was once Shelagh.

When they'd gone upstairs before to use one of the amazing bathroom mirrors to cut up more of the coke she'd put an even bigger amount out. He'd already had a huge one downstairs. When they snorted their lines, he felt as if his head was going to burst with her constant twittering and clumsy attempts at seduction. He'd asked her about her sons and she'd told him what little she knew, it was obvious that they'd told her nothing important. He then wanted her to tell him what Kay had told her. One of the only things worth knowing was that they were going to join up with Maisie Malone. That was good gossip, and he was pleased with something big to tell TJ. He would get more information from Pete, Michaels so called best mate. He'd get all the inside knowledge soon from him s he'd been manipulating him for a long time. He was ripe for the picking, as he'd been really careful to not tell him too much. It was amazing really but Stephen didn't even realise that the gossip he'd gotten had been around for ages. Lots of people knew, but as he was locked in his fantasy world, and TJ in his castle they didn't know as much as they thought. He had to stop then asking questions eventually. He'd slipped up when he'd mentioned Kay. She had started to get suspicious asking him in a loud voice. 'Why do you want to talk about them all of the time? How the fuck do you know Kay?"After he had kissed her to make her forget about her questions she'd groped at his penis and when she felt he wasn't very hard she got really angry. He had tried to ignore her as she was rubbing him raw, and when she fumbled with his zip and nearly pulled him free he'd pushed her away hard. He actually felt embarrassed and strangely vulnerable. She started to raise her nasally annoying voice, and started screaming how she was going to ring the boys, her big strong sons, and tell them he knew Kay so must be after something. When he hadn't reacted the way she'd wanted, she became even more abusive. Her voice drilled into his head, steel bands wrapped around his brain and squeezed hard. He knew that no one was around to hear them and the neighbours were too far. Then a voice in his head told him to make her be quiet. Her voice made him feel uncomfortable and even more paranoid. He kept seeing flashbacks, all the women he'd abused, their screams, their faces, their eyes after fear had passed. Then defiance replacing it in some, resignation in others. Everything looked red, he shook his head and all he could see was flashes of the bloody wounds he'd left behind, black and red. He could just about see Shelagh through the red haze. She'd been about to speak on her mobile phone when he'd just snapped. Knocking the phone out of her hand, he heard it shatter on his floor. He grabbed her hair and pulled her to him. She was trying desperately to keep looking cocksure, but for the first time that night he could see a real emotion in her eyes. Fear at last. 'Is that what you want bitch? Is that better you fucking whore?' Stephen had snarled. She'd looked scared and the penny dropped then that she wasn't as invulnerable as she thought. She looked right into his eyes, and seeing the madness there had started to scream and try to get out from his powerful grip. The more she struggled under his weight the more turned on he became, his head full of thoughts of Sara, her daughter. Then he saw the other souls he had hurt and tortured, the horror subsided and was replaced by a lust so strong he'd have given anything to feel like this forever. He was on the brink of coming, his erection strained against his pants. He was giddy with malice at being able to prove all the sluts wrong. He was a true man, he could get an erection easily. He was going to make them pay for all this. Shelagh first, she'd be screaming for mercy. His groin aching and his body naturally thrusting forward Shelagh took him unawares and kneed him as hard as she could. The exquisite ache in his balls changed to a hot, white lightening. While he was gasping for breath on his knees, she'd tried to run. He heard her clattering down the stairs, muttering under her breath, and he lay there gathering strength, not at all worried. The house was locked down, and she had no way of getting out without a code or the keys. He recovered quickly anyway, and he felt the familiar excitement build again, even after being kneed so hard. He felt his power building, the lust exhilarating and as his erection grew again so did his ego. He could still hear her muttering and squealing and now taking deep breaths he was sure he could smell her fear. He bounded down the stairs, and saw Shelagh struggling with the locks on the front door. Stupidly thinking she could open it. She pulled as hard as she could, but it wouldn't budge. She heard a strange keening noise and then to her horror realised it was coming from her. She stood back from the door and took in a deep but shaky breath. Her sense of survival and indignation kicked in.

'Listen you little shit you know who I am! My boys are the Moffats after all, I've told you again and again. If anything happens to me they will hunt you down. Do you get it?? So back off and ring me a taxi. Which you can pay for and you can pay me for the fucking coke too.'

Stephen come down the stairs and smiled at her, 'Of course it was just a little misunderstanding. Let me get my wallet. Come back to the kitchen.' He said.

Shelagh felt her confidence returning, and was lost in thoughts of how much she could screw him for. Just by promising not to tell the boys. So she didn't see that when Stephen came back in he wasn't carrying his wallet but a big brown leather wrap, the type butchers have. Unfortunately she realised what it was. She felt urine running down her legs as Stephen pulled out a boning knife and then stuck it in her throat. He grinned at her as she slid down the wall, clutching at the gaping wound in her neck. Stephen was smiling still when he said

'The amount of money I could make in the far east, and among some of our finest right here, if I had film footage of the murder of a mother and daughter to sell to some of my special friends! I wish I had filmed it, all those years ago. I might just film you when you're dead. How jealous they will be when I tell them I had the pleasure of loving you both with my knife. You see it's like this, I killed Sara not some piece of shit gangster. It was me, and I'll do the same to your bastard boys.' Spittle flew from his mouth, along with his insane laughter as he stabbed her over and over, slipping the knife in and out with relative ease, enjoying the loss of control eventually climaxing as Shelagh struggled with her last breath.

At first it didn't make sense what he said to Shelagh after all she was being stabbed to death, but Sara my daughter, how did he know her? She didn't understand at first, and then it hit her. This was who had murdered her; if only she could get the lads to her she'd be fine. Imagine what they would give her if she told them she knew for sure how Sara had died. How it was this weirdo who killed her, and hurt me. She no longer felt the knife going in and out of her body, she was unaware of everything, numb with the coke and adrenalin, and loss of blood. Her last thoughts were a mix of emotions, how angry and upset she was that she didn't get to take all her coke and spend her money. She didn't believe she was dying she wouldn't accept it, then a cold black fear grabbed her, out of nowhere, and as her life's blood left her, draining quickly out of her many wounds, an image appeared before her closing eyes. It was of Sara laughing at her, as clear and cold as a winters day. Soon it faded from sight, but she could still hear

Sara's voice talking to her. The fear she felt started to subside until she heard exactly what was being said. 'Hey Shelagh, now that the same man has taken both our lives, perhaps I can rest in peace. Especially knowing that you dear mother, are finally going to burn in hell.'

Chapter 16

Tiffany was finishing a work out in her front room on her yoga mat. It was important now she stayed in perfect shape. She had developed a plan called bag a Moffat the minute she heard the Moffats were joining forces with Mad Maisie and her crew. Excellent, she knew all about Maisie and what turned her on, as she had a hell of a reputation, always taking what she wanted from young women. She liked them young and pretty. Also with a good body and not very bright by all accounts. It was also known that she would probably never leave Linda her other half. She really loved her but couldn't stay faithful apparently, well the jury was out on that one. This gossip was all from the Estate of course. She often wondered how people found all this out, but everyone knew something or other. She brought her thoughts back to Maisie who would spoil her lovers with the usual trinkets such as diamond and gold jewellery, clothes, shoes, little holidays and she'd heard this from a couple of the girls who'd actually been Maisies bits on the side. She was as bad as any man, when it came to dumping them. She lost interest or her guilt got the better of her and she'd be straight back to Linda. Tiffany wondered if it was worth trying to go the full way with Maisie now. It was all part of her quest to bag a Moffat so she had decided it was. She'd flirted with her to get a job and it had worked, so in the future when the boys were around she could make her move. The chance to start her master plan had presented a lot sooner than she thought possible. She now worried she wasn't prepared hence the strenuous workouts. She was sweaty from her exertion so went to the bathroom to get a wash. She started to fill the sink, and get her toiletries together, and thought back to how easy the first part had been. She just hoped to God that the rest of her plan worked as well. If so she'd have a Moffat preferably Carl by the end of the year. She kept going through it in her mind, how Maisie had been, was it too easy? So as she had her wash she thought back to when she got offered her chance a few days ago.

On the day in question, after a nice lie in she'd decided to go to Maisies club to try her hand at getting some barmaid work. Maisie had dumped yet another one of her women. A barmaid so a spot had opened up. She was determined to try at least. After a nice long soak in the bath, a good lunch she'd had delivered, and a full hour on her makeup and clothes, she felt ready to try and start phase one of her plan. She dressed sexily but not too obvious, and picked a black low cut top with long sleeves and rhinestones. She paired it with tight red jeans and finished with black leather boots. They had diamante patterns on them to match her top. She toyed with the idea of wearing her black cowboy hat but decided it may be a bit too quirky for Maisie. Even a little too flirty, or obvious. Rodney had bought her the boots as they were super expensive. She found it easy to forget him, and he was pushed far from her mind. She timed it when she knew Maisie was about and she took a taxi to the club. She got out of the cab on Stanley Road, five minutes away from the club. She loved Bootle and knew it well. She threw a fiver at the driver and walked the rest of the way. She took a deep breath and re-applied fresh lip gloss after a final cigarette, before she approached the doors. The doors pushed easily apart as she went in, even though they were huge ornamental cast iron monsters. They had been expertly painted in a way to look old but not scruffy, but certainly eye catching.

Sure enough Maisie was there at the bar sipping a cup of coffee and reading the paper. Her club was always full of the local gangsters at night. It was the place to be seen, and she turned a blind eye to coke, weed, tabs and speed but she wouldn't of course tolerate smack. She didn't care about it morally, but it wasn't a party drug and she didn't want the local bag heads attracting attention and scoring in her club. Maisie also had a policy that there was only a certain type of staff who could work for her, mainly good looking, sexy and confident. They didn't know but she generally had them checked out first by word of mouth or even a local private eye if the job meant handling lots of money. One of the reasons their club made so much was they had something for everyone, mainly Linda's ideas. One that had turned out surprisingly lucrative much to Maisie's shock was an event for the older ladies disguised as a bingo afternoon for charity. In reality and they were catered to by several older but handsome and charming gigolos who flirted only with them. They had their favourites, the most popular an ex football player from the USA called Bobby who was in his 40s. He wore a cowboy hat and very tight jeans, and they'd poached him from a phone sex line he was working on after a recommendation from one of the other staff. He was hovering behind the bar now, with a pot of coffee waiting for Maisies instructions. God she was arrogant thought Tiffany, as she approached them. Watching as she lifted her cup and he rushed over and filled it. She didn't even thank or acknowledge him. Then she raised her head looked at him and pointed to the Staff Only sign with her chin so he left quickly. Nearly all the staff understood what every nuance from Maisie meant, and if you didn't after a week or two you were history.

Tiffany put on her best sultry look and aimed for the bar. She approached and as she got closer to her said 'Hiya, Maisie, I'm Tiffany Green, I was told you might be hiring staff so I thought I'd apply.' Maisie carried on reading not looking up, replied 'Who told you that? Don't listen to the rumours about me. They may be true. It also depends on whether you can provide what I want whether or not I hire you.' She chuckled to herself and looked right at Tiffany. 'Not bad, you may do, how are you at chatting up the punters?' She took another swig of coffee and then asked her. 'Hang on don't I know you from somewhere? Weren't you that prick Rodney's bit on the side? One of TJs men, you were the talk of the town. Your reputation precedes you Tiffany Green.' Maisie was doing one of her usual tricks, speaking fast throwing information she knew would make you feel vulnerable to gauge the reaction. Tiffany blanched; she hadn't seen this coming and wasn't prepared for it. She dropped her bag on the floor as a way to buy her some time to get her mind straight. 'God I'm sorry clumsy me' she said as she bent over to pick it up, taking her time and making sure her cleavage was on full show. She stood back up and Maisie stared openly at her breasts. She looked at her up and down and then stopped and took
in the expression on her face. Tiffany felt a small thrill as she looked back and noticed the naked lust in her eyes. She thought she'd take a chance and go for the sympathy vote with her. 'Yeah I was seeing him but he was a jealous knob head and he beat me up. I've left him now, and I'm never going back to the horrible twat.' She started to pretend to cry, her hands covering her face. Maisie knew what was going on, she'd done all this type of thing herself, but found herself intrigued by this sexy little minx in front of her. She got up and went over to Tiffany putting her arm around her. 'Aww come on honey I didn't mean to upset you. Tell you what, give me the gossip on TJ later, and I'll give you a go at serving drinks eh? Then we'll see if you're up to the job. Take your time.' Tiffany was glad her head was buried in her hands so Maisie wouldn't see the sneaky little smile that had appeared as she felt her plan working. She struggled to get back in control. Maisie pulled Tiffany closer and as she struggled to look sad again, held her gently by the shoulders, forcing her to look into her eyes. 'Now now girl no more crying. Go on behind the bar, and I'll ask you to make me a drink or two.' Tiffany's confidence started to grow knowing she'd do okay behind this bar. She'd been working on and off in pubs and clubs in Liverpool since her 15th birthday. She'd met many a rich dickhead who'd she'd taken to the cleaners. It was better than going out with a group of

screaming girls any day for picking up these type of blokes. Maisie held her while she pretended to sniffle and wipe her eyes. She had deliberately rubbed the mascara so it would look like she had cried more than the few crocodile tears she had managed to squeeze out.

'Right angel, when you've calmed completely, come and show us what you can do. I'll have a Manhattan; they love the cocktails the girls who come in here. They think it makes them look sophisticated.' Maisie laughed. Tiffany quickly assessed the bar and its contents going straight to the cocktail bar which was basically an alcove with a load of brightly coloured bottles with exotic labels. She looked round for the right shaped glass, and put in a measure of whiskey, some vermouth some Angostura bitters and pierced a Maraschino cherry with a cocktail stick and put it across the top. She turned round and put it by Maisie and said 'there you go boss, have a try of that.' Maisie threw back her head and laughed loudly. Tentatively she took a small sip then a bigger one. 'Mmmm that's good Tiff, you seem to know your stuff.' Are you that good all the time? Well you're hired for now. You can work legit or work on the side it's up to you.' Tiffany squealed, and then exclaimed in her best gushing voice. 'Thanks Maisie, that's great. I don't care as long as I can work here. What pays more do you think?' Maisie ignored the last question, thinking that was Linda's department. 'You can start in a few days, after the weekend so it's a bit quieter. Get yourself sorted girl, you can go on trial for a few weeks, make sure you like it. Okay?' Maisie replied, thinking I need to make sure I like you. She felt the familiar stirrings of lust at the thought of the chase, and she knew then she had to at least try to bed her, the straight ones were much more fun. Tiff could barely hide her excitement. She loved it when her plans worked, then she calmed herself down, she had a long way to go yet she thought, and she felt that it was working, but Maisie was too long in the tooth and saw it in her eyes, and wondered what she was up to. She'd planted a seed of doubt now, maybe Tiffany was a plant for TJ or something. Well two can play at that game. She'd make sure she warned the boys about her, not to tell her anything important, and then she'd feed her some false information. If it eventually got back to TJ then she'd know. Gossip was rife in the clubs with the staff, she'd soon find out if she was playing games. She knew that Tiffany was beautiful and had a raw sexuality a lot of women envied. Although she was young she already had a reputation as a gold digger, that's how Maisie had heard of her. Why else would she go with the likes of Rodney one of TJs major henchmen? Still she could do well better than him. He wanted to show her off to everyone. Usually that load of misogynist idiots were exceptionally secretive especially cheating on their wives. She also remembered listening to the talk in the club a lot of men knew all about her and what she was, and still they chased her, wanting her, as an escort and more.

Just then Tiffany walked back around the bar, deliberately provocative for Maisies benefit and it worked. Maisie followed her and grabbed her from behind and massaged her shoulders. Although she was being gentle Tiffany could feel the strength in her fingers and realised that she wouldn't stand a chance if Maisie turned on her.

Firm and with calloused skin, she could feel her hands through her thin top and to her surprise she quite liked the sensation. Although she expected to feel repulsion she didn't. Once she'd made the decision to play along she turned around and kissed Maisie hard on the lips. When they came up for air, Tiffany was okay because she'd pretended Maisie was Carl. The warm glow and tingles started in her

were even making her wet. She felt a little flummoxed at how her body had reacted just by pretending it was Carl. She'd acted out with women to turn men on in clubs and hotel rooms, but she hadn't ever felt aroused, but then she'd never pretended it was with a man before, she usually just went blank like the other woman who was acting with her. She never really understood why men were so aroused by them kissing and feeling each other's boobs, the furthest they went was naked on top. The men were so turned on they never had to do anything more, and if the odd man had asked her and most of the girls she had worked with it was always a no anyway.

She quickly put her doubts out of her mind and decided to just try and enjoy the moment, and how hot she felt controlling this powerful woman. That's when it hit her, she wasn't gay or even bisexual she was feeling this because Maisie was so powerful and she Tiffany was controlling her or so she thought. Maisie was sensing her reactions with interest, she was enjoying it of course, that's all these girls ever meant to her. Sex and fun and a bit of strange to have on her arm when she went on a binge. This one would be no different, but she could tell that Tiff was genuinely turned on, and that was a surprise. She was used to them putting it on for her, so they could access her money and drugs of course, some of them had been gay and enjoyed the sex genuinely but she didn't care as long as she got what she wanted. As Maisie pulled back to look at her, running her hands down Tiffany's arms and grabbing her hands so they were face to face again, she felt her stiffen.

Tiffany suddenly realised how out of control she was herself, and she felt her emotions running through her body and she turned red to her roots and felt angry. This was ridiculous, she loved controlling men, all shapes and sizes, that was her biggest turn on. Earth to Tiffany she thought , this was a woman. Could she really go through with it? What

62

would it be like to have actual sex, snogging and groping was one thing but naked sex? She suddenly felt repulsed at herself for being so turned on. Maisie sensed the sudden change and pushed her away, and stared at her, confused and now a little angry too. 'That was nice you horny little bitch. However I'm going home to my other half now.' She had to make sure that Tiffany was put back in her place, and as usual made a comment aimed at making her conquests feel cheap and used. It also sometimes made them more desperate to win her from Linda. As long as she was in control and got the last word in that was okay. 'Right Tiff, I will see you next Monday at seven o'clock. Don't be late and dress sexy.' Maisie said as she walked off leaving Tiff to wonder what the hell was going on. Where did she stand with her future boss now? God had she blown it. She'd have to wait and see. When Tiffany came back to the present, she noticed that the sink was running over. She'd been so lost in her thoughts about what had happened at the club, the water was an inch deep on the floor. Good job the old dear who'd lived here before had a wet room put in. So to sum up, well she didn't care where she stood with Maisie as long as she was working there when the Moffats came in.

Chapter 17

Stephen looked at Shelagh's body, his love of blood and gore competing with his practical side. He wasn't on the other side of the world he was at home in his beautiful house. He had sworn to himself he wouldn't do anything like that here in his castle, but he had. Not only that he'd really gone to town on the horrible cow. She had made him so horny when she'd started to show fear and struggled, then when she'd kicked him in the balls he had lost all semblance of control. Angry that he'd been aroused by her despite her disgusting lewd antics, he'd really seen red in front of his eyes. Therefore it was her fault. He didn't feel any guilt at all, just annoyance at having to sort it all out. It was too much hard work. Any fear had gone as the coke had cleared from his head. That's all it was, he didn't feel fear normally, the coke must have caused the paranoid feelings. Once he understood it, he didn't fear it anymore. He was positive he was okay. He didn't realise it was the meth speeding around his system that was making him feel okay. In fact he decided he could use a bit more now he was in control. His blonde hair was dark with sweat, and as he absently wiped his face he spread blood across it making him look like he was wearing some macabre Halloween mask.

He looked at the tableau in front of him, it looked like a horror movie, and a random chuckle came out of his mouth, as he thought of a joke, which had just entered his head. The only horror in this movie was that bitch Shelagh. It made him giggle again when he contemplated ringing TJ, and he imagined how it would sound.

'Hey TJ I've done away with the slag, sorry got carried away! The lads may be a bit pissed off eh? Still that's one less Moffat to worry about.' He went to the sink, grinning at his own thoughts, and washed his face and hair in really hot water. Then he found some evil smelling soap under the sink. The smell started to get to him reminding him of hospitals so he kept rinsing with cold. He set up a coffee for himself; while it was percolating he made his way to the outhouse where he kept all his tools and cleaning supplies. He grabbed a roll of bin bags, a big piece of plastic, rubber gloves, some discenfectant and a huge bottle of bleach. He also grabbed some brand new sponges and an old sheet for tearing up, and then he went into the kitchen. The bin bags were made for the new wheelie bins that had started appearing all over Merseyside. These were for garden waste so pretty big, feeling pleased with himself for buying them, he figured he could get Shelagh into one no bother after he wrapped her up in some plastic. He snapped on his rubber gloves and after putting the polythene on the floor he grabbed her body under the arms, and manoeuvred her off the table.

The blood had left streaks all over the table and floor, but he didn't mind too much. This was a mess he had learnt to endure, as it was part of his craft. Blood was really hard to get rid of he mused. He sometimes enjoyed the lack of thought when he was scrubbing and cleaning. He could switch off from the chore, and concentrate on some of the women he'd enjoyed, and fantasise about some he was going to enjoy. After he rolled her up he slotted her into a bin bag and tied the top. He then repeated this several times until he was sure she wasn't going to leak anywhere. He then thought about getting the body out of his house as quickly as possible. He then threw bleach all over the stains, put some of the torn up sheet on it and left it soaking. If it discoloured the floor he'd get it stained again, he'd just say he'd dropped a bottle of bleach or rather his cleaner did, even though he didn't have one. In fact he could do it himself, it wasn't on show and he had no intentions of letting anyone see in here ever. Hardly anyone but workmen came here. He just wanted to be sure in case the local pigs ever showed up. You could never be too safe, and being paranoid and careful in his line of work was healthy he thought for the hundredth time.

He couldn't take a chance getting a pull in his little Volkswagen golf, not in the early hours like this. He was reluctant to put the old boot Shelagh in his new boot, he thought smirking again. Well in the immaculate boot of his Jag. However he should put on a smart shirt and jacket, and use it, and if he got pulled over he could play the business man coming home late from a meeting in Chester or somewhere. The traffic police around here could appear spiteful. He was certain that some of them stopped you just because they were envious of the Jag. Spreading newspapers in the boot, his quick mind went through probabilities. He thought about getting a breathalyser for example, relief passed through him remembering he hadn't had much to drink. He had to think of every eventuality so he could be prepared. He put Shelagh's body in the boot. Laid a few bin bags of old clothes he had in the garage over her. Well they wouldn't be going to the local charity shop not now. Then quietly shut it tight. He would just get rid of them in the sea with her. The only reason he was doing it was he had his eye on one of the young girls who volunteered there and it was a way of getting to talk to her. He checked his reflection he looked smart in a new shirt and he put on a tie but loosened it so he looked the part of tired executive. It's now or never he thought as he started his Jag, she was purring like a kitten, which calmed him. As he turned out of his drive, taking a deep breath he took a left out on to Liverpool Road, heading towards the shore in Rock Ferry, Wirral. As he was driving down the road, he nearly swerved as he saw Shelagh sitting in the back. She had disgusting black holes where he had stabbed her, and one of the Thai girls was with her. It was the one called Dao he thought but she was rotten and bloody so he couldn't be sure. He pulled over his heart beating so hard again he thought he was going to pass out. He took a deep breath and turned his head awkwardly to look and a nerve twanged painfully in his neck, but they had gone. He steadied his breathing and then laughed at himself. He'd heard stress could make you see all types of things, but didn't think it could ever happen to him. His descent into madness had started and all the things he had done to innocent victims were starting to rear their very ugly heads. The coke mixed with meth was like a key that had unlocked a previously undiscovered part of his brain. He was a sociopath and his psychosis was unleashed and crashed over his brain like a tidal wave. The second bag of coke that Stephen found in Shelagh's bag well it wasn't the good stuff she'd taken off the Yuppie. No this had been dirt cheap, as the dealers struggled to get rid of it. It was a bad batch. They were practically giving it away, and of course Shelagh loved a bargain. It had been all over the press, warning young people to keep away from it as it was laced with rat poison and LSD. The body count was three but the casualties many more. Stephen knew nothing about this and thought he was taking the good stuff. As there was no one or nothing in his car now he dismissed it uneasily. He'd denied it was anything to worry about, and carried on to the old shore to get rid of Shelagh's body once and for all.

Michael and Carl were just getting their stuff together, they'd talked long into the night after Maisie had gone. Now it was getting late or really early, so they decided to go and wake Gez up. That's the way to interrogate your enemies, the police did it after all. They busted your door down in the early hours scaring you shitless and asking you questions while you were half asleep. 'What about Aunty Cathy Mick? Won't she start screaming about telling our Ma and all that?' Carl asked. 'She'll call us bullies, whinge to Mother dearest on the phone. Then forget when she gets pissed tonight on one of our bottles of vodka.' Michael replied. 'Don't worry we'll scare Gez so much he'll piss his pants but we won't actually cut off his fucking dick even though I'd like to. Maybe one of his balls for the dogs would do.' Michael chuckled as he said it. Carl laughed out loud, brashly as his adrenalin was kicking in. This is how he psyched himself up for the kill. A few lines of decent coke helped too.
They ran down the stairs and as they got to the door, Pete was there lurking. 'What's going on lads?' he asked.
'Nowt for you to worry yourself over Petey baby' replied Carl laughing. Pete felt his anger spike and clenched his teeth. Carl didn't notice but Michael did, and made a mental note to keep his eye on Pete. They knew someone close to them was giving out information and he knew that Pete thought he was his best mate, even brother. His anger was making him act like a dick. He didn't even bother to hide how jealous he was of Carl and him when they were together. He shook his head in disgust, and tried one more little experiment. He threw his keys at Pete, he didn't see them coming and they hit him hard on the arm. 'Do us a favour mate, lock up for us when the lads leave.' Carl burst out laughing, and said 'Goal! Right on target there bro. Next time aim for the head.' Pete had to struggle to keep calm, his teeth and jaw clenched together so tight it hurt his head. Michael saw the vein sticking out on his forehead and now knew in his heart that Pete was almost certainly behind the lies and gossip going round. His days were numbered but he would deal with him after he'd dealt with Gez. He almost felt ashamed, as it was his mate, and ultimately he felt responsible. Hey maybe it was all bollocks and it was just in his head. He was sure he'd find out one way or another.
They drove quickly to the Estate but not so fast they'd get pulled over. They lucked out as it happened because it was really quiet. They left the

car on the outside of a railway crossing and legged it to Gez's house. When they got there they saw his light was on and his mums' room was in darkness. 'Good boy Gez, we can see you nice and clear now. Let's not kick the door in, just let ourselves in quietly' Michael whispered. 'Good idea.' Carl replied. Michael kicked over a dying plant in a bucket and retrieved the key they kept there. He let himself in and Carl followed. They were hit by a foul smell; the hall carpet was sticky and covered in burns and cigarette butts. They headed up the stairs, and saw the light coming from under the door. 'That's his I hope.' Michael said and Carl nodded. Michael put his hand on the handle and swung the

door open. The scene that greeted them was Gez lying naked on the bed dick in hand masturbating over a porn film silently running on his VCR.

'Aaargggh!' screamed Gez, while the brothers just stood there horrified at the sight but not that shocked. 'We always said you were a wanker Gez, now we have the proof.' Carl commented. Michael wanted to laugh, but bit his tongue in case Gez had any misconceptions that it was friendly banter.

Gez put his hands over his penis and struggled to get up off the bed. Carl grabbed a disgustingly dirty striped dressing gown and threw it at him. 'Put that on now!' He snarled. His hands felt greasy and he felt sick, he looked at them and they looked clean but he imagined he had dirt under his nails. He felt bile rising in his throat. Gez's face was ashen. He sat on the bed and gripped the filthy gown shut as there was no belt or buttons. He knew for sure now that his cousins had heard he'd been slagging them off. Either that or probably about him dealing. He wasn't as frightened as he should be, at this point, as he knew they were family. His thoughts ran away with him and he thought he was probably going to get a telling off. Plus they'd fine him and it would cost him a few quid. He had plenty which he'd dossed away over the years. He'd stolen off his mother, taken off Michael and Carl. In actual fact he'd even gone through a phase taking it off the homeless when they slept in the entry at the back of Lime Street Station. That was his level of bullying. Pick on not only the most vulnerable but concentrated on the weakest ones. He didn't care about anyone but himself, and now he was in the shit big time and there was no one he could ask for help. He couldn't say about Pete, because he'd kill him no bother or torture him. Stephen Bentley wouldn't help him, as he was a real psycho. He was too worried to think about anything rationally. 'Aw come on lads, we're family do you want a cuppa?' Gez remarked trying to sound more confident than he felt. Michael and Carl looked at the disgusting room and looked at Gez in disbelief. 'It's okay I'll wash the cups in boiling water like.' He said his voice draining away. Carl did one of his most false and sinister smiles to him. 'Come 'ed lad get your clothes on, we're taking you for a little drive. Don't even think of waking your Mum up, it'll be worse for you if you do.' Gez started to panic thinking of a way out, but apart from a boarded up window and the door where Michael stood, he had no chance. He took a sigh to calm his nerves and grabbed his pants and a grubby t-shirt. Nearly falling sideways as he put one leg in his jeans he dressed quickly and put on trainers without socks. Carl and Michael averted their eyes, but still kept him in their peripheral vision.

They both thought the same thing the little weasel might decide to hide a weapon like a knife in his pants. Gez couldn't think straight he was so frightened. His fear had raised several notches when he knew they were taking him for a drive. He'd felt okay in the house but now he didn't know what to do. 'Eh lads why do we need to go out? Come on we can talk about this here. I know you're pissed off about me dealing a bit on the side but I've kept loads of the money in case you ever needed it.'

Carl winked at Michael none too discretely and said 'Aw eh that's great, but we need to discuss other things as well. If you want to give us a bit of cash now great, but it really isn't going to make that much difference. Anyway Aunty Cathy will need it for the funeral expenses won't she?' Gez went dizzy with fear and adrenalin and made a mad rush for the door. Michael caught him easily and grabbing him by the throat pushed him so he fell into Carl. Pinching his ear hard he said 'Fuck off you little shit, and try that again and we'll do what we're going to do to you here. A nice surprise for your ma to find.' Carl smiled sinisterly. Gez didn't know if they meant it or not. He just resigned himself to getting the beating or whatever was going to happen over and done with. He felt a tiny bit of hope then, maybe it was just a wind up about killing him.
They walked quietly down the stairs and out the house, back to the train tracks, and put Gez in the back seat like you would an errant child. Then they put the child locks on, just in case he had any more ideas of escape. 'Where do you want to go Mikey?' asked Carl. Michael pretended to put a great deal of thought into it said 'I know we'll go to the woods for a big surprise!' Carl grinned at his joke, and pulled out of the road towards the woods.

Chapter 18

Stephen was now on New Chester Road, nearing Rock Ferry. There were the other beaches such as Meols, Holyoake, and West Kirby, much closer to his house. They were more open and well lit, and had been well cared for by the locals. There was a good chance of being seen. Rock Ferry was different especially at this time, it was deadly quiet the only chance earlier of attracting attention would have been the odd courting couple. However as it was pretty chilly he doubted anyone would be around. He drove past Cammell Lairds, and down New Chester Road and carried on until he reached the shore. It was ideal here; it was by a row of big houses called the Esplanade, and the once famous Rock Park. He parked his car down the ramp to the actual beach and sat quietly after switching his engine off and waited to see if there was any sign of life. He sat quietly in the car looking at the famous skyline of Liverpool. The Liver buildings as proud as ever had been cleaned in the 1980s. They looked amazing when they were lit up at night thought Stephen as he stared at black water starting to get close to the shore. He was pleased his plan was going so well especially as the tide was coming in. He could carry the body onto the sand and leave it there to be washed out. His timing was impeccable and it just served to make him think that his good luck was down to something supernatural. He heard a voice clearly say ' the devil looks after his own.' It made him jump and woke him up from his stupor. He got out of the car, opened the boot and lifted Shelagh's lifeless body out with its shroud of bin bags, and carried her out to where the tide was rushing in. He got back into his car and was pleased that it was so dark on the actual beach that you couldn't see his handiwork, and as long as the tide came in quickly, he'd be okay. Reversing quietly up the ramp he turned out and skilfully manoeuvred onto the main road, and headed back home to clean up the rest of the evidence.

Gez was quietly snivelling on the back seat, as Carl slowed the car down, and they came to the outside of Woolton Woods. 'Beautiful here Gez, you know very quiet and peaceful.' Michael commented and then added 'we'll have to keep it down you know we don't want to scare any of the local wildlife. Anyway let's get out now and go for a walk.' They both opened their doors and stepped out, Michael clicked his key fob and the back doors opened. They grabbed Gez out of the back no longer worried about being seen, as it was deserted. Holding his arms either side they marched him into the woods, Michael used a pencil torch to guide them. As they reached a big Oak tree they stopped underneath it and Michael carried on. When he came back he had a metal box, wrapped in plastic.

'All our kit Gez, do you want to see?' Gez just shook his head, trembling in the dark. Michael unwrapped and opened the box. He pulled out a camping lamp, and put it on. 'There you go now let's put some light on the subject.' He pulled out a 12 gauge double barrelled shotgun, and a box of shells. 'Now then Gez we need to know exactly what you've been saying about us, how much money you owe us, and who are you talking to when TJ's men come to visit?' Gez chose this moment to lose control of his bowels.

'Ah for fucks sake! He's shit himself' said Michael grimacing. 'That's rank. God you'll have to shoot him Carl, I'm not getting near that.' Gez sobbed quietly in the shadows, frightened all the more by the sinister shapes of the dark trees because to Gez as they moved and whispered they were telling their secret messages about all the horror they'd seen, and had yet to see.

Stephen let himself in his house, suddenly dreading what he had to do as the events of the night caught up with him. This worried him as usually he didn't mind as he enjoyed reliving it, but then it was nearly all work, and again he felt resentment that he hadn't had the chance to enjoy her and had had to do the boring bit straight away. So that was it he thought feeling relief, then he cheered up even more when he remembered he still had Shelagh's coke. 'That'll do nicely to take care of the tiredness' he said out loud. As he walked in he got stripped off, removed all his clothes, he didn't want his new stuff ruined, and got his cleaning kit out. He looked at the blood and drying bleach, and felt nothing except irritated, then shrugged and started to do the job. After he had cleaned it up and filled a bin bag, he wondered what would be best to do. Burn it or dump it. The police were getting better and better now with forensics, there was progress with D.N.A and blood spatter that type of thing. Stephen found forensics fascinating, and kept his hand in, checking what research papers were available on the web. Sometimes it took hours to download but he didn't care, the knowledge was worth it. He had a top of the range IBM computer with Windows 98 before it was released everywhere and a half of a gig hard drive and 64 mg of memory, with a modem. He'd have to be careful though as some of the stuff he stored on it wasn't legal, his own stuff definitely incriminating. It wasn't password protected, as he had a floppy disk with a virus on that would wipe the hard drive in a minute, so it would slow the whole process down if he had to log in and put in a password. A bouncer he almost liked had given the disc to him. He was called Jay or Jason or something and Stephen knew that he also liked women in the same special way that he did, but he hadn't killed anyone yet. He had badly maimed an ex girlfriend. She'd got thousands in criminal injuries, and that had really angered him. That had put Stephen off him, as he couldn't control his anger over her and wouldn't let it go. It was a pity because he had real potential. What was his name Stephen mused, it come to him suddenly, Jake Stephens, he was glad he'd remembered him. When he took over TJs business he would ask him if he wanted to work for him. He could come in handy. He was processing all this when he saw a flash in his mirror as he passed it in the hall. He put it down to the lights in the corner of his eye. Then he saw it again. He jumped out of his skin as Shelagh Moffat waved to him and, behind her, smiling, was a thing that looked like Sara. They disappeared as fast as they had popped up. It was so real that Stephen checked the mirror thoroughly, and eventually managed to push the fear it was causing away, using a mantra he'd made up. He sang it to himself and the silence 'they can't harm me, the devil is my master, they are not real, I am so much faster, they can't harm me.' He knew it didn't make much sense, but it had stopped the crawling tarantulas of fear that wrapped themselves around his spine. He decided to have a drink and some more coke, little knowing the more he took the stronger the hallucinations would be, due to the ecstasy and LSD this batch was laced with.

Chapter 19

Maisie had been dropped off by Ginger Phil, and let herself quietly in. She crept into the bedroom and saw that Linda was asleep. Undressing in the dark she quickly slipped into bed and put her arm around her. Linda stirred and moaned. Maisie felt herself becoming aroused as she thought of the little tart Tiffany. Plus the warmth and comfortable familiarity of her long term partner and the security of their beautiful big bed, added to her feelings, which were altogether pleasant. She felt really horny but didn't want to wake Linda up and seduce her whilst thinking of Tiffany. It was disrespectful and she always thought that she made love to Linda opposed to the likes of Tiffany where it was just sex. Well it would be if she could persuade her. Her eyes finally closed and she let out a sigh, it had been months since her and Linda had done anything, no wonder she had to play around. Linda meanwhile waited patiently until Maisie's breathing slowed and then opened her eyes, having been awake all the time. Her brain was racing because she had to go to the hospital tomorrow and was still having trouble thinking of anything else. She couldn't cancel yet another appointment, she had to get the results about the lumps she'd found in her breast weeks ago. The hospital kept ringing and sending her letters, so she knew she had to face up to it. She'd hidden herself after the biopsy, making sure she wasn't seen topless. She couldn't feel sexy at all now, she knew Maisie so well, felt her heat when she'd gotten into bed.

Even despite the affairs and Maisie taking her for granted, she wished perhaps for the last time ever she could just turn over and make love. Just to feel normal. However the thoughts she'd buried for so long of being use, hurt and humiliated had finally caught up with her. Plus she didn't have the energy, so tried her best to stay still until Maisie was in deep sleep. A horrible thought went through her head, and lodged there. She realised she didn't want to make love with Maisie because she just didn't fancy her anymore. The affairs made her really angry. She had been so passive and forgiving, just to keep the peace. Maisie moved over and held her tightly burying her face into back of her neck, even in her sleep she was possessive. She wondered what Maisie would do without her? She knew that contrary to what people thought, she Linda was often the strongest one. She gently put out her bum and pushed Maisie away from her, she felt trapped and annoyed at her being so close. Also she didn't want her to touch her breasts which were extremely tender.

She eventually fell into an uncomfortable sleep, and it felt like an hour later when it was in fact four, so she groggily dragged herself out of bed. Maisie was still fast asleep and Linda didn't want her to wake up, and find out what was going on. The last thing she needed while she was feeling nervous about getting her results was a Maisie panic. Her screaming, stamping and throwing things were annoying at the best of times. She always put herself first and sadly she always would. What she needed was calm and kind, not someone turning her potentially fatal cancer into an excuse for a brat fit. So she shut the door quietly on their ensuite bathroom and turned on the shower. It had warmed straight away and she gratefully stripped off and stepped under the soothing torrents. She wanted to get out and not have to explain anything. Maybe she'd tell her later when they could sit down alone. After getting dressed in the bathroom she went to her jewellery box and took out her gold and diamond bracelet and hid it in her pocket. Then she went out into the room and wrote a quick note on their message board. '***Lost my gold and diamond bracelet at the club, it's been handed in, so going to get it, didn't want to tell you in case you were angry with me. Love L x***' She checked Maisie and she was still out cold, much to her relief. She grabbed her shoes so not to make any more noise she practically flew down the stairs, and stepped out into the bright sunlight. She put on her shoes and walked to the corner and went into the local café. As she walked in the girls Bev and Alicia who worked there, shouted hello. Linda smiled and asked for a milky coffee to go, and could they ring her taxi. As Bev's boyfriend had started the taxi firm a year ago with his business partner Joe she was always pleased when Linda used them. As everyone local knew Maisie and Linda. Being associated with them was good for business. 'Going anywhere nice Linds?' asked Bev, desperately making out to the customers that they were good friends. 'Not today Bev and I want to ask you a favour.' She said lowering her voice. 'Don't mention to my other half that you've seen me please. If she comes in asking.' Bev was ecstatic now convinced she had just become Linda's new confidant. 'No of course not Linda your secret is safe with me.' She said grinning like a fool. 'Cheers gorgeous, thanks for that.' And Linda gave her a sexy wink. Bev blushed the colour of beetroot and was secretly even more thrilled that she might be fancied by someone as important and powerful as Linda. It didn't matter to her that she didn't have a gay bone in her body. She liked Linda, but Maisie got on her nerves but she would never admit that to anyone but her fellah. Just had to make sure she didn't slip up and tell anyone that Linda had been in the café and confided in her. God it was so hard, she wanted to boast to the customers, and she'd have to tell Alicia to keep her mouth shut too. She heard Linda say to the driver where she was going as she was holding the door. She felt immediately anxious as it was a reminder that she'd been in the Liverpool Royal Hospital, herself with a cancer scare. The whole experience had been beyond awful. Then she had a funny feeling that Linda was dealing with something awful like that on her own. Why would she keep it secret from Maisie? Linda was a lovely person, Maisie was mad to play around behind her back. Everyone knew what she was like. With her expensive clothes, and flash jewellery and being driven round in her big cars by gangsters. Well no matter how tough, flash and independent she liked to portray herself, she wouldn't be the big I am without Linda. She was loved by everyone, apart from being beautiful, she was kind and generous. It was such a pity Maisie didn't see how fucking lucky she was to have her. She probably would when it was too late, Bev thought to herself. She was suddenly snapped out of her daydream by Alicia shouting 'Oi sleepy knickers, a little help please.' People laughed and Bev laughed along with them. She shouted her apologies sarcastically for leaving her for five whole minutes and walked over to the chaos of the kitchen, Linda and Maisie temporarily forgotten.

Linda wasn't enjoying the taxi ride, she was tightly wound and worried and could have done with someone to hold her hand. The taxi driver Joe was trying desperately to engage her into conversation, and she just couldn't do it. She kept playing with her coffee cup taking tiny sips through the hole in the lid. She'd known him for years, a nice bloke and well and truly divorced, his wife had cheated on him for years according to the rumour mill. Why had she remembered he was divorced? She was still lost in thought as they arrived at the hospital; Linda reached into her pocket to give him a tenner and told him to keep the change when it was only a couple of pounds.

However he told her it was on the house. She threw the money at him and told him to take it as a tip. As she got to the hospital entrance she felt her knees go weak and start to give way. Joe was pulling out of the car park when he saw her fall. Slamming on the breaks and putting on his hazard lights he leapt out of the car and ran over to her. Already people were gathering to see if she was okay. Joe got there and she was grateful to see an almost familiar face, feeling like a freak show with people gawping at her.

He knelt down and put his arms around her protectively, and for the first time in her adult life she actually felt a stirring of something she hadn't felt since her teens. She fancied him, a man! Her last involvement with a male in any way romantic had been a crush on an effeminate boy who had been a Goth. When she went to the gay clubs with him, she felt at home, and that only served to convince her she was, if not gay certainly differently wired to other women. Then Maisie had come into her life, and that was that.

She had occasionally when subconsciously eyeing up a man, thought she was bisexual but had only broached the subject once. Maisie held the view that if you were bisexual you were somehow greedy and kinky and just liked sex with anyone. She didn't agree but kept her mouth shut as it was easier than listening to one of Maisies tirades. Joe in the meantime had helped her to her feet and then picked her up, and carried her into the reception of the hospital. She pretended to object but was grateful as the situation gave her time to get herself together. He shouted a nurse who was passing, and told her how Linda had collapsed outside. The nurse ran off and returned with a wheelchair and told Joe to put her in. Linda was struggling as the emotions ran through her. She told herself she only felt all this because Maisie as usual wasn't there to support her. Joe had made her feel safe because he was so big and had rushed to help her. Then she laughed at herself Maisie wasn't there because she'd hidden it from her. God what was wrong with her, a few lumps in her breast and she'd changed into a heterosexual lunatic?

She laughed out loud at that thought, and Joe standing by her looked at her in a bemused way. 'Did you bump your head queen?' he asked. 'No you cheeky sod. I was just thinking about your face.' Joe grinned at this and retorted 'Are you sure you weren't looking in a mirror.' They both burst out laughing.

The nurse who had been to get a clipboard came over and asked 'How are you feeling now love? Will your husband be staying with you for your assessment?' Both Linda and Joe blushed at this remark and smirked like kids. Linda grasping her last bit of self control took a deep breath and explained that she was due for an appointment. She'd just had the wobbles with nerves and she was feeling okay now.

'Oh okay, give me your name and we'll see where you have to go.' replied the nurse. 'But you have to stay in the chair just in case, perhaps your big strong fellah can push you around.' Joe had never been more conscious of his six foot five frame or the fact he hadn't shaved and had on his jeans with holes in. He knew who Linda was, he knew about her and Maisie but he was sure she had flirted with him? She was a lovely woman who people always spoke highly of. It was never going to happen so he just smiled. Linda watched Joe and she could almost see the thoughts flitting across his face. She noticed not for the first time how good looking he was and best of all he didn't seem aware of it. He was acting awkwardly and didn't know what to do next. One good thing had come out of this, it had taken her mind off the appointment and her test results but now it was time to face it. Joe asked if she'd be okay as he had to move the car.

The nurse came back as he was about to leave and said 'Come on Linda time for your appointment it's just along here at the Oncology Department. Come on hubby you can push her.' Joe grimaced when he heard where her appointment was, and although Linda told him quietly it was okay for him to go he grabbed the handles and pushed her down the corridor. She decided to go in on her own. She felt too exposed and vulnerable so Joe reluctantly went to sort out the car and make sure he hadn't been clamped. He kissed her on the cheek and told her he'd wait for her. She felt wobbly again at the thought of what she was about to learn. Well here we go she thought this is it. Time to fly or time to die.

Chapter 20

Gez was coming round and found he could hardly move. Pain ran through his entire body. He couldn't see, he didn't know if he was blind or if it was just dark, he was so disorientated. One thing though he was alive, just. He felt motion in the claustrophobic space, and realised he was in a car boot. It all started to come back now, the Moffats turning up, the trip to the woods. 'Oh God' he mumbled out loud as he remembered, he had shit himself, even before they had done anything to him. The shame of that was bad enough he thought. That's before they'd tortured him, and got out all his secrets, the pain just wasn't worth it. He'd told them about Stephen Bentley and how he'd supplied the heroin to sell, how he'd asked him to find out information for TJ. Then when Gez thought they had finally stopped and he had taken the worst beating of his life, but had survived, frigging Michael spoilt it and asked about Pete. He'd tried to deny it but when Michael had eventually put a gun in his mouth. Then Carl had gone on and on about how he was going to make his death look like a suicide, he'd given Pete up. He owed him nothing as he was a slimy twat even worse than him. It was a huge betrayal as he'd been friends with Michael since they were at primary school together. Gez had always been on the outside of their little gang, his horrible fucking mother was to blame, as they always took the piss out of his clothes and his trainers. She had always been a cheap skate when it came to him and his clothes, getting knock off even when she had plenty of money, always carrying on with some rich married bloke. She was always covered in real designer clothes and some serious bling.

Then when the looks had started to fade she'd carried on with the men but not so rich or nice. Aunty Shelagh was even worse, a terrible mother who'd sold her daughter to the highest bidder. Pair of bitches he hoped they would die horrible deaths alone and scared. He was lost in thoughts of revenge on all of them when the car stopped. Oh God what now he thought? It was bright when they opened the boot, blindingly so, at least he could still see through his swollen eyes. He heard Michael say to Carl 'Grab him by the feet I'll get the top end.' To which Carl replied 'Why should I go nearer the shit? Who put me on brain detail? He said misquoting Jules from Pulp Fiction. 'You get him.'

'Oh stop it you puff' Michael laughed 'Come here I'll do it.' They lifted him out and dropped him on a piece of sheeting on the floor. They were in an underground garage by the looks of it, Gez just lay there not knowing what to expect or what was coming next. He looked up and Michael was coming towards him with a big Bowie knife. He flinched as he bent over him and cut the ropes that were binding his wrists and ankles. 'Right here's an old track suit, get yourself cleaned up there's a sink and lots of soap through there. We will have a chat when you no longer smell of shit okay?' Michael said in a no nonsense tone. Gez tried to get up but struggled. Michael held out his hand and Gez grabbed it, and he pulled him to his feet. He was suspicious waiting for the punch or slap to come. It didn't so he hobbled over to where the cleaners sink was and cleaned himself up with lots of blue paper towels and soap. He came back into the garage and sat shakily down on old chair. There was a packet of cigs and a lighter and he lit one greedily sucking in the smoke even though it made him cough and his ribs hurt. He noticed a can of coke and some tablets and he took a look at the bottle. Seeing it was dihydracodeine, he took four and swigged a huge gulp of coke. Michael said 'now you're ready so listen to us.'

'Me and Carl have decided that instead of killing you, now you have told us all we wanted to know that you can work for us. You can carry on meeting with Pete and Stephen, but you will tell them what we tell you to say. You can even deal but through us, and no smack, but you can keep the profit as payment.' Gez felt ridiculously grateful, he started to cry and Carl and Michael turned their backs while he sorted himself out.

'You understand this though, family or not, we could have killed you tonight in the woods and not one solitary person on the planet except for your ma would give a shit. So you need to start mending your ways. If we find out you have betrayed us again we will kill you. There are no second chances. Are you clear Gez?' Carl was the one that had spoken, usually it was Michael. It somehow made it far more sinister, so he nodded his agreement. 'Can't hear you Gez.' said Carl. 'Thanks guys, you can rely on me, I promise.' His usual snivelling tone was gone as he replied. Both Moffats noticed the change in his voice, and hoped that their plan had worked. Even after all he'd gone through, the fear, the beating and being tied up in a boot, he still felt ridiculously grateful to be alive and able to work for his cousins. The resentment was being replaced albeit grudgingly by respect. He thought that he had come close to losing his life. But knew for sure that if Pete or Stephen and especially TJ would kill him or put him in a wheelchair if he had tried to do the same to them. Now because of his double dealing, he had to do it to them anyway. He still felt safer because he was on the Moffats side and they would protect him if he proved himself to them.

Michael watched him with interest then he said 'you're free to go now, we will be in touch. Oh and one last thing. Tidy that fucking dump up. Use the money you've saved, that you owe us. Get it cleaned and get some new furniture. Pay for Aunty Cath to go to Blackpool with the girls or something and sort it. Gez no family of ours is going to live in a stinking pit.' He threw all his old stuff in a bin bag tied it up and put it in the bin as he left the lock up. He knew where he was now and he began his long walk home, the final test.

Stephen had cleaned up his mess, he was dog tired. He heard his phone ring and looked at the screen. It was TJ, and for once he genuinely didn't give a shit. He switched it off, and decided he was going to bed. He stopped on the stairs and looked down at this kingdom from a distance, it looked fine. You really couldn't tell a murder had happened here he thought with a weird smile on his face. It would do for now. It was clean he'd disposed of all the crap left over and burnt it in the garden. He switched off the light, now tired and smelling of smoke, a little paranoid from taking coke all night and with his teeth grinding he walked up the stairs. His jaw swinging wildly as the amphetamine still coursed through his veins. He looked forward to reliving the excitement of the night, oh God when the knife went in, that was how he made love, better than using his dick any day. For all his playing that was still his favourite part. Sara was to blame he'd never been so aroused when he stabbed her. Maybe he would do a random attack and do it quick.

He could go on a day trip to London where all the runaways gathered. It was a quick fix he could enjoy and better still could do it outside of his domain. It wouldn't be his mess to clean as long as he took gloves and things with him. He undressed and flopped down on the bed, lost in old fantasies and new dreams of his very special kind of love. As he felt himself growing hard, he decided to masturbate if he could. It was easy and he was surprised at how quickly he'd come. He then fell into a fitful sleep, despite the coke, and his dreams were strange and frightening. They were about all the women he'd hurt, loved and murdered in cold blood.

Linda had been told the results. It wasn't great but it wasn't as bad as she'd been dreading. Joe a man she had sort of known for years but hardly spoken to, had been there supporting her all the way. She was glad he hadn't come in because she'd done a victory punch and felt a bit stupid. The doctor who told her the results just grinned and assured her there wasn't much that could surprise him in this world anymore. She was so mixed up, she sort of still felt something for Maisie, she had been sure she was mostly gay and perhaps a bisexual but mainly into women, and now this. She'd felt so safe with him, and turned on when he'd picked her up and carried her! God she'd known prostitutes, housewives, business women who'd all stayed with their husbands for years, brought up the kids then, followed their hearts or sometimes their loins. They had left their men and gone to the other side, and been happy too.

What would it be like to do it the other way round? It was certainly unusual and she couldn't think of a single example. Everything about him had been right, his smell was amazing, his blue eyes, the stubble on his chin, and she'd ached to touch it. He'd was out of breath as he'd run all the way back to make sure he was there for her when she came out of the consultation room. Her eyes were red from crying more with relief than anything else. He was really concerned so she explained what the findings were.

There were cancerous lumps in her breasts but thankfully benign, and could be easily removed. She would be left with a bit of scarring but nothing drastic and a plastic surgeon was doing the operation. She didn't even have to take money out of the accounts now and pay for it without Maisie knowing. The good old N.H.S was doing it all for her. She decided she would make an anonymous and decent sized donation to Alder Hey Children's hospital to show her gratitude.

She was so grateful to be alive and relatively okay she had hugged Joe hard and he'd held her tight his eyes filling up at her news. Guiltily, she thought that best of all I don't have to tell Maisie. Her feeling bad was short lived as she remembered Maisies last affair when the girl Tracey had turned up pissed out of her head at the club shouting about it for everyone to hear. One of the members of staff, a bitchy bitter girl called Nikita had switched the music off so everyone could hear the sordid details. Tracey had walked up to Linda and screamed in her face. 'Oh my God look at you, you're nothing compared to me, I'm fucking gorgeous you're getting old. Let Maisie go she deserves someone like me.' She'd felt humiliated and hurt, but had as usual retained her dignity and walked off, head held high ignoring Maisies pleas to forgive her. She had walked behind the bar and pretended to leave through the kitchen, but stood back in the shadows to watch the fun. Tracey had run up to Maisie and tried to hug her, crying and then shouting 'We're free now to be together now the truth is out. The stupid cow's gone at last.' Maisie was so angry she could barely talk through her gritted teeth. She took a deep breath and spat in Tracey's face, and punched her hard, quick and with vicious accuracy. Tracey fell backwards to the floor. Maisie straddled her and pinned her down. Whatever she whispered into Tracey's ear made her struggle to throw her off, and when Maisie allowed her to get up, she looked haunted. She didn't say a word, just rolled over, got to her feet, and ran as fast as she could. Even when Jojo tripped her up and she fell hard snapping her wrist, it didn't slow her down she was so frightened. Then it came to Nikita's turn she was slapped hard by Maisie, frightened half to death by Phil and then thrown out by two big bouncers, none too gently.

Linda had known in her heart that she and Maisie had finished a long time ago, but had clung onto each other, as they were best mates apart from anything else. But she realised with her renewed vigour for life and with total joy that she could still feel passionate, loving and even sexy again. Feelings she'd damped down for years at Maisies side. So when Joe took her towards home she said she wanted to go into town.

He did a U turn in the road, and pulled over. Joe looked at her in the mirror and said 'I'm only a phone call away here's my private number for you,' and passed her his card over his shoulder. Then got out to open the door for her, ever the gentleman. Joe had dropped her in front of Lime Street Station and as there was no parking, and although he should hurry up, he stood frozen holding the door not knowing quite what to do next. Linda was bemused by his confusion so trying to reassure him for the kindness he had shown her, she hugged him. She stood on her tip toes so she could whisper in his ear. Joe shuddered as he felt her warm breath on his neck.

'I will ring you very soon, and we can meet up if you would like.' Joe just nodded dumbly and waved goodbye as she walked through the big train station to London Road. Then went and bought a new mobile phone from T.J. Hughes knowing for sure she was going to get in touch with him soon.

Carl and Michael went back to the flat, needing home again, they'd discussed the situation with Pete over and over on the drive home, but Michael had insisted it was his problem. Carl said he was there when he needed him, and when he was ready it should be known without saying he had his back. They were both dog tired so they went into their separate rooms, and got ready to crash out. 'Night Carl, I'm knackered from beating the crap out of Gez.' Carl lying on his bed already in just his boxers laughed out loud. 'Yeah know what you mean, night night John Boy.' He shouted through and closed his eyes, and was soon asleep. Michael lay there looking at the ceiling even not finding sleep as easily as his brother. His thoughts only with Pete, his mate since they were in junior school together. He was sick to his soul with the betrayal but tried not to show it. It was his problem, and he had to deal with it. At least Carl knew now and was pretty good about it, he hadn't made any snide comments or teased him. Michael hated that he was really hurt but couldn't show it. He closed his eyes and eventually slept fitfully.

When they woke up it was really late, so they ran round getting ready to go to the house and sort out their business. Carl was drying his hair in the bathroom, when Michael put his head in. 'Eh just had a thought. Where do you reckon mummy dearest is? She'd have been round on the scav by now wouldn't she? Or sent loads of texts, or bothered Kay, or got in some mess or other.' He said in a sing song voice. His brothers' words didn't bother him, he knew she was a walking disaster when she was on her own for a bit. Then it came to him, someone had seen her getting in a car outside Fat Fi's. She'd be alright if she was off with some bloke for a few days. 'Oi Mike don't worry lad, she's with someone from round here. They know who she is.' 'Not worried bro, just curious that's all I know we don't' see her for ages at a time, but usually when she's made contact she's around for a few weeks bleeding us dry. Usually until something better comes along, like one of the old knob heads on the estate. something's not right and I can't put my finger on it. It could be that card some prick left at Sara's memorial, and then Ma having one in her bag, who has the guts to do that?' Michael chewed on his nail as he thought it through. 'Well Gez's kept his mouth shut that's for sure or we would have Aunty Cath round on the warpath' smiled Carl. 'You know what you're right that's what it must be. I'm expecting a load of crap off the old slappers! God Shelagh and Cath together. Now there's a nightmare in the making. It's the peace and quiet making me jumpy, we'll ask next door, Kay is like the Oracle she knows everything and everyone, and all their business.' Michael stopped talking and took a breath.

'Okay mate calm down!' Carl laughed 'you're going to have an embolism if you carry on. It'll be okay we'll sort this out once and for all.' He added jokingly 'so get your make up and your knickers on and let's rock!'

Chapter 21

As he sat behind his huge desk, TJ realised how angry he was and it was all down to fucking Bentley and the stupid bastard Moffats. Ha! Bunch of dickheads, he'd deal with them soon enough. He knew how to play the long game that was another of his successful strategies. He'd tried so many times to get hold of Stephen and although he knew how insane he was, not once did it occur to him that something might have happened to him whilst doing his dirty work. His paranoia made him think that the minute no one did his bidding when he clicked his fingers that they might have turned on him. He watched Rodney who was hanging round like a big dickhead, sulking over some tart called Tiffany, and getting on his fucking nerves. 'For God's sake Rod go and either talk to the girl get her back or go back to your friggin' wife but stop stomping round here moaning about it.' TJ snapped. Rodney looked at him all hurt eyes and then to his surprise saw the glint of anger there. He was one of his only allies, and the nearest thing he'd had to a best mate while he was building his reputation and he was loyal, the years had proved that. It was because of mad bastards like him, he'd gotten away with murder and intimidation for so long. So he decided to put it right and said, 'alright mate I'm sorry, but don't tell anyone I said that. You're just doing my head in. Go and see her, have the rest of the day off, I'll be alright. TJ just wanted him to go now, he'd been angry at Stephen not him. Rodney brightened up and said 'Ta Boss I'll go now and sort it out once and for all eh?' He decided he'd go and straighten himself out while the wife was at her mothers. Then he'd go and see Tiffany and find out what she was up to. He'd forgotten how angry she'd made him when she pretended not to be in, and it never occurred to him that she may not want to see him again.

He had treated her like a possession like a lot of men in their fifties and sixties. They were the last true bastion of sexism on a wider scale. To Rodney, TJ and their ilk, their wives and girlfriends were property nothing more, and they expected the best of both worlds. The mistress was someone to shag and stick on their arms while they were out. The wife at home was also expected to look good, bring up immaculate children and clean and cook every day. In Rodney's world it used to be If the wife wanted to work she'd get a good slap, and then have anything from fifty to a couple of thousand quid slapped in her hand as a way of saying sorry. It was expected that she go and treat her and the kids and that was the end of it. That's how it was with the wife even in the 1990s. These new women like Tiffany could be a fucking nightmare, all attitude and if you raised a hand most of them well they'd fight back or get the police. He felt a twitch in his trousers, God he'd missed Tiffany alright, so beautiful, young and defiant but best of all so fucking sexy.

Maisie woke up and felt like a parrot had crapped in her mouth. That was the only way to describe it, it tasted rank. She stretched out and no Linda, she had sort of promised she'd take her out today. She must be up already with a hump on. She looked at the time, and it was pretty late. She noticed the note on the message board, and was rubbing her eyes to make sure she'd read it right. Linda had only gone and lost her gold and diamond bracelet the silly cow. She'd tear a strip off her later after all it had cost an arm and a leg, but then she read the rest of the message. Jesus Christ it was a miracle it had been handed in, she'd have to find out who it was and bung them a reward. God the person must be a saint. She thought of all the Scouse women like her who knew their gold better than any jeweller in Boodles. No matter how broke some of the women were, ones she'd known in her life had always had good quality gold necklaces, rings and earrings on, except her mother of course, she'd sold hers for booze eventually. The other women were covered in it, and they'd be buried in it before they'd take it off and sell it. If she'd have found Linda's bracelet when she was younger it would have been pawned within an hour. She started to wake up properly and remembered the Moffats last night, she was made up, lots more money to look forward to, but best of all getting rid of the prick TJ. She'd had enough of him being head man in Liverpool. He was a joke now, and everyone knew it was just a matter of time. Her lads were reasonably loyal, her best mates as well as her crew and she loved them all, but who would drop her if they had a better offer? As she was getting ready she noticed how late it was. Where the fuck was Linda? She usually didn't disappear for this long often unless she'd told her why. She went into the bathroom, and started the shower. As she stepped in she soaped herself and as she washed between her legs she thought of Tiffany, she rubbed herself as she thought of biting her breasts and licking her all over. Lost in these thoughts she climaxed quickly and then she decided she would have to bed the arrogant little cow for real. She had lost interest the other day, but now she wanted her more than ever because Tiffany had sort of rejected her. She would get dressed and try to find out where Linda had been, use her being out for ages as an excuse for an argument, and go and call on Tiffany. Her address was on the application form. She didn't realise how much her imagination was running away with her, her arrogance making it seem easy to seduce Tiff. Oh she'd buy her a gift something expensive that would do it, or if she still played hard to get it would at least get her defences down. She loved the hunt, she really did.

Maybe buy her an antique if she had the time to go and have a look in her favourite shop in Hoylake, on the Wirral Peninsula. She felt a renewed vigour now. It was thinking of Tiffany, she always felt like this when she was chasing a new conquest, and it made her feel alive. She jumped as she heard the slam of the front door, and heard someone coming up the stairs, it sounded like they were stomping their feet. It couldn't be Linda, she didn't normally make this much noise, then she remembered their door wasn't locked. Paranoid now, Maisie ran across the room and grabbed a brass model of the goddess Kali, and waited her heart beating hard in her chest, for the door to open. She lifted it above her head ready to slam it down on anyone who dared to come into her space uninvited. The door swung open and Maisie just stopped herself from braining Linda. She swung the brass icon and managed to make it hit the door instead. 'What the pissing hell is going on?' Screamed Linda 'What on earth are you doing?' Maisie felt her stomach churn at what she had nearly done. 'OH GOD ALMIGHTY!' she shouted 'what the fuck where you doing stomping up the stairs? You never usually make that much noise coming in. I didn't know what to think, woke up you weren't here. Then as I'm getting ready to look for you as you didn't think to ring me, you show up making more noise than King Kong with stilettos' on!' Maisie ran out of steam as she hadn't taken a single breath while shouting at Linda. She threw the goddess on the sofa and bent over and put her hands on her knees while gathering her thoughts. Then did a slow breathing technique she'd learnt when she'd had counselling for anger. She looked up and Linda was glaring at her. 'What is wrong with you?' Maisie snapped 'got nothing to say now?' Linda felt her temper rising, and hotly said 'I've got plenty to say, you nearly smashed my head open, because I happened to stomp up the stairs? I often do that, how come you only noticed now? Do you know why I do it? Just in case you're screwing one of your little tarts up here. So you can at least have a bit of dignity. What is going on Maisie? Why are you so bloody jumpy about me coming in? Is it TJ or have the Moffats sold you out or let you down?' Maisie stared at her taken aback by her newly confident, brusque manner. Then remembering she had her day planned around Tiffany now, she calmed down so she could get away quicker. 'Alright I'm sorry love, forgive me? Come here and give us a kiss.' Maisie cooed trying to look pathetic.

Linda would have normally laughed as part of the game. Not today though, she just wasn't in the mood to play along. 'Look Maisie, I'm not in the mood. I feel shite and am going to bed with a couple of pain killers.' Maisie looked at her then, as if she hardly knew her. 'Did you get your bracelet back then?' she asked. Linda felt a flutter of panic. She had to think where was it, and who could she say handed it in? She decided to bluff it out until she felt her head was working properly. 'Yes it's fine, I've got it back.' She snapped and went into the bedroom. She frantically searched her pockets for the bracelet and felt it in the lining. She made a lot of noise putting it in her jewellery box as Maisie came in. After making sure she'd seen it in her hand she slammed down the lid and then started to get undressed, after grabbing her pyjamas from the cupboard. She crossed her arms and turned her back on Maisie, making it clear she wasn't prepared to get undressed while she was there. Maisie was confused and didn't recognise her normally easy going partner.

'Oh okay' she said 'I won't care about you any more then, I am going OUT!' she stormed out of the bedroom and into the main living area. She was sort of pleased with what had just happened, but Linda's behaviour was definitely unsettling. Oh screw it she thought. This would blow over, and now she could go and try and persuade Tiffany to see things her way. First she'd call Ginger Phil to take her over to the Wirral so she could buy something nice and expensive for both women. She had no worries with time, the shop keeper lived above his little treasure trove and would always open his doors for her. The amount of stuff she bought from him meant she could call in at 3.a.m if she so chose. She loved the power that being rich brought.

Linda got into bed and heard Maisie getting ready then she slammed the door on her way out. Queen Maisie has left the building. She muttered then breathed a sigh of relief and smiled. Giggling a little with nerves and joy she thought of the nonsense she had gone through to cover her tracks, including the bracelet. God she could have just left it where it was, but she knew how Maisie could be. She'd have checked it was missing while she was out, and then interrogated her. If she hadn't been so keen to get to wherever she was going. Whoever more like, her smile waned and she sighed a little sadly. Not so many years ago if Maisie had tried to smash her head in with a brass goddess well then she'd have begged her forgiveness and booked a holiday to somewhere hot. But the way she had dismissed it so easily was the final nail in the coffin.

She had only stomped up the stairs because she was happy about her news and being with Joe. Also she thought Maisie would be out. She could kick herself. She couldn't let Maisie have any inkling what was going on. She knew that when Joe got in touch she would have to see him, she could barely wait. She couldn't believe she felt this way about a man. A MAN! She shouted out loud. It was so enthralling the way the feelings coursed through her body. It was so fast her head spun, but God it felt good. She also knew that she couldn't live the lie anymore with Maisie, and her stomach flipped at the thought. Well tough they were finished; she knew Maisie was either with the next one or chasing her relentlessly. The last one Jill or was it Jane or Gemma oh who cared? It was someone beginning with the J sound. Maisie had sat there pleading with her to give them another chance. She'd heard it so many times in their relationship. Why couldn't Maisie be honest and let her go? For the first time she realised for sure that they didn't have any future at all, even just as friends. She thought about the money in the business. There was plenty, her needs had been few over the years, she'd scrimped and saved as much as Maisie had thrown her share away on drugs, clothes, women and anything that took her fancy. She looked at herself in the mirror. Being brutally honest she was attractive with a few laugh lines and the odd grey hair but for her age she looked okay. She was a little shocked at the woman who looked out at her. Where had the girl and all the years gone? She'd given them totally to Maisie who no longer deserved her love and loyalty. She felt brave and ready to face life on her own, she had secretly thought about it and in the bad times it helped to keep her sane. She just never believed it could or would happen. She lay down thinking about this. Her tummy flipped over every time she thought of him picking her up. She was sure the thoughts going round in her head would keep her awake, but her exhaustion took over. Wonderful fantasies of Joe played before her eyes, now closed, as she drifted off content in her dreams of something better to come.

Chapter 22

Stephen woke up, stretched and then slid out of bed. He felt refreshed and ready to face whatever shit the day may bring. Immediately he thought of Shelagh and "the" situation, but he didn't feel a thing. He thought of TJ and knew he'd pushed his luck by not answering his phone for ages. He went downstairs put on some coffee and went over to his mobile. Twenty eight missed calls he almost laughed, and then he felt really annoyed. What the frigging hell was TJ on? He snarled out loud 'you stupid little shit, get one of your other twats to run round for you.' He went through the call log, and every one of them was from him. His reasonably good mood started to dissipate, and the day he took TJs Empire couldn't come soon enough. He went over and swigged his coffee, and prepared himself to face TJs annoying questions. He had to get it right about Shelagh, he had to prepare his story of lies, and he knew how to do this as long as he wasn't caught on the hoof. The phone vibrated and rang and fell off the counter, smashing on the floor the battery skittered across his laminated floor. He groaned and picked up the dead phone, and messed around putting the battery in. He waited for it to switch on, and when he saw that the new call was from TJ he nearly threw it in the sink, and then imagined smashing the phone on TJs head with a huge lump hammer. He prepared himself and pressed TJs number. He answered straight away not with the expected hello but with 'Where the fucking fuck have you been? What the fuck do I pay you for? I wanted to talk to you about something, and wanted specific information off that tart Shelagh Moffat about her precious sons? Then you tell me you are with her then nothing else, I hope you got some decent information for me?' TJ had been growling without realising it and Stephen could hear his teeth grinding together. He smiled then, his hatred of the man making him immune to any insult the fat bastard cared to share. After all he had so many saved already and was going to enjoy discussing them with TJ one day soon. Him and his torture kit. He may even hog roast the dickhead. Now that would be funny.

He would make him pay before he killed him and took over. 'Yes sorry about that Mr. Murphy. I decided to go and get some food, and I ate it in the car to be honest I wasn't feeling too well after eating it. I did it after I dropped the Moffats mother off, and it was very late, I went to that 24 hour chippy on the Dock Road. Anyway she was boasting a lot about how much the boys were now worth, that they owned at least three properties, probably many more and had lovely posh cars. How they owned all the videos and now DVDs were coming in, they had all them

sorted too. I mean I know it's not much information there, but I got a real gem, apparently they're joining up with Maisie Malone
. They're taking over the dealing in her club, and supplying the ale for her bar, the cheap stuff from France.' He said pinching himself to act like an arse licker and not lose his temper. 'I mean the age of them too, owning all that and having a decent amount of money coming in. You have got to do something soon Mr. Murphy they can't be allowed to get away with it can they?' TJ listened silently then replied now he had calmed down a little as he thought through what Stephen had said. 'Alright, you didn't do bad getting all that from a few hours, and you didn't report back because you were sick. One thing the Maisie Malone union is common knowledge. What I need to know is it real? Anyway it might not have been food poisoning. Are you sure the old bitch didn't make you sick sitting that close to her?' He chuckled then and Stephen knew he'd won again. 'One thing though Stephen, what the fuck is a DVD?'

Stephen smirked at the question. TJ was as ignorant and arrogant as usual and his refusal to learn anything new verified just how fucking past it this idiot was. He then told TJ all he knew. They have amazing clarity and sound and are easy to store. Its stands for Digital Versatile Disc or some say Video. They are exactly the same to look at as a CD, and they will probably bury the video tape. The CD has nearly wiped out vinyl and cassette tapes.' TJ was silent as he took all this in, he wasn't quite as stupid as people thought, but was exceptionally lazy. He was so used to getting others to do everything for him he felt it didn't matter if he didn't take it in. 'Ah I see so we can sort out getting DVDs pirated then in the next few years, and if we do it properly we can take it back from the Moffats if they're still around, which I doubt, as they're too cocky by half.' He said his mood blackening again. Stephen sensed his boss's moods kept changing and were all over the place, and wondered if he was heading for a breakdown. He seemed to skip from one thing to the next, say the same things over and over, and Stephen hoped he really was losing the plot. 'I need you to get over here anyway we have things to discuss now Stephen, and I don't want to do it over the phone. The landline is okay but they can pick you up loud and clear on the mobile.' TJ commented.

Stephen smiled even wider now, relishing his paranoia. 'Okay Mr. Murphy what time do you want me to come?' he said. There was the usual silence TJ and his games, thinking that by making you wait proved how powerful he was. Then after what seemed like an eternity both of them playing a game of chicken. Waiting to see who would give in first. The silence was excruciating for TJ but not for Stephen who was far more qualified to play mind games. TJ eventually gave in and shouted 'NOW!'

Stephen held the phone from his ear after he was nearly deafened by him. For doing that you can wait even longer he thought.

Maisie decided to go straight to Tiffany's after coming back with two beautiful carved ivory Japanese figures. One was a mermaid and one was a Geisha girl and she had bought them in her favourite shop in the Wirral. She had bought them for Linda and for Tiffany of course but she might keep them herself. She played with the little figures caressing them and wasn't sure if she could part with both They were over a hundred years old and therefore perfectly legal. She knew Linda wouldn't touch anything made out of ivory unless it was really ancient. The Land Rover rattled through the Queensway tunnel, it was made for the country roads after all, not going under the Mersey in a tunnel full of fumes. She had bought it for Phil as a present last year and he loved it dearly. So it was used no matter what for. It was a vintage army one. Cheekily purchased from the local police auction. As they made small talk Maisie was planning how to deal with Tiffany. She hoped to try and catch her off guard, always a good way to try and seduce them, when they was at their most vulnerable. She knew Tiffany was a calculating little bitch but God was she sexy. At the moment it didn't matter if she wasn't Mother Theresa or Saint Bob after Live Aid. She just didn't care she wanted to have sex with her not marry her, she told herself repeatedly. She had so much guilt about Linda but because Linda wasn't interested in making love at the moment, she justified her cheating ways. Little did she know that Linda had planned to leave her, such was her belief in her power over her, and she was convinced it would never happen. She turned round to Phil and told him roughly what was happening. He smiled fondly but a little sadly at her and asked. 'Where to boss lady? Have you got her full address or do I have to knock on doors looking for her?' Maisie burst out laughing, giggling she answered 'You cheeky git, you make me sound desperate. Poor Phil, but seeing as though you have done it before for me, I will treat you to the address!'

Phil laughed too 'what are we like eh queen Maisie? You're worse than any bloke I've ever known for the birds.' Maisie punched him on the arm 'Quack quack' she said, 'don't you let any normal woman hear you call them birds. These are the caring

sharing nineties, and just think a new millennium is coming soon, we will have flying cars, and spaceships!' Phil burst out laughing at this and slowed the Land Rover down. 'Oh you are priceless you loon, what drugs are you on tonight? God I nearly crashed me action man jeep!' They both laughed, comfortable with their banter, Maisie read out the address and they headed towards Tiffany's flat. As they pulled up to the front of the high rise block where she lived, she saw Rodney one of TJs men getting out of a taxi, and knew instinctively he was going to Tiffs. He went up to the front and she saw he was waiting for someone to let themselves in so he could get past the front doors. Maisie watched him, and said to Phil, 'look there's that sad bastard Rodney, he used to be someone him didn't he? Now he's just a sad old git, he's only in his forties or early fifties. These days that means nothing but he looks so much older.' Phil remembered that Rodney had got away with murder, a few times in fact. God two he knew for sure, the first was a poor family who burnt to death, leaving only a son who'd been at a mates on a sleep over. Then secondly a young mother in front of her kids. He felt anxious for Maisie but much more for Tiffany so he decided to stay and turned the engine off. 'He may be getting on Maisie my love but do not underestimate that bastard, he's got away with murder and everyone knows it. He didn't do much time for what he did, and some things they just couldn't prove. TJ got him the best brief in the UK and he walked. He only served a fraction of it because of good behaviour. In other words TJ had the judge in his pocket, the whole thing was a fucking joke, so be careful love. I'm going to see you up to your girl's door at least. Anyway he might not be going to Tiffs he may be collecting some money or even going for a score.' Maisie smiled at this but she listened to him, he was on the ball and had her back. Just then a young lad in a hoody approached the flats, he ignored Rodney and went to the intercom and pressed a number, a tinny voice rang out, and the lad spoke into it. Then they heard the buzz, and the lad grabbed the door and went in, Rodney moving fast for his size went in straight after. 'Right that's it' said Maisie 'lets' go in after him and make sure he's not going to do something to Tiffany.' She had had a good idea if she could be seen to protect and stick up for Tiffany she was sure to get her foot in the door at least. This is what made her feel alive the anticipation and pursuit of a sexy younger woman, and especially if they weren't gay. That made her feel like a goddess complete with magical powers when they eventually gave in and she convinced them that she loved them.

Rodney went into the flats and the young hoody looked around at him ready to ask what he was playing at, but thought better of it when he saw the size of him. Even though he was a bit soft round the middle, he was still a formidable character. Rodney approached the lift as the lad disappeared into a ground floor flat. Pressing Tiffs floor he went up muttering under his breath. He had a few too many vodkas on the way here, and the way TJ had spoken to him had really aggravated him. As the lift slowly went up and he had time to think he got more and more angry and aggressive. He kept feeling for the crowbar and gun both concealed in his jacket. The lift juddered to a stop and he stepped out and looked at

Tiffs door. Then he decided to smoke a fag while he worked out how he was going to punish Tiffany for making him look a twat in front of everyone. The weapons he wouldn't use but they'd scare the shit out of her. Scrap that he'd fucking use it on any men there if he wanted.

Maisie and Phil had both followed his lead and within a few minutes were working out which floor she was on. After following a young mum in who was carrying her baby. As they all got in the lift Maisie asked the girl what flat Tiffany lived in, and she just stared blankly at them holding her baby protectively. Maisie took out a 20 pound note from her pocket and held it up. The girls snatched it greedily and said '47A.' The girl stopped the lift at the next floor and got out, not daring to look back. As the lift progressed slowly up they both heard banging noises, 'Looks like we may a little late.' Phil said ominously. Maisie glanced up at him and pushed out of the opening doors. She ran round the corner and Tiffany's door was hanging off the hinges, and both of them could hear screaming. When she went in with Phil just behind her they both stopped suddenly and took in the scene in front of them. Rodney had Tiffany by the hair, he had wrapped it around his fist and he was holding a gun to her head. Maisie just stood there but Phil grabbed her from behind and moved her out into the hall. Maisie objected and then Rodney noticed them. 'Ooh if it isn't the lezzy lover from Liverpool and her fucking gorilla, sorry Orang-utan you ginger twat.' Phil just smiled at him and said 'well I'm not called Ginger Phil for nothing am I? Put her down mate you don't know where she's been.' He was trying to lighten the situation, but inside he was fuming. If he didn't have the gun in his hand he'd have butted him by now. Rodney laughed at this, spittle flying from his mouth, and you could tell he was having trouble focusing. 'You're right lad, but she's a fucking lying tart and she owes me money. So if you don't mind this is private.' Phil put his hands up in mock surrender and aimed to try and get Rodney to empathise with him so said 'Whatever mate, just I'm bursting to have a piss and a drink of water I have a terrible hangover, can I just go and do that?' I mean I have been on a three day bender because of my bitch of a wife, and you know how that feels don't you?'

Rodney was so drunk, angry and confused he didn't think that Phil and Maisie were a threat now because of what Phil had just said. Maisie was peering around the door. She hadn't taken her eyes off Tiffany, who was sobbing quietly mascara and tears running down her face. Phil strode up the hall and looked at Rodney and said 'go 'ead lad I really need to get down there before I piss myself, do us a favour eh and move over.' Rodney still not sure what was going on tightened his grip on Tiffany's hair and she squealed in pain. He dropped his arm as he went to move and the gun was pointing at the floor, and that's when Phil saw his chance. He grabbed him sideways by the neck and bit his ear as hard as he could. Rodney stood perfectly still and then roared in pain, bringing his arm up with the gun trying to aim it at Phil, but because the hall was so narrow he could hardly move. Phil spat out a bloody glob and grabbed his wrist tight, jerking Rodney's hand so that the gun flew out of his grip. Maisie saw her chance and ran in and picked it up quickly. Aiming it squarely at Rodney she told him to let go of Tiffany. Rodney still had hold of her and grinned despite his bleeding ear and throbbing hand. Phil stepped back to let Maisie handle it. She instinctively knew that he didn't see her as a threat, so she looked at the gun and said 'oh it's a Smith and Wesson Model 5906 a Yankee cops gun eh?' she said holding it steady. Rodney was no longer smiling when he realised she knew about guns and by her stance how to fire one. As if she could read his mind she inspected the gun and then pointed it back at him. 'Better make sure the magazine is in properly or it won't fire didn't you know that Rodney?' He knew he was defeated so he let go of Tiffany's hair and she stumbled and fell into Phil's arms. Surprised at how he liked the sensation he instinctively held her close and looked at Rodney and said   'I thought you were hard mate, being TJs right hand man. Not any more though eh? Now he's got that psycho Bentley to replace you.' Rodney trembled and started to cry, and sniffle. Maisie looked on bemused, working out how to deliver the final blow to the big fat bully, when Tiffany who had been silent pushed away from Phil, went into the kitchen, and came out with a baseball bat. Screaming like a harpy she ran at Rodney and hit him square in the face, his nose exploded like a rotten tomato, blood flying everywhere. He screamed and clutched at his face as blood poured from his ear and his nose. Maisie looked on and felt not a shred of pity for this vile bastard. Phil focused on Tiffany who stood holding the bloody bat panting and making funny little noises in her throat. 'Come on queen give us the bat, you don't want to kill him do you? I mean he has made enough mess on your carpet.' He said and gently took the bat off her. Speaking in a calm voice he told her to go put the kettle on. As Tiffany went into the kitchen Maisie still had the gun pointing at Rodney. She winked at him and Phil grabbed him by the scruff of the neck and walked him out the door.

He then said 'Right you snivelling bastard, you deserve everything you get in life. Everyone knows what you've done so get the fuck out, and if you try anything like this again I will kill you make no mistake.'
Maisie laughed and said 'Thanks for the pressie Rodney, give my regards to TJ won't you? How much are these guns worth now on the black market? Tell him some gossip too, I Maisie Malone and the Moffats are like kin now, so he'd better watch his ugly hairy back for a change. I mean what a man? Threatening and beating up dads in front of their kids. Oh I

bet that was you wasn't it Rodney the plonker? Very brave we heard all about it, oh and women too, but you like killing them too don't you? Well come and have a go at me you nasty little turd.' Rodney just stood staring holding his ear and nose, blood seemed to be coming out of everywhere. He stumbled off down the corridor to the lift, trying to outrun the terrible words as they were the truth. He had never felt so humiliated in his life, and he knew there was fuck all he could do about it. His ear was half gone his nose smashed and definitely broken, he'd never been a looker, one of the reasons people were scared of him was because of his size and menacing ugly face. Now they'd probably laugh at him when news got round that Maisie and Phil had whipped his arse. He spat out a blob of phlegm and blood and stumbled into the lift. He'd have to go to A and E, well at least the coppers weren't involved plus TJ had access to a bogus doctor who'd been kicked out from medical school. He got addicted to morphine and nearly killed two patients when he was a resident. They usually used him for anything like this, but if he went there he'd want paying and he'd be sure to tell TJ. He didn't have the money he used to have that went to Bentley the little queer, he thought bitterly. The more he thought about Stephen the more he felt his rage returning. As his heart race increased the throbbing pain in his nose and ear increased, and he screamed and shouted in the lift. Hurting himself more by punching the walls as hard as he could stand. He ran out of steam as the lift reached the floor and he wandered out of the main door into the night.

Maisie and Phil stood looking at each other grinning. 'Well I didn't expect that did you Maisie?' Phil said and burst out laughing. 'Christ I hope he hasn't got anything nasty. I'm going to brush my teeth and rinse my mouth out.' Maisie went serious for a moment she hadn't thought of that. 'Fuck Phil, say he's fucking HIV positive or got Hep or something. You daft bastard biting his ear, which by the way is stuck on the skirting board over there so we'd better pick it up.' Phil was still smiling, 'what was I suppose to do Maisie he was going to hurt the girl and he might have shot her, and us into the bargain. It was all I could do with the dickhead not to squeeze his neck and keep doing it until he stopped breathing. Rumour has it that it was him who did Sara remember. If we remind Carl and Michael about that they will stand with us against TJ and all his hired lunatics forever.' Maisie went up to Phil and put the gun she'd been holding in the back of her jeans, and then smelt her hands. They smelt of cordite so she went into the kitchen to wash it off. Tiffany was cowering behind the door. 'You okay love?' she asked. Tiffany still trembling and holding the kettle in her hands just nodded, and looked at the floor. Maisie didn't ask, just took the kettle off her filled it and put it on. Then she washed her hands as thoroughly as she could and kept sneaking furtive glances at Tiffany, saw the tears rolling down her cheeks, and went over and put her fingers under her chin. She lifted her face gently up, 'come on love it's all over now, me and Phil stopped him and he won't coming back.' Tiffany sniffed loudly and nodded. Maisie put her arms around her and pulled Tiffany to her, she was so grateful that Maisie and Phil had come when they did, that she just held on to her. They stood like that until Phil came back from the bathroom. She stood back from Maisie and went and hugged Phil to her muttering thanks over and over. Phil smirked at Maisie and she just rolled her eyes and shook her head. 'It's alright girl,' he said 'it was a pleasure to beat the crap out of that big bullying pile of shit.' Tiffany who was barely holding it together said 'I don't suppose that I could come with you to yours could I or if someone could stay here with me? I'll be okay soon.' Maisie felt like all her Christmases had come at once, she couldn't quite believe it, she must have the luck of the devil. A vulnerable Tiffany and she could sleep with her maybe even in the same bed, so she wouldn't try it on with her just yet. That could keep until tomorrow she thought grinning to herself, but tonight well it was a good start.

Chapter 23

Michael and Carl drove back to town both lost in thought about what they were going to do. They'd seen it with their own eyes, what Gez had told them about Peter Jones, best friend, to Michael who had trusted and known him most of his life. He was a complete and utter Judas, a back stabbing bastard. Peter meeting Stephen Bentley was as good as getting I love TJ tattooed on his chest. Michael was struggling with it obviously in pain. Carl had never bonded with him, but had tolerated his fawning over Michael because they'd seemed close. He still sometimes felt the green eyed monster, but it soon passed as of course as he loved and trusted Michael as much as he had Sara. So as Michael snapped out of his silence and started to reminisce, the words flowing out of him, Carl kept quiet and just let him talk to get it off his chest. He started with how they'd all got into trouble while attending infant school, when they were little more than babies They'd been caught picking all the daffodils in the gardens by their school. They then took them into school for the teachers and some for Sara and peoples mums of course. Every card, calendar and pasta picture they made, every ounce of love they were shown, or showed was from Sara or for her. Michael and Carl had to accept the painful truth eventually. Even when their bitch of a mother had made her do things she didn't want to, she'd done it for her boys, to buy them school uniforms, shoes and feed them.

Part of what made Michael strive so hard to be successful was he just couldn't get his head round what she'd done for them. She'd sold her beautiful body to all types of perverted scum. It made him so angry, and he and Carl had met some of the men who'd forced themselves on her, and some of them couldn't walk anymore, not without a pair of crutches or a walking stick. One rich bastard had tried to buy them, and they'd played along and taken his money, and then they kicked the shit out of him anyway. As Sara had been underage there was no chance of anyone going to the police. The Moffats would get done for GBH, maybe even attempted murder, but the perverts they beat would get done for raping a minor, so they got away with it all, as no one would press charges. including a senior police man, and a High Court Judge or two. A few times Michael had to stop Carl before he killed some of them, and Carl had stopped him once or twice. They talked about the night that Shelagh turned up drunker than usual, it had been really late, and it had been the anniversary of Sara's death. As she stumbled into the flat she had seen their looks of the repugnance and disgust aimed at her. So to pay them back she took great pleasure informing them rather smugly that their precious Sara didn't have sex at the beginning she wouldn't allow it. All she had to do was get Sara to dance and sing for the punters who liked little girls. It was enough, and for that alone she earned good money. She then added that Sara was the one who eventually wanted sex, just to see the hurt on their faces. She didn't tell them that it was her who had escalated it from getting Sara to sit on their knees and being kissed and groped from no touching at all. The boys knew all about it as the women on the Estate had told them a long time ago, and they had it stored away for the day they would make their mother pay for her cruelty. When Sara was 14 she was caught having a gentle kiss in the alleyway with Sammy, a boy from school who she had a massive crush on. She was being a normal teenager and couldn't wait to go out with him. He was a nice lad whose dad was a well known smack head, so they had a lot in common. A camaraderie born of neglectful parents. Sara was looking forward to taking her babies Michael and Carl to the park so it would seem all four of them, were a little family. Sara asked the boys to keep their eyes out for their mother but only being small, Shelagh had appeared from nowhere and pushed them both out of the way before Sammy and Sara had even finished their kiss. Shelagh drugged up on speed and vodka had run into the alley way screaming like a banshee grabbed Sara from behind and dragged her by her hair into the flat. The boys had retaliated screaming and attacking their mother so she'd get off Sara. Poor Sammy didn't know what to do, he wanted to pull Shelagh off but didn't want to hurt a woman even this evil bitch. He shouted 'Get off her you mad cow.' However Sara had had enough and easily shook Shelagh off as she was so angry and full of adrenalin. She grabbed the boys and Sammy then locked them all in their bedroom. She comforted them holding them tight, trying to distract them from the disgusting language and threats their mother was screaming on the other side of the door. Sammy helped too, and Sara's heart was full of joy and felt lighter for it. Shelagh full of speed and vodka was immune to the pain from the boys who'd bitten, kicked and punched her. She'd feel it tomorrow. Sara thought of this and realised they'd have to go and stay at Fat Fi's until Shelagh went away. Her thoughts went to the knife she kept safely away from the boys in the heating vent. She realised with horror she was prepared to use it too, often fantasizing how good it would be to get rid of their mother once and for all. She wouldn't hesitate if Shelagh looked at the boys the wrong way, never mind trying to give them a beating again. Sara remembered it was a few months ago when she had been at a friend's. It was so she could get to know Sammy, and had been two hours late home. She wasn't worried because Kay was supposed to be looking after them, and she loved feeding them and putting them to bed. The boys ran to her the minute she got in, terror in their eyes that were red and swollen from crying. She then found out that Kay had gone to the bingo as Shelagh had convinced her that she would watch them for twenty minutes until Sara got in. As she was late in by a few hours, they were hungry and tired but Shelagh had ignored their pleas for food. Starving the boys had fixed themselves something to eat, cereal and milk. They had made an almighty mess and tried to clean it up making it worse. Sara would have just laughed at them and tidied up. Shelagh however decided they'd been doing it to punish her so she had grabbed them both by the hair and dragged them into their bedroom. There she had beaten them both on the legs and bum with a whip she kept for sex games.

Their little legs and backsides were red raw and sore, and Michael had a clump of hair missing, and Carl a swollen lip. Sara felt dizzy with anger, and although usually a little scared of her mother, her outrage at what Shelagh had done to her two small brothers had depleted any fear she may have felt. She soothed the boys and put them in their room with the sweets she had stolen on the way home, and then confronted Shelagh. It had resulted in Sara getting the upper hand and dragging the evil cow out by her hair to see how she'd like it. She had pushed her down concrete stairs outside. Shelagh had been drunk of course so apart from scraped knees and bruises she was okay. Remembering that she won gave her the courage she needed to carry on. Sara couldn't understand why as she soothed the trembling boys, what was bugging their disgusting mother so much. All the things she was expected to with men and she made her do more and more each day it seemed should be enough. Forcing her into doing things like sitting on their knees while they pawed at her body through her flimsy school dress. It was disgusting and just having a kiss with Sammy was much more innocent. She knew her mother was paid well for her humiliation. So as she was the one that earned it, she took money for them when Shelagh eventually passed out. Perhaps it was that. It wasn't and she soon found out the reason for her mother's behaviour. Shelagh had sold her virginity already, promised it to one of the rich Arabs she sometimes brought home from the casinos. He'd given her two hundred pounds and promised her another five as soon as the dirty deed was done. He was really excited at the thought of breaking in Sara. She knew him and she hated him, he was sweaty, hairy and fat. His breath stank and he was always calling round and asking her to sit on his knee. Oh my God it would only be a matter of time before she sold the boys too, Sara felt weak with fear even at the thought. If a finger was laid on her little brothers she would definitely use the knife if her mother let anyone near them. No she wouldn't be that stupid, the women on the Estate would lynch her if they knew. Shelagh had been sleeping with men since she was barely 12, using her body to her advantage even then. As far as she was concerned her daughter was ready to earn them some more money and she would do as she was told. She was two years older than her, when she started. Sara was so disgusted at the thought she made a promise to herself she would lose her virginity as soon as she could, and hopefully to someone gorgeous like Sammy that would show the horrible old cow. She couldn't wait to be 16, and then maybe she could get them the fuck out of dodge.

Michael and Carl when talking about their mother often as was the Scouse way, used humour to try and make sense of it all, but they had never admitted to each other until recently just how evil and selfish Shelagh had been and still was. Everyone knew what she had done to Sara and in their hearts they'd known for a long time. Shelagh had actually shagged the social worker allocated to them and he'd given them a clean bill of health. People couldn't get their heads round the pain she'd willingly inflicted on Sara, and her little brothers. As well as Michael and Carl the people on the estate actually hated her. For the brothers it was an act when they gave her money or were seen to talk to her. It was for others benefit not theirs, because they didn't want anyone to know she was their weakness and that she had truly screwed them all up. Both men felt shame, for what the rancid old bitch had done to Sara when they were too small to stop it. Of course it wasn't their fault but they felt like it was. When they'd realised exactly what Shelagh had done when they read the reports from the police a while ago, it'd been very hard not to go and spit in her face tell her to fuck off and wash their hands of her. If it wasn't for their public face they would never have spoken to her again. But they appreciated the long game and as a couple of hard men which was the reputation they were aiming for, you just didn't kill your mother. It just wasn't done, so they pretended and acted and waited, and one day they'd pay her back. When they were really powerful and owned TJs Empire, they'd make sure she was cut off with nothing, and no one, if she hadn't died of cirrhosis of the liver by then of course. Then they wouldn't give a fuck what anyone thought of them and how they treated her. In fact they'd make sure she ended up homeless drinking methylated spirit and sleeping rough, they both agreed that death was too good for her.

They'd been to see therapists from their Church when Sara died, and they were taken in by their next door neighbour Kay on the sly. A gang of women from the estate all pitched in to help, because Shelagh wasn't around very often. They had looked after themselves and even at their young age they were used to it. They were careful as school because if they went into Social Services care, lads of their age would be split up and put into a home no foster families for them. Besides Shelagh was still their legal guardian and she turned up randomly with food for them, and to offer a few quid for Kay, so she could keep her freedom. She wouldn't give up claiming for them but when Kay demanded her child benefit she got it, Kay needed it for the boys' food and spent every single penny and more on them. Eventually although Shelagh moaned about losing the few pounds a week it was a situation that suited them all.

As they got near their town house, they talked about what else they were going to do for Kay for all the things she had done for them. They had set her up with satellite television, a few thousand in an account, and a holiday for now. They wanted to give it to her now so they could see her face.   So they changed direction and decided to go back to their flat. There was plenty of food in the freezer, and Kay was bound to have got them stuff in. Then they planned to talk about Peter and Shelagh. Carl had kept quiet except now and again nodding his head and agreeing with Michael, so as they pulled up to their flat, he noticed the police car outside. 'Oh shit Michael what now? Do you think one of the lads has been pulled dropping off some merchandise or do you reckon it's a drunk and disorderly again with mummy dearest?' Michael said 'Christ not in the mood for this, I wanted to talk about what we're going to do with Pete. And I'm starving.' Carl just shrugged and said 'well we're not going to find out sitting here, let's get it over with. You haven't got anything on you have you? I haven't thank God left it all at the house in the safe and outside the flat in our secret stash.' Michael nodded and smiled 'well thank the Good Lord for small mercies.' He did a fair imitation of an American preacher based on Kenny Everett's show which they had loved when younger. Carl laughed surprised at this show of humour and Michael carried it on shouting 'Oh Jeeezuzzz, my brothers and sisters must listen to You Lord and pay for their wicked ways and for being in league with the devil. Maybe them there holiest police are here on the side of the righteous! However me and you know Lordy Lord them there coppers mostly belong to Beelzebub.' For some reason probably as their emotions were running high after discussing their past. Add that to Michael talking honestly about painful memories, they both burst out laughing. The more they tried to handle it the more they giggled. The police who had been on the stairs waiting by the flat looked at the Moffats in surprise and yet they didn't say anything. Michael went first and Carl was right behind. 'What's up, are you waiting for us?' he asked the female PC who was with a man in plain clothes. They recognised him as DS Frank Maher from CID. She nodded silently and smiled. He'd never seen the police constable before, she was really pretty, with a full mouth, startling blue eyes and a flash of white blonde hair that peeped out from under her hat. She seemed quite tall and filled out her uniform well. Michael found himself wondering how long her hair was and what it would feel like to run his hands through it as he kissed her. Then he grinned to himself at the thought of asking a copper out. Carl winked at him, and he knew that he was thinking something similar. However as they grinned at the two police, they both seemed to avoid their eyes, and as their smiles faded they both knew this was something serious. So many thoughts went through their heads, had someone been bust and grassed them up? Maybe they had someone for Sara's murder, but one thing for was for sure the coppers were being nice to them.

The blonde as if reading their thoughts said 'I'm PC Dana Byrne this is DS Frank Maher and I'm afraid we may have some bad news for you.' Carl took the last few steps up to the landing and got out his keys, as Michael said 'Well come on we'll go and put the kettle on and you can tell us what this is about.' As Carl was letting himself in their front door, Kay came out to see what was going on. 'You okay boys? I put some fresh milk in the fridge today for you and a loaf and butter. You're stocked up on everything else.' Michael gave her a hug and took a twenty pound note out of his pocket and put it in her hand. 'Trust you to have a twenty I'll get you some change. It only comes to a few quid.' Michael gently led her to her flat and said 'That's a little bit extra for you for looking after the place and us. I'll let you know what the police have got to say when they go okay?' Kay was pacified by this but there was genuine concern on her face. 'Do you think it's to do with Sara? Have they found something out?' she said. Michael kissed her on the top of the head and replied 'We don't know a thing yet Kay, be a good girl and like I said we'll tell you it all later. I doubt even though I'd hoped it myself. But if it's to do with Sara it's an old case and they wouldn't call this late, it would be in the morning. Do us a favour, keep your eye out and if anyone goes to knock at ours tell them to go away okay? Oh and you can be our new secretary tell them to leave a message with you if it's important.' Kay was overjoyed that the boys were including her in something so important. She couldn't wait to rub it in to that stupid cow Shelagh when she saw her. Oh and boast to all her mates of course.

Michael knew exactly how to please Kay and she was always thrilled when he gave her some responsibility. He allowed himself a smile when he thought of how excited she was going to be when they give her some presents. He went in the front room as Carl was in the hall by the kitchen door, and he saw that PC Byrne had taken over making the tea. 'Who wants milk and how many sugars? She shouted.

After a couple of moments with no replies, she shrugged to herself and put the cups on the tray with milk and sugar and an assortment of spoons. She followed Carl into the living room where the others were waiting. Sergeant Maher was standing looking out the window, and Michael was on the couch. After the drinks had been sorted, and everyone was sitting down Sergeant Maher cleared his throat and announced the reason they were there. 'I'm afraid to say that a body washed up yesterday on West Kirby beach, unfortunately some children found it. It was still wrapped in plastic and the poor little buggers thought it was treasure. They were very upset after they realised that it was a person as you can imagine. We have reason to believe it may be your mother Shelagh Moffat.' Carl blinked in disbelief as Michaels jaw dropped open. 'We would like you to come down to the morgue and identify her if that's at all possible. Just one of you can do it, or if you don't want to you can get another relative or friend if you wish.' Michael struggled to take this in and asked why they thought it might be her. Also Carl said not to hold anything back. DS Maher told them straight that although she had some contusions and lacerations she had been wrapped in a tight plastic shroud so she was partly waterproof. Add that to being found quickly and the cool temperature decomposition was minimal. They got her fingerprints and then they followed procedure to the end. After confirming with the forensic dentist it was definitely her only then did they go to the Moffats flat to tell them. Michael and Carl looked at each other, they were shocked

99

and a range of emotions were running through both of them, especially after they had been talking about their disgust for her not half an hour ago.

Detective Sergeant Maher sipped his tea and like PC Byrne he was watching their reactions. Carl spooned extra sugar into his and Michael's drinks and passed it to him. Maher coughed uncomfortably and then said. 'After we've identified the body and we're sure it is your erm....mum, mother, we will need to question you about when you saw her last Are there any known enemies that type of thing. A couple of hours should suffice at the station.' Michael stood up rage running through his body, his complexion getting redder by the minute. 'Now listen here YOU! We need time to process this, and you should show some fucking respect. So watch your fucking tone, and be careful how you proceed. ' He pointed straight at DS Maher. Carl went over to his brother and put his arm around his shoulder and sat him down.

'I'm sorry son,' the DS said 'It's just routine in a murder inquiry; I know you've just lost your mum, and I know about you losing your sister Sara when you were both young boys. If I come across as uncaring I don't mean to.' PC Byrne who tried to break down the tension in the room said 'It's true it's just the way he speaks, he's not so bad when you get to know him.' She smiled gently at Michael and Carl. This seemed to pacify Michael he leant forward Carl still with his arm around his shoulders and put his head in his hands, and stared at the floor 'Come on then Mikey lad let's go and see if it is her. If you don't want to I'll do it while you wait in the car.' Carl was surprised at himself and how calm he felt. Maybe it was because he couldn't wrap his head around the fact that their horrible mother may be actually dead and gone, and he didn't know how to feel.

Sergeant Maher drained his tea, and put his mug on the tray 'Thanks for that, it was a nice cuppa. Do you want to come now with us and get it over with or have some time to get adjusted to it? Then if you really don't want to come to the station we can come back here and do the interview if you want. But of course we understand if you want to leave that too. Come on PC Byrne let's go outside for a fag while they have a think.' She smiled and said 'didn't think we could smoke on the job Sir.' Sergeant Maher smiled and said 'there are always special circumstances and this is one.' They both left and went and stood on the landing outside the front door.

Michael waited until it was quiet and then said 'Fuck the police Carl if it is our mother we will have to go and kill the bastard who's done this, won't we? You know we're may have to get rid of everything while they're sniffing around.' Carl put his finger to his lips in the universal sign that meant be quiet. 'Ssshhhh, they may be able to hear you 'he whispered.

'I'm sorry bro don't know what the hell I'm saying or doing.' Michael mumbled, 'Do you want to go now and see if it's her, but I have a feeling it is. Listen if we have to get rid of anything in the big house, let's get in touch with Maisie she'll store it for us.' There was a gentle tap on the door, PC Byrne stood there and smiled. 'Well have you had time to make up your minds?' Or do you need a bit longer?' she asked.

'No queen, we will do it now, get it over with, thanks for looking after us. If you want to tell your boss that we'll be ready to go in a minute.' Carl replied to her last question. PC Byrne smiled a little sadly and nodded her head going back out onto the landing. Michael finished his drink and grimaced at the mouthful of sugar. 'Good for shock that,' smiled Carl. They both stood up and patting themselves down and checking their wallets and keys they locked up the flat and started to walk down the stairs. Kay popped her head out and when she saw their faces knew it wasn't good news. 'Hey boys you okay? Do you need anything, what's happened?' Michael smiled sadly at her, and kissed her on the cheek. 'They've found a body Kay and they think it may be our Ma.' Kay reeled at the news, even though she couldn't stand Shelagh she wasn't prepared for that. 'Oh my poor boys!' she exclaimed. 'Come here and give us a hug,' Michael stood by her and let her hold him, and she then said 'you too Carl come on son,' He bent over and she almost disappeared between the two big men, but she held them fiercely with her eyes shut, tears streaming down her cheeks. They stood like that for a few minutes, until they gently drew away, and took her to her flat and settled her in. Kay cried out loud and even in her grief she was crying for the two men who she had just held. Not a single tear was for Shelagh, the rest were for Sara who if she had lived would have finally been free of the wicked bitch.

Chapter 24

Maisie stretched luxuriously in Tiffs bed and looked over at her sleeping form, she was so close. Her beautiful hair was spread all over the pillow and she had her thumb in her mouth, which she found endearing. She really was working hard with this one, lying there in the bedroom she thought back to the night before closing her eyes and reliving it all in her mind. She thought back to the last few hours and thought that she was nearly there. After Ginger Phil had gone she had run a bath for her and sat on the toilet listening as Tiffany told her everything about the abortion. How she'd slept with Rodney at first because he made her feel safe, and of course for the money and the bit of prestige as he was one of TJs main men. Then when she'd found herself yet again throwing up in the morning and feeling like shit, she'd felt nothing but repulsion for him. She'd also slept with another of TJs men a dickhead called Buffy because he was a bouncer and looked like a great big buffalo.

She didn't even know his real name. She'd enjoyed him for a while but omitted lots of things when telling Maisie. She had lied through her teeth why she'd come for a job at Maisie's club. She couldn't tell her the truth that town was full of gossip over how Maisie was the Moffats new best friend and she was letting them the club for all sorts of things. She left out the bit out about how she wanted to bag a Moffat and didn't really care which one. Maisie had nodded sympathetically at what she was saying; somehow knowing she was keeping something to herself. She didn't care as she washed her back gently being especially tender where Tiffany's bruises were worst. Maisie did her best not to get turned on, she just wanted to look after her for a while and build up more trust. As she caressed her firm soft skin in the bath with the sponge she was amazed at her will power not to just lean over and kiss her neck and although she wanted to use her fingers instead of the sponge, she didn't do it. Holding out made it even better. Truth be told she was dog tired, emotionally drained from Linda and her nonsense and the fight had used up all her adrenalin. She looked forward to resting for a while. She always carried a bit of coke and weed with her in a cigarette packet, and it crossed her mind to do a bit of Charlie, but she must be getting old she couldn't be arsed with a stimulant. Not that she needed anything to be the life and soul. Instead she'd make a big fat joint to smoke instead then she would relax and so would Tiffany if she could get her to participate, plus this weed made you horny.

She got a fluffy towel out of the cupboard in the hall, and held it out for Tiffany as she stepped out of the bath. Maisie even made a point of averting her eyes, every bit of her behaviour carefully calculated so that she didn't scare her, or give her true intentions away. It made it so much more exciting. She went and put the kettle on as Tiff got dressed in clean pyjamas and a dressing gown. Maisie made them some drinks, and sat in the tiny kitchen, waiting for Tiffany to come and join her. She was skinning up on the table as Tiffany came in.

'Caught in the act, I hope you don't mind love but I need to wind down a bit.' Tiffany laughed then, and pulled a bag full of weed out of her pocket and shook it in front of her face. Maisie threw back her head and laughing said 'Excellent you've got more than me, here give us a bit to put in let's make it a mixed double!' Tiffany threw the bag on the table and sat down grabbing her tea. She took a sip gratefully and then got up went to the cupboard and got out a giant bar of chocolate. 'Munchies are prepared, hope you like chocolate Maisie.' Tiffany grinned.

'You are joking of course lovely, all females love choccie even us dykes!' replied Maisie and grinned at her and then finished rolling the joint. She lit it up inhaled greedily and passed it across to Tiffany. Who took a huge drag, and promptly coughed her guts up. Maisie got up to get her a glass of water and was struggling not to laugh. She tried to keep her face away so she wouldn't see her but couldn't contain it any longer. She put the water on the table and saw Tiffany was also giggling now her coughing had stopped but tears were streaming down her face. They both made eye contact and then fell about laughing together. When they'd calmed down, they drank some tea and ate some chocolate and discussed the nights events yet again. 'God you don't think he'll come back do you Maisie?' commented Tiffany. 'Nah he won't be able to stand the shame when Phil goes and tells everyone at the club what happened, and he will,' said Maisie still smiling. 'It will be fine queen I promise, and I'll stay tonight, and if you want tomorrow, you can go and book in a nice hotel in town I'll pay. I'll be around don't you worry.'

Tiffany knew she was being seduced, enough men tried, they all showed her kindness at first because they wanted her, and then she'd get bored of them or them her because she wouldn't commit to any one person. They'd either get nasty and stalk her for a while, or give up and go when the sparkle wore off. She always sold the jewellery she got, none of it meaning anything to her except it was a way to buy her weed, clothes and pay her bills. She found it was easy to dismiss these men, and never look back. She was almost the same as Maisie in the way she could delete a person from her brain. Plus Maisie had tried it on with her when she'd gone for her job. She realised she had been dumped only once, a prick called Frank dropped her like a ton of bricks because his wife was suspicious, or so he said. Funnily enough it was when she said she wanted to go out and be wined and dined. He was a copper and she started to think that maybe he didn't even have a wife, and that he was trying to get information out of her about some of the dealers on the estate.

Tiffany felt another little part of her harden. As far as she was concerned rich people were there to use until she bagged the one who was going to rescue her and give her a good life. She still wanted a Moffat, probably Carl more than Michael because he wasn't as serious or as involved in the business as Michael she'd heard. When she imagined one of them when she masturbated as she came she always thought of Carl, so he was the one now. She smiled at the thought she had made her mind up. So back to Maisie, what should she do? I may as well at least experiment. She had been really turned on when Maisie had kissed her in the club, and then felt repulsed with herself for reacting so easily, but what the hell? It will turn out okay and if Linda's not around she may as well play up to her. She'd done a bit more research about Maisie after the kiss at the club. She had a bad reputation as a womaniser and was worse than any of the blokes at the club. She was known to go mad over a girl, spoil her rotten then after a few months she dumped them, and grovelled around Linda. The girl of her affections sometimes went mad for a few weeks trying to get back in with Maisie, and then disappeared. These women had given up boyfriends or girlfriends convinced they were her true love gay or bi, but it was the money and the power that was the real draw. Everyone used to joke she'd killed them especially the most recent one who'd been screaming blue murder at the club, who had not been heard of since. She had been a little embarrassed when she had fell into bed exhausted and still tearful, and very stoned. Maisie smiled and got in beside her, making sure she wasn't touching her. Tiffany fell asleep quickly, and Maisie lay there looking at her, thinking how easy it would be to fall in love with this one. She was beautiful and although had proved to be far from innocent she had a vulnerability she found very appealing. Maisie put her head down and fell into a deep sleep as for once she wasn't thinking of Linda and the twisted self made guilt that sometimes wouldn't allow her rest.

Chapter 25

The drive into town was surprisingly quick, Michael and Carl concentrating on the route to the mortuary, rather than what was waiting for them there. DS Maher and Dana were discussing their reaction to the news. 'Well what do you make of them Sir, do you think their reaction is normal?' Asked Dana who really enjoyed playing the role of apprentice, and was really eager to find out as much as possible about the brothers.

'Well we both know our boys have a bit of a reputation, and have built up quite a little empire considering how young they are, but they have nothing to do with their mothers 'death, as far as I'm concerned.' He answered, and then he added 'Shelagh Moffat had been done for prostitution, fraud, neglecting the kids when they were young. She actually put her daughter Sara on the game, who was murdered when the boys were little. They worshipped the ground their sister Sara walked on, they still do. Every year on the day she was murdered they go to where she was found and put some flowers and a message, as do most of the Estate where they live.' Dana looked surprised, and thought deep down that she rather fancied Michael and was intrigued by this bad boy despite her new career. 'It sounds like they have a lot of respect around here Sir Did they find the person or persons who murdered Sara?' She said. Maher just glanced at her sideways and shook his head to indicate a definite no. Dana took this as a sign that their conversation was over for now, and looked out of the window. She made a mental note to look up the file the minute she had the chance.

Michael and Carl pulled up to the Liverpool city morgue, it wasn't far from their townhouse, and hadn't taken long to find. Most Scousers had a subconscious map in their heads of the whole city. As it was at night there were plenty of places to park, and they were sitting on the bonnet of the car by the time Maher and Byrne pulled in after them. They walked over to their car and Michael opened the door for Dana, and he and Carl followed them in. Maher went up to reception and signed them all in, grumbling under his breath about the security guard who was missing off the desk. He led them down a long corridor under ugly overhead lighting. As they approached the office DS Maher turned round and told them to wait a moment, he knocked then entered. Michael, Carl and Dana stood around and feeling awkward she reached over and caressed Michaels arm, and then Carl's. 'It won't be long now, then hopefully you can go home and we can leave any further questioning until tomorrow or the day after.' 'We'll see how we feel when we get out won't we bro' Carl said to which Michael replied 'Yes Carl we will have to wait and see. I'd rather get it over and done with to be honest, but I feel exhausted.'' Suddenly Maher came out of the office with a woman in a white overall, 'This is Dr Mottershead the resident pathologist at Liverpool University. She consults with us all the time on cases like this.' The doctor was a pretty brunette woman probably in her early 40s but looked much younger. Whatever her age she radiated a professional calmness that comes with experience. She smiled at the brothers and said 'Come this way we've arranged a viewing room for you.'

She walked briskly to the left and they approached a door marked suite no.3. The doctor opened the door and there was a window that took up half of the wall. There were curtains drawn across and a microphone set in a stainless steel square with a few buttons.   Dr Mottershead said 'Excuse me a minute I just want to make sure that everything is okay.' She left quickly and she was gone for around two minutes, and then came back in. She approached Michael and Carl and asked if they were ready. They nodded and she tapped gently on the window and the curtains pulled back.   Both men took in a deep breath and looked at their mother in death. Her face looked like it was made of plastic and had some horrible wounds. She was covered right up to her neck, but there was no mistaking it was her. Her blonde hair looked dark and wet and was brushed back flat off her face, everything about it was wrong.   Michael thought she looked like she was breathing, and shook his head to let the reality of the situation sink in. Moments passed but to Michael and Carl it had seemed like hours, it was too surreal for their brains to take in or make sense of at that moment.   Michael faced the Doctor, 'I've seen enough thanks, how about you Carl lad?' Carl just nodded, and looked at the floor. 'It is most definitely my mother Shelagh Moffat' said Michael quietly 'Carl would you agree?' said Maher. 'Yes it's my mother Shelagh Moffat, but she looks weird, all wrong somehow, is it because she's been in the water or what?' Dr. Mottershead who had been quiet came over to Carl and grabbed his hand, holding it she looked up into his face and said 'I hope you don't mind me saying this but your mum has been in the water for a while. However as she was wrapped up, she looks okay considering what her poor body has been through. She also has injuries all over her upper body so I don't want you to see any of that.   You seem like men who can take the truth so as long as you are okay with it, I will be doing an autopsy to gather evidence to help find the bastard or bastards who did this to her.' Michael felt a sob catch in his throat and coughed to disguise it, Carl sensing his brothers' discomfort took his cue to speak on their behalf.

'Thanks Dr. Mottershead it's a great comfort that you are so dedicated to your job. I think we need a bit of time to take this in, so we'll be going straight home now, any questions can wait until tomorrow night when we've sorted ourselves out.' DS Maher nodded as he had given Dana permission before to tell them they'd leave it until the following day. He was trying to build a relationship with them, hoping they would drop their guards and let something slip about who they suspected. The police including him had a few ideas, starting with Mr. Prick himself TJ Murphy. Of course he wouldn't get his hands dirty but he had a fair few working for him that would. The police intelligence had known for a while about TJ and about the Moffats going after his little empire. Also they knew that Maisie Malone was joining up with the Moffats, not sure why yet but it would come out in the wash. He mentally slapped himself to wake up and take in the situation with their mother dead on a slab in front of them, they might drop a piece of valuable information without realising. He thought they were coping well, but they were covering what they really felt, and that was the same emotions as everyone else who had lost someone brutally to murder, no matter how much violence you were brought up with. Detective Sergeant Maher followed the two men as they walked out of Pembroke court mortuary keeping to the shadows. He knew that if they found out who'd done this to their mother no matter how they'd felt about her they would be putting the word round that if anyone knew anything there would be a big reward. While no one would be grassed up to the police. They wanted it their way, and to get to who was responsible before they were safe in police custody. Well they'd be safe for a while anyway.

Chapter 26

Linda wondered where Maisie was, she hadn't been back for ages and they kept missing each other which suited her fine. She was so used to her going off with her latest girl she had trained herself to ignore it even when she had still cared. She really didn't anymore but was a bit annoyed because she usually got in touch. Even through Phil or one of the guys to give her some bullshit message. She just didn't like not knowing where she was, in case she sneaked in and caught her getting ready to leave. She was probably at a two day rave or something then off to her new tarts house for sex. Linda had enjoyed her time alone, as it gave her time to sort out her mind and also what stuff to take to Joes. She got a fluttering sensation in her stomach as she thought about going to his flat later.

She hoped to God he hadn't changed his mind or bottled out. She had imagined it at least twenty times, but she knew that come hell or high water she was going to meet him, and if he did bottle out she was still leaving Maisie. She even felt okay about having her cysts and lumps removed the way she had chosen. She knew it would be sore and she'd be feeling off after each operation but it was okay as long as she had Joe to look forward to. Luckily the surgeon was amazing, she could see just from the one procedure how it was going to look. She felt pretty lucky all in all, and keeping this from everyone had given her a quiet confidence in herself. It wasn't keeping it a secret it was that she had dealt with something huge on her own. It also put her priorities in order too. She knew that Maisie was definitely chasing her next conquest, due to the lack of contact. It confirmed what she had once feared and now celebrated, she was definitely with another woman again.

The business was in both of their names of course, Maisie the public face, the party girl, thrill seeker. She had an entourage before they existed for the likes of Lady Gaga. They were a bunch of two faced hangers on, who you wouldn't see for dust if something went wrong. Linda the one in the background who did all the hard work was the kind one. if you had a problem you could go to Linda who'd always try to help. Of course she was liked she paid the wages she thought to herself, sighing in annoyance at herself and her negative attitude. She would leave Maisie what was hers and the club. She was just going to live on her savings , her investments and some profits from the club. They were plentiful. If Maisie expected her to do the books and paper work she wanted a weekly wage on top of her share from the profits. That was fair enough, plus if she and Joe made a real go of it, and stayed in his flat for the foreseeable future, then she wouldn't have to be involved hardly at all. What it really meant was she wanted to avoid Maisie as much as possible, she wasn't ready for it yet. She was going to buy a better computer so she could communicate if she needed to. You could talk to other people all over the world now if you both have the software as well as the comp and your phone line, so up the road shouldn't be a problem. Her stomach was knotted and thrills of excitement both good and bad ran up her spine. She was just missing the ugly. She was sure that would turn up. The thought of actually making love to Joe instead of their snatched kisses were the good. The thought of Maisie's almighty tantrums smashing things up and her screaming obscenities were the bad. She smiled as she thought Maisie could also be the ugly one when her face was screwed up. Well it's now or never to leave her and go with him, she pretended to ponder but she knew she'd made her mind up days ago.

News spread quickly through the estate, and everyone was doing their best to seem not interested in the best piece of gossip for a long time. Shelagh Moffat was dead; the vile horrible cow had finally got hers after all she'd done to her own kind and her own kids. The rumours spread thick and fast, one thing was sure though, everyone knew she'd been murdered, and there were so many who hated her. They speculated, was it TJ, or a dealer she'd crossed once too often? Or was it an enemy of the Moffats or some out of town firm trying to move in? One thing was sure. It was exciting and it would be really exciting when they found out who had done it. It was a matter of principle now, the Moffat boys would make someone pay for this no matter how much of a low down skank their mother had been.

Michael and Carl were exhausted, and they sat in their car outside the flat wondering what to do next. 'We need sleep and rest Michael lad,' said Carl. 'Too right bro, but where? If we go to the town house the lads will be there waiting for us, I've already had about 40 missed calls 20 off Judas, not to mention the 18 texts.' Answered Michael 'The little shit wants you to know he cares,' growled Carl. 'I know we need time to think about him and mother dearest. Well I know one thing if we go in the flat we won't get peace even Kay won't be able to stop all the well wishers calling, and maybe the frigging press. So we're pretty much screwed all round.' He thought for a while 'I know we'll go and get some cash out of one of the accounts and go and get a luxury hotel for the night. Then we can rest get some good scran and in the morning go through what's next. Does that sound good?' Michael asked. Carl nodded and smiled at his brother, and they pulled out of the Estate and started to drive towards Chester.

Joe was a bag of nerves. Tonight was the night that Linda was finally leaving Maisie Malone, one of the hardest women he'd ever come across, or most men had ever come across. She was fearless and known for it, he knew he was even risking his life doing this, but he couldn't help it he loved Linda and she was worth fighting for. She was leaving Maisie and he was just providing a place to stay. But he now believed in love at first site.

He didn't care if she walked out and left the club and all its money behind, he just wanted to wake up with her, nurture her and when she had healed both inside and out from her surgery, make love to her. If she didn't want that he was so besotted with her he'd be happy just to have her as a flat mate for now. He had visions of Maisie coming after him with bloody Phil and her minions, shotguns in hand, and he still wasn't put off, so he knew it was love. Also he had two crossbows and was a pretty good shot, he loved going to the firing range, where he had made some good mates, even if they were nutters who did war re-enactments. Besides all that, it kept his arms strong. He had one safely stashed under his seat in the taxi and the other hanging on the wall by the front door. It was easy to reach and it was loaded, dangerous he knew but only if you were an idiot who didn't know how to handle them. Anyway it was time to go and pick her up, fingers crossed, he checked his flat it was clean and tidy and smelt nice. That would do for now, and the bed was changed with brand new bedding. If she felt like him then their surroundings wouldn't matter at all as long as they were together. He looked at the clock and decided he'd waited long enough, grabbing his car keys and with his heart in his mouth, he locked up then got in the car. Say she wasn't there?

Michael and Carl had gone to the Grosvenor Hotel in Chester. It was an old hotel surviving many years and a fixture of the city. It was expensive as a London hotel as it h five stars, and their room was big and beautifully decorated. The food ridiculous prices but the customer service flawless. The brothers were also great tippers so they were pretty popular amongst the staff. It did really well when the Chester races were on. It was also the type of place where as long as you could pay your way, any eccentric behaviour was tolerated as long as you weren't rude to the other guests. This suited them fine, they loved staying there. They checked in, ordered sandwiches, some tea, two bottles of water and a bottle of Jack Daniels. Michael threw on a robe and threw one at Carl, who smiled. 'What we're so rich now we pay for our robes? Do you remember when we used to nick them in the plastic from the Adelphi so we could sell them or give them to Kay and the girls?' he said. Michael laughed out loud a deep belly laugh rich and strong. As their room service arrived, they tipped the porter and then locked the door with a do not disturb sign outside. 'Right let's get some sleep after our butties, then we'll take it from there.' They both ate their food silently watching TV and then both nodded off in their luxurious beds, exhaustion finally taking them both down into deep dreamless sleep.

Maisie went into the loo with her mobile phone and sent a text to Phil. Within twenty five minutes he was there. He knocked and she looked through the spy hole. He was standing there with a box of coffees and cakes. As he came in he said 'hello your highness I have brought refreshments for you and your concubine.' Maisie laughed and replied 'don't push it serf." Phil laughed and asked 'well did you get what you wanted or not?'

'You are of course right Maisie we shall meet up again later and decide his fate. Do you want me to take you home now?' He asked She stood thinking then said. 'I don't know whether I can face it Phil. Is Linda about or has she asked where I am?' Phil looked at the floor and didn't answer. Maisie realised something was up. 'Go on spit it out I've been waiting for news' she said, for once afraid. 'She didn't come home last night, one of the lads kicked your door in this morning worried that something had happened to her. I hate to say this but the flat was empty. Everything was cold, the bed was made and some of her clothes were missing.' Phil mumbled.

Maisie struggled to take this in as what Phil just said didn't make sense. 'Well ask the lads to go and ask round and find her please Phil, I will pay them over time.' She started to walk away chewing at her nails thinking where she could be, but Phil said 'Maisie honey there's something else happened, I think you should know. Shelagh Moffat the one and only has been murdered. She was found dead and cut up, wrapped in plastic on the shore in Birkenhead somewhere.' Maisie's head already filled with thoughts of Linda lying dead somewhere just stared at Phil trying to take it in. 'Christ Maisie you look like a bag of shite are you okay, you look like you're going to faint.' Phil asked concerned. 'I'm okay you daft git Phil you know me, tough as old boots just a bit of shock you know. Tell you what ring Michael and Carl when you can and leave a message of condolence. Let them know anything they need, to ask us and we'll do our best to give it to them. Okay?'Phil nodded his assent and went over and hugged Maisie too him, enjoying her warmth and vulnerability in those few minutes. 'Right I'll get off and go and try and get in touch with the Moffats. I'll pick you up in a few hours so we can decide what to do with the other twat Rodney.' Phil said as he walked towards the door, Maisie nodded and went into the hall to find Tiffany just coming towards the kitchen.

Tiffany had woken up with a banging headache and a fierce hunger in her belly. Both down to the skunk she'd been smoking all night. She heard voices in the kitchen but smelt something wonderful, like coffee and cakes. She got up and as she was going in to see Maisie and who her visitor was she heard what they were talking about and stopped in the hall. She recognised Phil's voice and caught most of what he said. This was interesting they had something planned for Rodney eh? Good kick the prick in the balls. But then a creepy thought got in there. Maybe it would be something worth noting and maybe it would bring some rewards in the future. She hated herself in a way for thinking like this after Maisie and Phil had saved her neck, but she was so determined to get the life she wanted she would do anything she had to. Even if it including blackmailing Maisie. Then her heart hardened when she thought of all she'd gone through to get here. The abortions, the beatings, the perverts, sucking men's cocks, and even worse when they hadn't washed. The false smiles and dressing up when all she wanted to do was put on her PJs and have a hot water bottle resting on her aching stomach. Every little bit of being used, the indignation and hatred poured out of her and she felt a sense of excitement, and wonderment at how strong she felt. Her new determination came to rest within her, comfortable and warm in her belly. She couldn't hurt Phil though, he made her feel safe, and she liked him, pity she had her heart set on the big time. She had no idea what the future held, and she hoped she would have a change of heart eventually. But just for now she had to stay strong and focused.

Fuck it she'd even play with Maisie if that's what it took, as long as it wasn't too kinky. She was on the up and her plan was coming together. Maisie thought she had her now, but she knew that it was the other way round. She was so lost in her own thoughts she nearly got caught listening to them. She managed to step back a couple of feet and make it look like she was just approaching the kitchen. She'd also registered that they'd been talking about Linda going missing and she wasn't sure but was it Shelagh Moffat who was dead. So what if she was, that would be even better news for her. She could maybe plant the seeds and get Carl with both sympathy and sex.

Chapter 27

The night before Joe had picked up Linda and they had gone to his flat, she had been touched and delighted as it was obvious he had cleaned and tidied. She was over the moon with its simple taste. It was the type of flat she had wanted when she was young and single. She'd forgotten how nice it was not to be surrounded by stuff, Maisie's mountains of stuff. She had been pleased again at his joy over her bags, which meant she was staying for a while. It was so crazy the way it had all happened so fast but when you were getting on you didn't hang round like you did when you were young and immortal. Joe had carried her bags in and was in the kitchen making tea. She took in the brown leather couches, the coffee coloured walls, the simple coffee table and the wall mounted fire. They must have cost a fortune, they hadn't been out long, so they were super expensive. He had a big TV massive big black plastic square with a flat screen but it was a huge lump of plastic. A few simple throws in gold and cream, matching the curtains. She really liked it here already.

She actually dared to hope that this could work out. He brought in a tray on it were two mugs a tea pot, some biscuits, sugar and milk. She had to hide a smile at his seriousness, but her heart swelled with love as he prepared her tea, not asking because he remembered. This simple act meant more to her than any of the huge gestures she had been offered over the last few years by Maisie. Her and her money now meant nothing. She thought of her and the men she had grown up with, and how everyone would be looking for her soon. Well until Maisie got home and read the note she had left for her, then surely she wouldn't be missed. She was going to live in the now, and lying back the most relaxed she'd felt in years, she dozed off. The stress, worry and surgery had taken their toll, and her body as exhausted as her mind, had said enough is enough. Joe moved her cup now empty from her hand, and kissed her on the forehead and once on the mouth, and was rewarded with a little groan of pleasure and a contented sigh. Smiling he went and got the blanket from the closet and gently laid it on her. He flicked on the TV and put it on low, and he couldn't quite hear it, so he turned it off, grabbed his book and he too fell asleep after two chapters like a contented cat.

Maisie was confused her feelings were all over the place. She kept smiling at Tiffany who fussed about getting dressed and cleaning the flat, hiding from her how she felt. She had to wait for Phil he would find out what was going on with Linda, but she knew in her heart that she'd probably lost her. Unfortunately her head refused to accept it. She'd been so lucky with her true love, but had blown it chasing skirt all over town. She was so self destructive. She looked at the clock it could be hours before Phil was due back. She decided that she needed to feel a woman in her arms. She wanted Tiffany underneath her touching her naked skin, the thrill of a new body to taste and experiment with. She stood up and walking calmly over to Tiffany, took her in her arms, and kissed her. She kissed her long and hard and Tiffany who had made her mind up to endure anything for her long term plans seemed to respond. As she slipped her hand underneath Tiffany's silky top, she felt a kick she hadn't felt in a long time. She whispered in Tiffany's ear 'Hey hope you don't mind me doing this, do you want to go to bed?' Tiffany looked up into Maisie's eyes, and enjoying the power of the moment made her wait for what seemed an eternity, and then in her best seductive voice breathlessly replied 'Yes.'

Carl and Michael woke up after a long sleep, they'd expected to fall asleep for a few hours but it was daylight outside. They were both woolly headed from their long sleep, but they'd be okay after some coffee and the full breakfast they'd ordered from room service. The bottle of their favourite whiskey lay unopened on the chair, sleep helping them both more than that could.

'So what now Mickey lad eh, what now?' Carl asked. Michael said sadly 'Let's just get the funeral sorted for ma, and take it from there. Remember revenge is a dish best served cold, so Pete will wait for a bit. Let's wait until we've arranged the funeral, then he won't see it coming.' Carl nodded his assent as they heard a knock on the door. Both men looked at each other, wondering who it was who knew there were here, then Carl let out a barking laugh. 'Room service you dick, and I'm a dick too!' he shouted laughing. Michael laughed too relief making his knees go weak. Never again would they rush off and do this without their guns, or even a decent baseball bat. Although they were reasonably safe at the moment. News would have spread no one would try and take them out for a while, not while their mum had just been murdered. The old school gangsters who they aspired to be like wouldn't. However they knew when it come to the likes of TJ and some of the others they'd do it all the more. Michael said 'I think our paranoia has moved up a notch because basically someone has murdered our mother.

Then we find out that fucking twat Pete is in with Stephen Bentley! My supposed best mate, so then he must be in with TJ! Sometimes we aren't the brightest in the bunch but they are as good as any other reasons. So let's stop pissing about and make sure we get the lads to cover our backs. At least until we find out who killed ma. Until that day comes we will just have to be extra careful eh?' he finished. Carl nodded his assent and then added 'You're right of course but it's going to be fucking hard trying to be okay with Pete you know. For all we know he may have been the one responsible for ma's demise. I mean he loves you so much it would make some type of perverse logic to him. He knows you hate her, maybe it was a parting gift to you.' Michael gave thought to this and then said 'Well if it is him, we'll find out soon enough, so let's just get back into the thick of it and sort it out. Got to get the death certificate and then sort out a funeral parlour to take her that type of thing We need Jonna's uncles Freddy, Tommy or Danny to help us. We can ask now even though it may be ages before they release the body. So let's get moving, the sooner we do this the sooner we can carry on with our plans.' They finished their breakfasts and stood up, and got ready to face the world and his wife.

Linda opened her eyes, and it took her a moment to register where she was. She was on Joes couch, but for a tiny moment she wondered whether or not it was real. She looked over and he was snoring softly with a book on his chest. He looked so sweet and at peace. She stretched and sat up, went into his kitchen which was sparkling. It was very up to date chrome, red and black. She liked it and thought how easy it was to keep clean. She was so excited, the year two thousand wasn't far away and she would hopefully start the next millennium with Joe. Stop it she scolded herself and thought I must take it a day at a time. I'm only supposed to be staying here for a bit. She made the coffee and took it in; she nudged him gently, and then in a fit of daring kissed him full on the mouth. He woke up and smiled, laughing he pulled her onto him where they kissed and cuddled for the next twenty minutes. 'Christ we're like a pair of teenagers' Joe said grinning.

'I know it's wonderful.' Sighed Linda 'I feel I'm getting a second chance as I missed out on a lot of this when I was younger' she said. 'Me too' Joe replied. Joe kissed her on the top of the head, and asked 'do you want to phone for takeout or go out do something or just stay in now and I'll cook? Your wish is my command missus.' Linda knew going out was a definite no, Maisie and the lads could be looking for her everywhere. I wonder what she will do after she reads my letter. I hope she doesn't find out about Joe for a bit just until we are so strong she can't touch us, she thought worrying.

'Why don't we stay in and have a real English breakfast no matter what time it is? Ooh and how about just for now, today in fact we just enjoy being a new courting couple?' Linda asked Joe looking straight into his eyes. His gaze didn't waver from hers, and he looked deep within her and answered 'That is a great idea gorgeous, we have some good DVDs off the Moffat lads, they are pretty good for pirate copies.' Linda laughed out loud a nervous high pitched giggle, Joe jumped at the sudden noise and then asked her what was wrong. She smiled and told him how Maisie even had a presence here in her sanctuary. Even if it was indirectly through the Moffats. Then her determination returned 'Nothing to worry about you daft git, just a random thought.' They smiled at each other, Joe sensing Linda's fragility. He suddenly realised he had never felt so protective towards anyone for a long time. In fact since his child was born.

Maisie had made love to Tiffany and she had been gentle, skilful and kind. She liked it rough herself, but there was plenty of time for that she thought to herself. 'Well what did you think of that then, as good as with a bloke?' She looked Tiffany straight in the eyes when she asked. 'Better more satisfying' Tiffany lied, careful not to show any true emotions. She had sort of liked it, she had two orgasms. Mainly because she had fantasised it was Carl not Maisie who had pleased her with his tongue and hands. Add that to the amount of weed she'd smoked she had found it easy to pretend. She still felt wrong though, she missed the weight of a man on her and the feeling of him inside her. She also couldn't shake the mild repulsion she felt and was dreading having to go down on Maisie. 'Do you want me to take care of you Maisie?' Tiffany asked in a quiet voice. 'No love plenty of time for that, I just wanted to show you how good letting another woman make love to you felt.' Maisie replied. Tiffany buried any feelings of regret under her smile and pretended shyness. She had after all actually come twice, it had felt very good, even if it felt wrong. She was still unsure of what to do to Maisie. She could handle the snogs, the caressing of breasts even the kissing her body. It was whether she could do to Maisie what she had done to her. She was quite happy to be pleasured, and have someone do all the work, it made a change. She would just have to grin and bear it after all it was just another way of getting closer to Carl, wasn't it? She'd turned down many an offer to star in a porn film, purely due to feeling she couldn't do the business with some of the men she had seen in them. There was a new craze and it was really violent rough porn. She knew a few porn actresses. They had told her it hurt for a bit but was over quickly. A couple of them were her friends and tried to talk her into it. They pointed out that she only had to work for a few days a month it was so well paid. Tiffany said no, she didn't want to be recorded on film going down on anyone to be fair. Say she was asked by Carl to marry him, and actually kept one of her pregnancies for him, no it wasn't worth it. She snapped out of it suddenly and sat up, she had a lot to plan, now Linda was out of the picture. Maybe when she had Maisie wrapped around her little finger, she could pick her moment and then she would go for Carl. Her plant was to go to him for help. Act that she was so scared of Maisie that she would do anything she asked her to do. Then when he comforted her she would seduce him. It should work after all Maisie couldn't say too much after what she'd done to Linda. She could then tell him her version of the events that started all this, of the jealous old boyfriend who came round to kill her. How Maisie and Phil had saved her so she felt obliged to keep Maisie company when she asked. She was surprised but Maisie had forced her to do things, and how the thought of sex with another woman repulsed her. She'd beg him to keep quiet and then for the finale go off crying with shame at having told him her dilemma then move in for a kiss. Perhaps persuade him that the only way she'd feel better was if she was fucked by a man.

Maisie brought her back to earth with a loud 'Oi dozy, do you want to make us a coffee then as I did all the work?' Tiffany felt a little flash of anger but swallowed it down and replied in a quiet voice 'Of course if that's what you want. How many sugars again?' This was aimed to give her ego a little slap. She knew damned well how many sugars she took. Maisie looked at her and frowned, and replied in a stiff voice 'Two you daft mare, head like a sieve' and Tiffany knew she'd hit the mark.

There was a loud knock at the door, Tiffany jumped but to show she wasn't scared went to answer it. Relief flooded through her when she saw the red hair through the spy hole and realised it was Ginger Phil, so she opened the door. He grinned at her in a lecherous way, when he saw her messed up hair. Tiffany felt the flash of anger again, but was proud of how she ignored it. She deliberately said 'she's in there Phil' and pointed to the bedroom to let him see she wasn't bothered. His smile disappeared and he stood at the door embarrassed and Tiffany marked up another small victory. 'Come on then honey we got loads to do and sort out,' Phil said to

Maisie who was lying on the bed. She sat up and pulled on her shoes which had been on the floor. Running her fingers through her curls she said 'Alright mate. Let me just say good bye to Tiff,' and winked at him and Phil winked back out of habit. Tiffany had stayed in the kitchen knowing they probably wouldn't say anything worth hearing now as they were going. 'Come here and give us a kiss gorgeous' Maisie almost shouted so Phil would know for sure, and Tiffany took a deep breath and smiled as she prepared herself. Walking over she kissed Maisie and felt bile rise in her throat as she could smell herself on Maisie's face. She swallowed and tried to look serene. 'Bye honey I'll be back soon but if not I'll give you a ring okay?' Tiffany felt relief that it wasn't tonight by the looks of things, 'That'd be lovely Maisie, I look forward to it,' and she smiled shyly. Maisie slapped her on the bum and blew a kiss as she left. Tiffany said goodbye to Phil and shut the door behind her relieved it had been fixed so she could lock them all out. She wanted to have a hot shower and wash the smell and the memory off her. Going through this just made her more determined she would get Carl to fall for her, and on that happy thought she forgot about everyone but herself and the life she wanted.

Carl and Michael had stopped for petrol on the way home, both spotting the Liverpool Echo's headline of 'woman found dead on Birkenhead shore!' The Daily Mirror had a small bit on the front page, with more on page five. They bought two of each as Michael had paid for their petrol and they sat on the car in the forecourt reading it. 'Doesn't say anything we don't already know does it?' said Michael. Carl grunted and said Ssshhh as he hadn't finished his. 'Well if we'd have wanted to keep it quiet we'd be fucked now wouldn't we? Christ Almighty how do they find all this out, and so quickly? I wonder if it was our Dana otherwise known as PC Fit or the Frank the wank?' Michael said and Carl despite himself laughed out loud. When their chuckles had subsided they grimaced as they both thought of what lay ahead. Not wanting to appear in anyway weak, to each other, they pulled out of the petrol station quickly. Turning back onto New Chester Road on their way back to Liverpool. They filled the silence with benign conversation about the correct change they needed for the Mersey Tunnels and hoped the Queensway one was open. The Kingsway was in Wallasey and it would take ages to get home from there. It was and all went smoothly through the tunnel and soon they pulled up to the townhouse. The day was really dark with storm clouds overhead so all the lights were on. 'We've got a full house by the looks of it Mick lad' Carl commented. 'Unusual seeing how early it is.'

'Probably be Pete playing dutiful best mate, knowing him' replied Michael. 'God give me strength to not show him how pissed off I am.' Carl smiled sadly at his brother, reminded of how hurt he was by Pete's actions. They got out of the car and locked it up, and approached the front door, which was wide open. Feeling very freaked out by this they walked in slowly. Carl going in first cautiously covered by Michael, who was right behind him. He went to the umbrella stand in the hall and grabbed the baseball bats in there. He tapped Carl on the shoulder and he turned around quickly and snatched the bat. He felt the reassurance of the warm smooth wood in his hand. He immediately felt better and just hoped the intruders didn't have guns. An icy snake wrapped around his bowels as they made their way down the hall, and checked each room. They started to relax as all seemed clear on the ground floor. It was short lived as they heard groaning coming from one of the bedrooms. Taking two stairs at a time both of them stopped at the top and saw Jacko lying on the floor. He was groaning which meant he was still alive. 'You with us mate?'Michael asked him as he knelt down. 'I'll live Mick me old mate, I am so sorry I've let you down.' Carl was watching this and noticed blood pooling on the floor around Jacko's head. 'Quick Michael' Carl barked 'he's bleeding to fucking death.' Michael stood up quickly and saw his pants were covered in blood. 'Jacko stay with us mate, just going to get a towel and that to help you out. Trust you to make a mess all over the floor' he said smiling as reassuringly as he could. Jacko smiled back but his eyes were glazed. Carl rushed to the bathroom and back with a clean towel and gently lifted his head to have a look, there was a nasty looking wound and he stemmed the blood quickly by placing the towel there. 'Don't move mate, just in case it gets worse, Michael lad have you rang 999 yet?' Michael was mesmerised by the blood but stood up quickly coming to his senses. He patted his pants to find his phone, and then rang for the ambulance.

Carl smiled down at Jacko and tried to engage him in conversation to keep him conscious and also wanted desperately to know who'd hurt him. 'Do you know who did this mate, any ideas?' Jacko nodded and groaned at the pain this caused. 'I can't believe it Carl but it was Pete I am sure of it. There were a few of us sitting round waiting to see you two. You know to make sure you were okay as we had heard about your Ma, We were so angry and we'd had a few to drink and didn't know what to do so we all decided just to hang round and wait to hear. Pete as usual was gobbing off what he'd do to the twats who'd hurt your Ma, and how he'd known before all of us, and so on. Then he gets a text and goes all weird. Disappears for a bit, tells the lads you've texted him and we had to meet you at Maisie's. Of course Jonna goes mental, worrying about you, and then starts gathering heads on the phone. Then he starts shouting down to the basement where the rest of them are waiting. Everyone comes running up and noisy as hell start discussing what they're going to do to anyone who'd hurt you and yours. Then they tool up and head off into the night to Maisies.' Carl leant down as Jacko's voice was growing very faint, and he kept coughing. 'I know you're not supposed to drink anything or that mate but do you want some water?' Michael had rang the ambulance, and had gone to check the rest of the house. Apart from some stuff turned over in the basement and the room where Jacko was it looked like everything was still there. He ran back upstairs to them both making sure the front door was locked until the medics got here. 'The ambulance is on its way mate how are you doing?' Carl looked up at his brother his eyes giving away how worried he was for their friend. 'Do us a fave and get us a drink of water for him please.' Michael nodded and went to the bathroom and came back with a tumbler. He passed it to Carl who carefully lifted Jacko's head a little so he could take a sip. He took a few gulps and then put his head back down. 'Ta mate.' Jacko whispered, and then he carried on telling them what had happened. 'It was weird so strange, I was the only one left so I thought I'd stay here and lock up before I followed the rest. I thought Pete had gone with them. I got up to lock the doors and as I look outside there's Stephen fucking Bentley and Pete together talking like they're best mates. They obviously thought I'd gone with the lads, I didn't know what to do so I went inside to grab a weapon and as I was searching where we stash them, I feel a really mad pain in my head. I started to pass out and as I fell I saw Pete behind me with a hammer and Bentley standing in the doorway grinning. I knew it was him as it reflected in the glass part of the door, they had no idea I'd seen them. So I thought I'd play it safe and pretend to pass out, but I needn't have bothered because he hit me again.' He laughed weakly.

Carl had heard more than Michael and resolved not to lose it while his friend was relying on him. Anger like bright sparks started to go off in his head and he felt rage flush through his bones. No he said to himself, I have to keep it together, what good would it do any of them to go into a berserker rage now. All of them heard the sirens getting closer so Michael ran down to the street to wait for the ambulance to make sure the paramedics got the right house. He kept tight hold of the bat. He hadn't heard yet what Carl had, but he knew by his brothers face whatever Jacko had told him hadn't been good at all. He'd heard him mention Pete and Stephen Bentley.

The ambulance was going slowly up the road looking for the address, so Michael stood in front of them and waved them in. As they got out, Michael took them upstairs to Jacko who was struggling to keep his eyes open. After a brief explanation of what they wanted the paramedics to know, the medical workers told them to wait outside while they worked on Jacko. Carl told Michael straight away what Jacko had said, and he was struggling not to scream in anger and frustration. Michael felt a cool detachment take over as he calmly took it all in, and he knew for sure now they'd have to wait just a bit longer to get him. A good beating was one thing but they both knew now they might have to kill Pete and make an example of him. Otherwise no one would take them seriously again, they'd just have to be careful not to get caught. The paramedics had strapped Jacko into a stretcher and were carrying him slowly down the stairs. With a grim face Michael asked how he was, and the woman paramedic replied carefully that he was lucky to survive, and that they'd injected him with something to slow his blood loss and a painkiller, but they said they couldn't comment further as they had to wait to see what the doctor said. Michael nodded and said 'We'll be right behind you in the car.

Maisie sat simmering with anger, as Phil drove her back home. 'So she's just taken off and no one's seen her, after me paying all the staff over time too, for fucks sake. Phil what's going on? I hope she's left me a note or something.' Phil smiled used to Maisies total audacity, and said 'What do you mean Maisie after they way you disappear for days. Then there's all your affairs come on girl, you must admit it's amazing she didn't disappear years ago.' Maisie wasn't in the mood for the truth, so she replied 'Look I know you're being honest and mean well but shut up Phil! Shut UP I don't need another lesson okay?'Phil smiled to himself, enjoying her anger and discomfort as she always had to come out on top. Then there was today, where she just wasn't going to. He had spent so many years in love with her, other women never lasting long as they weren't her, and now it was turning into a sort of hate. He thought he would always be loyal he owed her that, but he knew she would never be his for sure now. Lately he felt bitter about the years he had missed. All the women he'd let go the kids he could have had, and the ones who had loved him and he'd ignored. He saw a child he had fathered, a boy called Phil Jnr. The mother had been desperate to keep him, so she'd called her son after his biological dad. He'd quite liked it in a way when he was little but the boy was annoying now he was older. Ginger like him, but no guts, and all he did was whine. His mother Natasha was one of those women who had to get up the ladder. She had a mediocre job, where she'd been promoted to line manager and she took great pleasure in bullying those below her. Especially disliking gorgeous, intelligent women. That's all she would talk about one of the other staff an older woman who was liked by everyone. She hated her, she was intelligent and beautiful, and comfortable in whom she was so Natasha hated her with a vengeance. She bullied her relentlessly even when she knew her sister was dying of cancer. That just made her vulnerable and she and Joe her little robot had made the woman so miserable she'd told them to shove the job up their arse and walked out. She was obsessed with work. Phil decided to leave her after listening to her go on about all this for weeks. Natasha eventually worked out he wasn't for her, and never would be, after his third affair. So she had taken up with Joe a talentless and stupid diabetic who worked for her, and as he had no balls he was the perfect partner for her. Natasha thought she was way better than anyone and she was as dumpy as a haggis and ugly inside and out. She lied and pretended she had gone to a good school, and had a degree and neither were true. She even drove a BMW now thinking she was the perfect example of style. Most Liverpool women he knew dressed really well. Wearing all the latest fashions and using knock off if the real thing was too expensive, or not available. He loved that about some of his ex girlfriends. Not Natasha, she couldn't do it. She was too chubby with huge thighs and no boobs. God what was he thinking she was just horrible and God alone knows what he ever saw in her. It no longer mattered how clichéd that sounded, if it wasn't for his son he'd would gladly never see her again.

'PHIL!!!' Maisie screamed as he nearly tail ended a car in front of him. 'What is wrong with you?' 'I am so sorry Maisie' he said. 'I was lost in thoughts about that bitch Natasha. Just thinking about my boy. It was how that horrible cow is making him into a whining git like that ponce of hers Joe.' Maisie calmed down and was as forgiving as usual with Phil straight away. 'Sorry my old mate. I'm being a right cow I know, sorry.' She looked down at her hands and Phil knew she was actually unsure what to do next, as he pulled up to their place by the club, this was a first he thought, the tough as nails Maisie Malone was frightened to death of life without Linda.

Chapter 28

Pete Jones who was once thought of as quite a hard man, and who belonged to the Moffats clan, was no longer that. He wasn't hard underneath as his reputation came with and because of Michael. It was hardness by association. Usually Pete could be seen hovering near the back whenever there was trouble. Jonna and Billy who'd known him forever saw it, but they wouldn't say. They joked he was like Rimmer out of Red Dwarf the comedy. Now they both wished they had. Pete was now on TJs side and he had no choice, there was no going back ever. It was too dodgy to go back to the Moffats house now, someone might have seen them. Stephen was sitting next to him in his car and taking in the situation. He was feeling a calm rage at everything that had gone wrong tonight, but this was a good consolation prize. The taking of Michael Moffats best mate and turning him against them all was a coup all right. He was proud of that aspect. He just couldn't believe that when he'd come round and met them that stupid fucking Jack the lad was still there. Pete having panicked had hit him at least twice. When he'd run off and Stephen reluctantly had to follow he was very disappointed. He wanted to cut Jacko at least, make sure he was either maimed or dead. Then he was going to leave the Moffats a nice little message in Jacko's blood across the wall. Pete was snivelling besides him now, about having to kill Jacko and hitting him twice when he was down. 'Forget it Pete it's over now, stop sniffling like a woman.' Stephen said trying to keep the annoyance out of his voice.

Pete struggled to stop but at least he'd shut up Stephen thought. 'Sorry Stephen I was just getting me head round what has happened like. It's harder than I thought. Now if it was Carl I had to kill it wouldn't have been a problem.'   Pete replied in a gruff voice. 'That's better Pete that's the spirit, now what do you want to do? Mr. Murphy told me to look after you and make sure you have everything you need. I've got some money for you so you can go to hotel and buy some nice togs, and a decent pair of the trainers you Scousers love so much. Me I'd buy a good suit a few nice pairs of pants and some smart shoes, none of that tracksuit crap for me, besides they're really flammable. Not good for people in our game.' Pete looked puzzled for a minute then asked 'what does flabbamle mean?' Stephen had to bite his tongue to prevent him reaching over and breaking his nose and decided to reply calmly, 'it's flammable and it means it can catch fire easily, so it's best not to wear them if you're out on a job. Take my advice and get some decent pants and things Pete, if you want to fit in with me and TJs firm okay?'

Pete looked at him and nodded his agreement. Stephen took out an envelope and handed it to him. Pete thanked him and looked in it. He could see a wad of fifties and some twenties, Michael had paid him well but nothing like this in one go. 'Jesus how much is in there then?' he asked and quickly put it away so no one could see, even though where they were was deserted. 'Two grand as a little thank you for coming over to TJs side. At first it was a thousand but when I told him you'd killed one of the Moffats gang, he was delighted with you. There is a condition. He has given you the extra to lay low for a bit. Go to a nice hotel out of town, where no one will think of looking. Go to a hairdresser if you can get your hair dyed a different colour. If you change the way you dress, then you can be invisible for a while until it dies down. Then if you're a good boy, maybe you can start coming around with me when I go and collect our protection money, that type of thing. Tell you what I'll drop you off at the Thornton Hough hotel, it's not far from me and it's only in Wirral. They'll think you've gone Manchester way especially when I tell Gez to tell them. Now there's a little shit, their own flesh and blood and he hates them.' Pete looked surprised, at this news he remembered Stephen mentioning it before but he'd forgotten all about it. He was so wrapped up in his own hatred for Carl he was surprised all over again.

Stephen started the car, and said if they wanted to go and get any stuff from his place they had to go soon, as they were bound to start looking for him. Little did they know Jacko was alive, and had seen them both, and the Moffats knew too by now. Pete said 'Well I need a suitcase and some stuff so I don't look suspicious in the hotel.' Stephen looked at him sideways a little surprised at this as he was perhaps a little smarter than he thought. He still indicated even though the roads were empty, being extra careful just in case there were any coppers hiding parked up the lane. They headed towards Pete's house.

Michael and Carl were at the hospital with little Joey, Jonna and some of the lads. Ginger Phil was also there, after taking Maisie home. She'd told him she wanted to be on her own so could he go and see if the Moffats were okay? Then he must offer help on behalf of her and the rest of the lads. They were all waiting around to hear what was happening to Jacko, and the staff were trying to avoid them. Tonight they looked exactly like what they were. A bunch of gangsters out for revenge. Their public faces hidden as they were too worried about their mate. Even Phil got caught up in it all, and said 'So who did it then? I want to kill them too lads, first your poor Ma now this mess. If this is TJ we need to fight back and hard. Do you reckon Pete is hiding somewhere local? Shall me and the lads look for him? He might have tried to stop who raided the house and got taken by them or hurt and dumped somewhere.' 'No thanks not yet mate' said Michael and looked at Carl who nodded yes to the question he asked him with his eyes. 'I'm going to tell you something now and I want it kept quiet for the time being. Pete is no longer welcome at our house, or in Liverpool or indeed on the fucking planet. It was him that tried to kill Jacko from behind. Jacko saw him in a reflection and guess who was with him?' Silence had taken over the room, the only noise was dishes being scraped and groans and murmurs in the distance. The expectation was awful and as names ran through all their heads, most had guessed who it was. 'Yes Stephen fucking Bentley was with him. He was behind him egging him on, as Jacko fell pretending to be knocked out, then the

123

bastard hit him again. That's why the wound is so bad as he hit him twice, perhaps three times in the same spot.'

Little Joey stood up his 6ft 8 frame seeming to suck all the space out of the room, he so was red in the face that Carl wondered idly if he was going to hit one of them. 'So let's get this right? Our Jacko has had his head kicked in by one of our own? It doesn't make any sense to me, just because Stephen the psycho Bentley told him to, well he's fucking dead that's for bastard sure. I'm going fucking looking for him right now who's with me?' Little Joey roared. The lads all agreed. Which made Michael and Carl both feel better being surrounded by the rest of their mates. Their anger at one of their own being hurt, was made ten times worse because Stephen Bentley had such power over Pete. Michael found it incredible that he could manipulate him to do this to friends who'd known him all their lives. Everyone in the room got louder shouting what they'd like to do to him. A brave nurse entered and asked them to be quiet. She was petite and pretty and had big brown eyes, her auburn curls contrasting with her rich coffee coloured skin. Carl despite all that was going on felt a tug in his heart and in his pants. She was fucking beautiful he thought, I'm going to get her number but not in front of these lot, they wouldn't understand. Everyone went quiet and looked at the floor. 'I know you're angry about your mate getting attacked lads, but it is a hospital and there are lots of other people here who are ill too. I'd really appreciate it if you could keep it down. Thanks.' They were respectful and kind, and there were mutters of sorry from around the room. Carl smiled at her, his hazel eyes sparkling with what could have been tears, she wasn't sure but also something else she couldn't quite place. Then she was surprised when she realised she knew what it was. It was mischief she was sure of it, she didn't know what to think of him. 'Can I have a word please, in private?' he asked. She felt a little flutter when he looked right at her. 'Yes that would be okay, come outside into the corridor' the nurse answered. As they both left the room Michael watched interested wondering what Carl was up to. He didn't wonder long, when he come back in and with the nurse who was called Suzy's phone number.

Maisie had let herself into the flat, it was quiet and cold. She could already feel how empty it was without Linda. She shivered and walked over to the beautiful coffee table, one of the antiques she had bought for her when they'd got a good deal with a brewery. It was a unique arts and crafts celebration piece Linda said in her pretend posh voice, making Maisie laugh out loud at the auction they'd been at. She nearly bought some horrible 1970s retro monstrosity she didn't want because the auctioneer had taken her laughter as a bid. It made her smile as she thought back. Yet it felt bitter sweet like she was filled with love but a huge part of her was missing. She saw the letter on the table. Linda's Catholic school script clear and concise her name printed on the front. She picked up the letter and took it through to the kitchen, putting on the kettle, she made herself some tea using some coffee whitener as there was no milk of course, as she never bought it. It started to sink in just how much Linda had done, from making sure they always had milk for their tea to running the club. She wouldn't allow the fear to grip her that the thought had caused. She concentrated on the tea which was nice when she put sugar in, and she went into the bedroom. Everything was tidy but she could see gaps in the wardrobe where Linda's clothes should be. Fucking hell she thought she really has gone, and she felt herself going dizzy. Sitting on the bed she opened the letter and began to read.

Hello Maisie,

This has been a long time coming as you well know. I don't love you like I should anymore but I will miss you after all the things we have been through, and the years we've been together. Usually at this point I'm supposed to say it's not you it's me. Well honey I would say it to make you feel better I suppose if I were acting like I usually do, but I'm afraid the old Linda has gone. I decided a while ago there is no way I was going to allow you to keep treating me like a dickhead, and you have Maisie, for someone who's supposed to love me. You have shit on me once too often. I have shown you love and loyalty over the years, don't you think some of the little tramps you go off with haven't tried it with me first? Bet that hurts the old ego doesn't it queen? But it's true and I wish I'd have stood up to you years ago. Maybe then you would have treated me the way I deserve to be treated. I have said it so many times, threatened you. I've said if go with another one, I'm gone. Of course I didn't go anywhere. So that's partly my fault for letting it go on for so long. I've had some serious things to deal with recently and you weren't around for me when I needed you most, and that's when I knew it was over. You think you can buy me, or seduce me or whatever it is that made you have power over me for so long now? No I'm afraid this is for good. This isn't a ruse to get

125

you to look for me and beg for me to come back to your bed Maisie it is a final goodbye. I will have to see you I'm sure in the near future to sort the practical things but not for a while yet. I wanted this letter to be full of meaning and I hoped it would make you realise that you can't go on the way you do by treading all over people who love and care for you.

Did you know Phil has been in love with you since we were kids? How else do you think he puts up with all your crap. The other guys tease him and call him your bitch. He just takes it. Well he was in love with you. Just like I was and I don't know if he still is, but give the guy a break and make him realise that you will never be with him. He is pretty smart, if he hasn't worked it out for himself by now I'd be surprised. You may be in for a shock but I have found someone else too, and I have not been this happy for years. I ask you to do the decent thing Maisie from the bottom of my heart, and not cause trouble for the person I love or their family when you find out who it is. Please I beg of you, let me go you've been wanting to be free for a long time. Be honest with yourself now and I hope you will find happiness with your latest conquest. Who knows she may be the one, because as sad as it makes me to say it, I'm not and now I know I never was.

Take care and be safe   Linda xxx

Maisie screamed and screwed up the letter as if it were alive, she threw it away from her, the tears were streaming down her face and she had never felt so upset and angry at the same time. The little bitch to do this to her now of all times, and she couldn't get over that some of the little tarts she had seduced had tried it on with Linda and then used her when they couldn't get what they wanted. Her selfish nature wouldn't allow her to take in the basic truth of Linda's words. So she concentrated on what made sense to her, she would find out who and kill the little slags. No torture them first, and then she would find who Linda had gone off with and fucking kill her too. Or at least maim her and hurt her family so she would never go near Linda again. It never even crossed her mind it was a man that Linda had gone to. What difficulties did she have that she'd ignored? She felt bile rise in her throat and ran to the toilet, throwing up her tea. She washed her face in cold water and started to think a little more clearly. Christ what a day for her to leave, when the Moffats were in potential shit, and she needed to back them up. What if half her boys left her for Linda what would she do? But they wouldn't because they'd been with them both for years and they knew what side their bread was buttered. Maisie knew too and took a little comfort from that. Her thoughts were running amok, and she knew she was being paranoid. This day had been coming a long time, and now it was finally here it was worse than she had ever imagined. She was so locked in her selfish bubble that she was now worried about people feeling sorry for her. That bothered her more than anything. She wouldn't be pitied. She had to get Tiffany to come to the club and be seen with her out and about, just to save face. Then when Linda came crawling back she would do the decent thing and let her move back in. That sounded like a plan, and in the mean time while the boys were out helping the Moffats she had the place to herself. She decided then that she was going to build a big fat joint, and smoke it in the bath. Then put some decent sounds on, and order some scran from China Town for this afternoon, and maybe get the clubs limo to pick Tiffany up and take it from there. She was starting to feel better already, because as far as Maisie was concerned it was just a matter of dealing with it. She had Tiff to keep her company for a few weeks, at least, excellent eye and arm candy. Oh boy was she looking forward to discovering her body properly. The thought of controlling her turned her on. She would teach her how to pleasure herself and her. She felt fine now that she had Linda sorted in her head. She went in the bathroom to run the hot water in her big Victorian tub. She built a joint while she waited for it to fill up. She wanted to feel like she'd washed all her worries away. She was so sure of herself that she didn't even feel that upset anymore. She was Maisie Malone, reinvented from Shirley Jacobs and could do anything. She knew Linda would be back eventually, and she had Tiffany to distract her until then. So she relaxed and lay back in the scented water. She'd found herself thinking about Tiffany a lot she could see her as her new girlfriend perhaps. Then the minute she thought about Linda she dismissed it as a stupid thought.

Tiffany would never measure up to Linda. No, her and Linda well they belonged together forever, pure and simple.

Chapter 29

Tiffany had been on her own all day, and wasn't feeling at all happy. For once she felt unsettled in her solitude because she wanted to know what was happening. She liked her own company, but with Maisie and Phil being gone for hours. As she had messaged them both with no reply from either, she felt ignored. She knew instinctively that something was going on and she hoped it was something exciting as she was bored off her head. So she made a decision instead of waiting for something to happen she'd get a taxi to Fat Fi's. She liked the old girl she'd been kind to her when Tiffany was just starting out as an escort.

She got ready quickly and left a note on the door for Maisie to call her, just in case she showed up. She got out at Fi's and noticed the usually noisy and busy bar was quiet. Even the girls weren't outside trying to sell their wares. She had a hunch something big was going down. It would distract her from how angry at fucking Maisie she was. No matter what she could have sent her a text at least, considering she'd given in to her. Bring it on she thought the more you use me, the more comfortable I am ripping you off. I'll enjoy taking your money and using you to bag Carl. As she approached the doors she saw some of the lads who worked for the Moffats hanging around. All these were lower level, all trying to work their way up into the Moffats inner circle. She went into the smoky bar and saw Fi polishing glasses. 'Christ what's got into you, are you actually cleaning?' she shouted at her, to which Fi replied. 'Oh my God hello my love, have you had a head injury or summit? Mixing with us common folk and coming in here like.'

She laughed loudly and asked her 'usual is it or do you want one of my fancy cocktails, they've even got tinned peaches and pineapples in them.' Tiffany laughed out loud, but with horror saw that Fi was serious. She saved face by saying 'they sound lovely but I can't handle the drink like I used to, so thanks my love but I'd love a cuppa and a gossip.' Fi smiled and shouted to one of the girls hanging around the bar to stick the kettle on, and come and take over from her when she'd done that.

Fi beckoned to Tiffany to follow her and they went into the kitchen together, the smell reminding her of the past. The freezing nights and waiting for her punters to pick her up when there was no escort work. Even though it was grubby and careworn, there was a part of her that missed being here. The banter with the girls and talking about the men they'd slept with, how much money each punter would pay. Crying with laughter at the weird requests and hilarious ones such as dressing as a cat and meowing as you did the dirty deed. Then the serious stuff like warning each other who to keep away from, especially if they proved to be violent and cruel.

She snapped back into the present and looked at the girl Michelle making the tea. Then she said 'So come on then Fi if anyone in the world knows what's going on it's you so fill us in.' Tiff asked smiling. Fi busied herself finished their cups of tea. She sent Michelle to tend to the bar so she could talk freely. After heaping about six sugars in hers, she grabbed some biscuits and put them on the table. When they were both sitting and dunking their digestives she started her tale.

'Well one of the reasons it's like tales from the Crypt around here is the bizzies have been in here all the time. You have heard about Shelagh Moffat of course?' Tiffany nodded and asked what exactly had happened. 'Well the soft mare had come in here, showing off because Michael and Carl were in here sorting out some business. It was the anniversary of Sara's death so they weren't in the best of moods. They were having a gab to me, and we all know how they felt about the mother but as they're on the way up, they were being respectful to her. I said I'd smack her face in for them.'

Fi grinned slurping her tea and munching on a custard cream, the digestives gone. 'They seemed to like that, and laughed with me. Anyway Tiff she was as usual off it, so they bunged her some money and she went off shouting about getting a taxi. That was the last time she was seen alive by anyone round here. Of course had to be my fucking bar.' Tiff didn't say anything as she knew Fi was warming up and the rest of the information she was after would come. Fi finished the packet of biscuits and asked if Tiffany wanted to have some from a fresh packet. She shook her head to indicate no, so Fi didn't get too distracted. She found herself holding her breath as she waited for her to carry on. 'So they found Shelagh's body in the Mersey the poor soul well she'd washed up on the Birkenhead side, in New Ferry, the old shore. The police have been asking all the girls if anyone recognised the car or taxi she got into. I don't know why they're bothering because they'll go straight to Carl or Michael if anyone knows anything about it. They won't go to the bizzies. As much as she was a total bitch to those children she was still their mother. They probably want to reward who ever did it but they have to be seen to be on the lookout for revenge. Everyone was saying it's probably TJ. Also after we heard about the amount of times the poor cow was stabbed, it could be the same person who killed Sara. Or it could just be some pervert picked her up and as she was always off it she didn't stand a chance.' Fi stopped to catch her breath then carried on. 'I heard about you too you know Tiff. News travels fast round here.' Tiffany who had been sipping her tea, felt her stomach flip a little asked 'why what have you heard Fi?' she managed a weak smile, but dreaded what Fi was going to say. 'Keep your g-string on love, I mean no harm to you. I will tell you now. I heard that Rodney tried to kill you and that Maisie and Phil saved your bacon. I hope it's true you gave him a broken nose. The big dumb tit thinking he could do that to you. God the sooner someone takes TJ's bunch of dickheads out the better. Be a better city or town as we call it, too. So don't sweat it nothing bad's been said about you. It's all about your ex fellah, who to be fair was batting way above his average ducks.' Tiff started to feel okay. Well as long as no one knew about her and Maisie yet. She smiled at the compliment thinking that was the thing with Fi she could always make you feel better, even if it was her who upset you in the first place. Then the canny old girl proved she was way ahead and she felt a flutter as Fi said next 'I also know that Maisie Malone is after her next catch, and I have a horrible feeling that might be you. You be careful love, she isn't right in the head. I've heard Linda's left her so she'll be more of a head case than usual. Please make sure you know what you're getting into. Right are you ready for the next instalment? Do you remember Peter Jones, Michaels bessie mate from school?' Tiff nodded that she did, and went to fill their cups up as Fi carried on talking.

She needed a minute to try and digest what Fi had said, and the little cold part of her took over. Then she felt the icy calm again. She was silent as Fi gabbed on. 'Well he's missing and no one knows why exactly, except it's got something to do with Jacko the lad. He's in hospital apparently, he's badly injured. This might have something to do with Shelagh being murdered too. I reckon TJ would try and kick them when they're down, so he probably sent the psycho and his mates after them. The Moffats lads had all gone looking for anything or anyone that may know who killed Shelagh apparently. Jacko stayed behind to lock up and someone came up on him from behind the cowardly bastard. They hit him hard and he's got a serious head injury. Everyone was saying he was dead. So the lads have been here looking for Pete, a couple of them were sitting in the bar in case he turned up. I said it's alright but you're making me punters nervous so lay low and be friendly. They left and then the next lot arrived, but I know those lads and their mothers so not that bothered by them. They're all trying to get in with Carl and Michael so they're keen to impress.' Fi stopped as she had run out of breath again. Then to Tiffany's amazement she lit up a cigarette and then had a coughing fit. 'Phew' remarked Tiffany grinning 'that was the fastest gossip sharing ever, Fi are you on the old drugs or what? Been smoking crack have we?' Fi pretend slapped her on the wrist, and replied to her, 'naughty girl, how dare you give cheek to your superiors.' They both laughed and enjoyed their closeness for a little longer. Janelle one of the girls who used to work the streets popped her head round the kitchen door and announced that Gez had just come into the bar, asking to speak to Fi. She looked puzzled and raised her eyebrows to Tiff but said to bring him through. When Gez come in Fi nearly didn't recognise him, gone were the bowl haircut and the scruffy hoody. He seemed taller, which he was now he didn't walk round in a constant stoned slump. He seemed to be holding his shoulders up. Even his complexion looked fresh and clean and virtually spot free. 'My God lad have you been on one of those new makeover programs or what? Gez actually blushed making him look even more human. Knowing he was feeling uncomfortable and he was after all Carl's cousin, Tiffany spoke up in his defence. 'Aw leave him alone Fi, he's looking so nice he must be in love.' Gez suddenly found something really interesting on the floor but then realised what Tiffany was doing, and he smiled shyly at her. 'Well before I have to ring the local priest and hire a hat for the wedding, what are you doing here Gez? What is it I can help you with?' Fi asked. 'I'm working for Carl and Michael now but keep it quiet please Fi.' Gez blurted out. Fi looked surprised and Tiffany kept quiet as she felt they'd forgotten she was there. 'Had a change of heart then lad? I knew you didn't like your cousins much, so why are you suddenly on their side? Have you stopped dealing for TJs men?' she said. Gez now blushing completely answered 'Let's just say they helped me to see what a dick I was being and they were pretty fair to me, so I'm trying to help them out and me Aunty Shelagh getting murdered has knocked me ma sick, so I just want to do the right thing. I come to see you 'cos I was hoping you'd be able to tell me what Shelagh was up to the night she was here, see if I can find anything out for them.' Fi smiled and said 'funny enough love I was just filling in my lovely mate Tiff here about all that, and to be fair lad I can't tell you more than I told her and the police, she was in here off her head and then she went out to get a taxi and that was it.' Gez looked disappointed but thanked her none the less. 'Please keep it quiet about me Fi, I'm going to meet Stephen Bentley later and he thinks I'm still working for him, but I'm shitting it. Another reason I come in here is I can't get hold of the lads, so I want someone to know where I'm going just in case.'

Fi grimaced at this, and then had an idea. 'How about when you go to see him you record him on your phone? Have you got a decent one like a Nokia? I've got a 638 it's a cracking little thing, that way you can cover your back.' Gez nodded and said it was a good idea. Tiffany had been taking all this in, she was surprised, thinking that as Gez was family he was bound to be on the Moffats side, to find out he'd not been was a shock, and to think he was in with TJ, it just showed how careful you had to be and to trust no one but yourself. He kept giving her shy looks but Tiffany was used to men doing that. She decided then that she would keep him sweet in case she needed him in the future to get close to the big prize Carl. She smiled at him and he looked away quickly. Fi noticed this and wondered what Tiff was up to, she knew her well and was worried about her playing around with Maisie, and didn't want her to get involved with Gez as he was at risk now he wasn't working for TJ anymore and it was only a matter of time before TJ found out he was back on his cousins side. Still she was a tough girl considering her stature, and could look after herself as she'd proved by breaking that big ape Rodney's nose. She giggled out loud at this and Gez and Tiff looked at her in surprise. 'What's going on, what has got into you, you nutter?' Tiff asked smiling herself. 'Absolutely nothing queen just imagining you fighting with Rodney the plonker, the size of you too.' Fi replied. Gez looked amazed at this, and thought he'd have to wait to see Fi on her own and ask about this. He liked Tiffany she was so pretty and she'd been kind to him so now he was hooked, and he looked forward to being on his own later so he could imagine what it would be like to be her boyfriend and to be able to bed her. He felt himself getting a hard on so he mentally slapped himself and brought himself back down to earth. 'Right Fi thanks for all your help, our Michael and Carl think the world of you, so I know I can trust you to keep my secret quiet can't I? I know I hardly know you Tiffany but you won't tell anyone will you? Seriously I would get my head kicked in if TJ knew.' He was almost whining again like old Gez so Fi stepped in. 'No lad, she won't she's a good girl our Tiff so you've got nothing to worry about. Go on go with you now and sort out that arsehole Bentley, find out what he knows, but for fucks sake be careful.' Gez smiled and nodded at Fi and took a deep breath, he felt a new confidence now and he knew he'd go and face that bastard Bentley and find out what he could for his cousins, and he might even impress Tiffany with his bravery.

Gez left Fi's and decided to go into town grab a burger; he had time to do that and then go and meet Stephen. He had his money sorted, he'd got a few mates to clear out the place, hired a pro to do the decorating. When his mother pretended she was fed up with all the mess when she come back from Blackpool, she was thrilled. He felt good getting his place sorted. He had got some nice stuff, and his bedroom was now immaculate, new bed, new stereo a decent TV and video combo. He'd done loads for his mum, and he'd donated a big amount to the homeless. When he'd taken money off some of them he felt deep shame now. Apart from that negative side he was feeling really pleased with himself, and then he remembered that Stephen would know something was up. He thought of how to get round it, and he was going to pretend he'd smartened himself up because of Aunty Shelagh dying, and that his mum had come into some money from an insurance policy. Yes that would do, he'd have to just wing it he smiled to himself. Piece of piss he thought. The man was crazy.

Tiffany had watched Gez go, and said to Fi 'He's almost cute him isn't he? Do you think it's because of who his cousins are? That was a bit heavy you telling me not to tell anyone, I love a gossip Fi that's why I come to you because you do it so well, and there's not a vindictive bone in you. But I'm not soft in the head I know when to keep my mouth shut!' Fi blushed crimson on hearing this. 'Oi stoppit with the attitude Tiff, I love you and I will tell you what you want to know, just ask and if I don't' know I'll ask some people who do okay? I'm just an old slag with a weakness for biscuits and good television, the odd film and I'm happy lovely, so make sure you start appreciating life like it should be when you're young and beautiful. Go on home and avoid the ones who drag you down, and look for a good man to keep you safe. If you can't do it yet then try and keep your head down in case you get caught in the crossfire. You can't avoid it if you're involved with any of them TJ Murphy, the Moffats and Maisie Malone. You just be careful, she will drop you like a ton of shit if Linda shows up or if she gets bored. Remember that, I'm telling you the truth for your own good.' Tiffany nodded to let her know she'd heard what was said, and for the first time felt real anger at her old friend, and snapped at her saying 'Do you know what Fi you're pissing me off; you don't think I'm capable of turning it round on the horrible cow? I know what's she like, and I've shagged men from every walk of life so I can put up with most things, it's not her I want it's someone she can help me meet OKAY?'She shouted the last word to make her point, turned on her heel and went into the ladies loo to calm down. Fi sat there fretting, hoping Tiff would realise that she was trying to protect her, she could read her like a book, and knew that she could have most men she wanted, but seemed to be drawn to the bad boys, like herself and most of the women she knew. While Tiffany was in the Ladies toilets resting her forehead on the cold glass of the mirror cooling off, she heard her phone deliver a text, it was from Maisie, asking her if she was around later as she'd like to call and see her. Tiffany decided to take a gamble and say no, she just hoped she wouldn't blow it so soon, she knew it was all part of the game but she just couldn't face Maisie and sex with her tonight. She sat on the loo and thought for a good five minutes, still a little unsure and just as she had changed her mind and decided to get it over and done with, another text off Maisie came, and made her mind up for her. It was easy to decide now, the stupid bitch could wait. She had sent her an order and not a request and one thing Tiffany had always prided herself on was she wouldn't be told what to do by fucking anyone, especially from an aging power crazy dyke who treated women worse than most of the dickhead men she knew.

Chapter 30

Stephen had sorted out Pete, and dropped him off at the hotel then much to his annoyance had to pick him up again. TJ had insisted he kept him near him as word spread of Pete's betrayal. Although the Moffats had tried to keep it in house TJ had been the one telling everyone, he didn't give a shit that he was risking Pete's life or Stephens's safety, he could look after himself of course and it was just another way to get one over on Michael and Carl. He'd also found out that Jacko wasn't dead, and that Pete had nearly killed him but not quite. He found himself disappointed, but at least he wasn't wanted for murder, GBH he could get dropped if he could get the right coppers and judge on it, if he still needed his services then of course. He wanted Pete so he could what was that word...... monopolise him, was that it? Anyway who cares, when he'd wrung every little bit of usefulness out of him he was gone. After all if he could betray someone he'd been friends with most of his life, he could turn on him in a minute so yes he was going to get his money's worth.

Stephen was angry and a little bit tired, and so he decided to kill two birds with one stone, after picking up Pete which had pissed him off having to spend more time with the imbecile he would go and see what information Gez had and score off the little twat at the same time. He had some coke stashed but after the good stuff off Shelagh it hadn't hit the mark, and he needed some to get through the next few days of shit with this tosser in tow. They hadn't had time to get Pete's stuff from his place so Stephen thought it could be fun to go to his house. After all he knew now that Jacko wasn't dead like they'd thought. The Moffats and the police would be looking for him, but it wasn't with the same urgency and he could go and take his time. Maybe Pete's wife was tasty someone to look at and review as someone to play with later. He took a sly glance at Pete sitting next to him in the car, he could see and smell his fear and was about to tell him Jacko wasn't dead. Pete caught him looking and trying to be funny said 'you a bum boy or what Bentley lad? Do you want a snog or what, stop staring at me you bent bastard?' Pete laughed at his own wit, and Stephen nearly leant over and bit him. It took every little bit of strength he had not do lose it and so breathing deeply he focused on the air conditioner swinging from the mirror. They had been sitting in the hotels car park, so Stephen started up the car and said 'come on stick on your seat belt wouldn't want you to go through the window now would we?' Pete even then didn't pick up on the menace in his voice, his stupidity a shield to the more subtle threats that had a habit of flying past him. 'So come on then Pete do you want to go and see your missus and the little one, and get some of your stuff or come with me and see Gez or both? Stephen asked feeling calmer now at the thought of amusing himself with Pete's girlfriend at a later date. Lately his fantasies, daydreams and memories were blurring into his reality, he was starting to wonder what was real and what was in the past sometimes. But he wasn't that worried, as long as no one but him knew so what? He enjoyed it all so it didn't really matter. As he was thinking he had automatically started driving towards Liverpool so he put his foot down and headed for the tunnel. As for Pete he'd let the bastard suffer thinking he'd killed Jacko until he saw fit to tell him he hadn't.

Maisie she was furious, Tiffany the little tramp had turned her down, saying she needed some time to herself. Maisie had enjoyed a long bath some weed, good food and had given herself a top to toe going over. Full body moisturiser, face pack, shaved legs and underarms, manicure and pedicure and had finished touching up her roots. She had felt great and it was cathartic in forgetting Linda and looking forward to Tiffany all the more. Now the little bitch was crying off, probably scared of enjoying her fucking self with another woman. God how dare she ignore me she thought, no wonder Rodney the plonker had lost it with the little bitch. She took a few deep breaths and sent out texts to the lads asking if anyone had any news on Linda, the Moffats and had they found anyone to blame yet? She put her phone down then decided to go and see them since Tiffany had pissed her off. She dressed in black, stylish top with flared sleeves and subtle diamante around the neck and, black dress pants. She looked good and as she applied her makeup rang Phil and asked him to pick her up. She'd go to the Moffats town house or where ever they were now and show her support however she could. Then she'd go and see Tiffany, that's why she had spent ages getting ready, just for her, so she'd better put out the cheeky cow. She rang Phil again to see where he was, then feeling antsy and impatient, ran down the stairs and waited for him to pick her up. Phil pulled up ten minutes later, he'd been on the prowl all night and day. He'd organized their lads to look for Pete, had tried to find out information on Shelagh and was tired out. Maisie saw he was exhausted, so said to him 'Aw look at you honey you're knackered doing our dirty work, it's okay I'll get one of the other lads to drive me round.' Phil smiled tiredly and said 'Maisie I'll drive you down to the town house where they all are, and will go in with you and show my face for an hour. Then I'll take you to Tiffs I assume, then home for some well deserved sleep.' The truth was that Linda's letter was still resonating in her head, especially the bit about Phil always loving her. It made her feel flattered in a way, but she didn't want to ruin their relationship, so she vowed she'd never tell him she knew. She'd noticed lately however Phil had made little digs about her love life, and she'd caught him looking at her and not in a nice way. She wondered if she'd gone too far with him as well as Linda. She would sort it out and buy him something nice. That was her way out, easy to solve any problem just throw money at it. Thinking of buying presents she could take one of the little Ivory carvings she'd bought for Tiffany as an extra excuse to see her, and suss out what was going on there. She still couldn't believe Tiff had blown her off, she had to be patient and find out why she had done it she supposed. She was lost in thought and didn't notice that they'd pulled up outside the Moffats town house. She said to Phil, 'God that was fast. How did you get us here so soon?' Phil shrugged and said 'It's because you were lost in your own little world. So I left you too it.' Right she thought, I need to focus. So she mentally prepared herself and got out waiting for Phil to lock the Land Rover.

Michael and Carl were in their study at the town house, they'd all been back for a while and had ordered a load of pizzas, kebabs and chips for everyone. They had taken theirs upstairs while they caught up, and were just finishing up when Little Joey come stomping up the stairs. 'Visitor for you lads, shall I show her up?' he gasped out of breath. Michael laughed at the big man, 'sure can if you tell us who it is you dozy git.' Carl laughed too, and Joey pretended to be hurt, but couldn't hide his big grin. 'Maisie of course you pair of divvies, and they call me thick!' Joey said. Michael threw a chip at him and he ducked and started to bounce down the stairs, Michael shouted after him so he stopped and looked up. 'Joey bring her up pretty please' he put up two fingers and gestured towards Carl, and then carried on thumping down the stairs. Michael and Carl laughed at him and Carl shouted 'now play nice and stop titting about.' But he'd gone. 'He can't half move for a big man him can't he?' said Carl. 'Yeah at school anyone who took the piss out of him, after a game of rugby or footie they never did it again remember? Michael replied and then looked up as he heard footsteps on the stairs and there was Maisie. Joey was just behind her, and kept a respectful 3 steps behind. "Hiya lads, how you doing?' she said and put her arms out for them. She hugged and kissed them both and then when they started to sit down grabbed both their hands. Then kneeled down so she could look up into their faces. "Of all the times for this to happen I am so sorry about your Shelagh. I know everyone says that, and I know you're probably sick of hearing it, but I do feel for you. Your mum was the same as my mother. They should never have had kids, but when she died I felt so angry and upset, even though she left me years before to be with her one true love vodka.' Maisie pulled herself up and then asked 'talking of booze does anyone fancy a drink, cuppa or something stronger?'

Michael stood up and hugged her and then said to her and Carl 'it's okay to be pissed, angry, happy, laughing as long as you feel something, and believe me I've felt all of those over the last few days. It's okay Maisie I will get the drinks sorted.' She sat down in Michaels place as he went to get their drinks and after removing her shoes put her feet up. "So how can I help Carl? I hope you're happy with Phil and the boys looking. We'll find them, who murdered your mother and where Pete is hiding. The traitorous little shit, I pray none of my men would do it to me, but you know what greed is like, everyone has a price don't they? It's just a matter of timing.'

Carl sat thinking of Maisies words then replied. 'The pity is Maisie love is Pete, hates me, that was and is part of it. He thought he was more important to our Mick than he was, and then he realised he wasn't. Sad thing is TJ probably gave him more money than he can count, so he went.'
Maisie nodded and said 'I'm having a hard time myself you know, Linda's left me. Between us I deserve it in a way, but she'll be back we're solid me and her, we have been for years. She's put up with me having a bit on the side all these years. I don't know what's going on in her little head but she will realise what she's missing and be back.' Carl looked at Maisie and for the first time saw the vain arrogant bitch she was famous for being. Although he didn't feel good thinking like that he still saw it, and felt himself reluctant to tell her too much. Michael came back up the stairs carrying a tray with cups of tea and the standard bottle of JD. Carl gave him a sly wink and he knew that something had changed.

The three sat talking about how Pete had nearly killed Jacko and how could he turn on someone he'd known most of his life. Michael said he felt he had to be the one to sort it as he'd trusted him. He'd thought the world of him until a few months ago, when it had all changed. Maisie wanted to know why and Michael then said ' not long ago Joey had seen Pete's missus out shopping with the little one, and both of them had cuts and bruises. She had a black eye and cuts on her face. The little one on his arms and legs. When Joey asked what had happened she ran off mumbling.
Joey may not be the cleverest as we often tease him, but even he knows abuse when he sees it.' 'Fucking hell Mick!' shouted Carl, 'when were you going to share that one? The prick doing that to his girl and his own flesh and blood. You know people have told me for years he's a wrong one, but I always gave him the benefit of the doubt because he was your mate. I knew how much he hated me but I let it go because I thought he was loyal

to you. If I would have got even a sniff of him hurting a woman and kid I'd have killed him, or at least made sure he couldn't do it again.'

Michael stood up and it was obvious to Maisie he was hurting inside and felt shame over his involvement. Maisie stood up to and walked over to Michael and hugged him again, and he said to Carl. 'That's why I didn't tell you I wanted to make sure first, so I went round to see Sylvia and Jay, and the fear I could sense was real. It's just makes it easier to sort him out.' Carl shook his head in disbelief and glared at Michael. He felt his phone vibrate in his pocket so he grabbed it and flipped it open. He couldn't believe what he saw, and he wanted to tell Michael but for some reason he couldn't explain he didn't want Maisie to know. 'Is it anything important lad?' Michael asked glad for the focus changing from him and Pete to something else. 'Nah nothing important but something private about Jacko and his ma.' Carl said, letting him know something was up and he didn't want Maisie to know. 'Oh okay tell us later.' Carl snapped his phone shut and then pretended it had gone off because it had run out of power.

Chapter 31

Tiffany was back in her flat after leaving Fi's, relieved that Maisie hadn't showed up. She'd sent a snotty text about seeing her later or something and then she sent one saying she was going to the Moffats. Tiffany was furious she'd missed her chance to see their inner sanctum, and to bat her eyelashes at Carl. Still she needed this time to prepare for the inevitable shag with Maisie. God the thought of going down on her still bothered her. She couldn't understand why she was so reluctant as she'd put up with worse. She'd also had her share of disgusting sexual experiences, but then that was one of the main reasons she'd left when she had. Instead of having loads of punters, she exchanged that life for getting a few mugs like Rodney, and it was just as tedious. Really dull and boring and then she still had to shag them occasionally. She wanted good looking, young and rich, not ugly, old and scary. Yes Carl now he fitted the young, handsome and rich. He was so good looking; he was gorgeous, with a beautiful mocha complexion, and a knockout smile, his eyes full of mischief. She'd only ever seen him from a distance at a few parties etc. and usually she was with someone who would kick off if she'd so much as looked at him.

Not only that she was ashamed of some of the men she'd been with, she was glad he hadn't noticed her. Especially if he'd have seen the likes of Rodney, God she could do without him that was for sure. She doubted he'd come back now, not after her hitting him in the face and breaking his nose. God it had felt good and she wasn't even sure how she's managed to do it but she had. She decided as she'd missed her chance for tonight at least, she'd put on her pjs, grab a few munchies and go to bed and watch TV just to switch off for a while. Yep nice big joint of grass, and then she'd sleep well too.

She loved this as it was still a luxury to get some time just for herself. She'd hated it when she was waiting for Maisie or Phil previously, she'd been on edge waiting for news. It wasn't the same as now when she had some luxuries, and she didn't have to answer the door. This was different, at the moment no punters and soon she'd never have to think of that part of her life ever again. Ahh! True bliss she thought, it really was compared to the night before when she was still shaking from the fear that Rodney had caused, then having to rely on Maisie and Phil. She quite fancied Phil, she just didn't like the fact he was Maisies lackey, it was horrible to watch. She was so sick of sex and having to please others, she was glad she was working on bagging a Moffat, and Maisie may tide her over financially until she was ready. She didn't want to use her savings. She may have to still do the odd job or maybe just do some proper escorting even though it didn't pay nearly as much. Still a hundred quid just to have a nice meal or the opera, and be on some ones arm was good,. Then her savings were safe and they were already pretty nice. It was mad when she thought about Maisie making her come, but then she was stoned and imagining Carl doing it, so having an orgasm was pretty easy. She missed being fucked after though, after she'd come she enjoyed that. She could sometimes come again if she was with someone she actually fancied, and he had a nice dick. To be gentle with her too counted. She'd been hurt too many times. Plus girth was all that mattered for a lot of women and yet men were obsessed with length when it wasn't that important. She could shut her eyes and she was with anyone she chose. She giggled at her thoughts about dicks, grabbed her clean pjs and supplies and smoked her weed on the balcony, and then she crept into bed. Some daft program was on late, a couple of students cooking or something, and then the Divine David some very strange TV indeed. She decided to watch a video, and went for one of her favourites, Scream. Then she thought better of it the last thing she wanted was to fall asleep listening to that. She got up and went in search of Romeo and Juliet. She loved this video, although she didn't really understand the Shakespearean language, she had the hots for Leonardo Di Caprio. Ooh she liked to fantasize about being with him. Her

139

last conscious thoughts were of Leonardo and Carl and who would be the best kisser. It was so comfortable she soon dozed off and went into a deep sleep.

Maisie was drinking with the Moffats and although Michael and Carl were trying to calm her down she didn't care that she was losing it. The drunker she got the more anger she felt towards Tiffany. She'd tell her and fucking Linda what she thought of them. The pair of bitches weren't playing by the rules. For a start she needed to find out where Linda had gone and who with. She racked her brains and couldn't think of any woman Linda would run off with. It must be someone she didn't know. Then she went on about a Tiffany who was straight but she was going to turn her properly and make her lick her feet. She kept going on about it and Carl had had enough. 'Come on Maisie love, I know you're pissed and angry but come on stay positive hey? You were telling me before how Linda always comes back so why is now any different?' Maisie glared at Carl and he held her gaze, she eventually looked away and Michael saw his chance to get rid of her as he wanted to find out what was bothering Carl. 'Come on queen you've had enough why don't you get Phil to take you home or to the club?' He opened a wooden box and took out a sandwich bag.' Here you go, some E's, coke and a bit of weed. Take your pick it will mellow you out.' Maisie stood up and looked at them both. She snatched the baggie of drugs that Michael was holding out, and then started shouting at the top of her lungs for Phil, who despite being knackered had waited for her instead of going home for some sleep.

'Right lads I'm off as you suggested. You know the score if you need anything let us know.' Phil nodded to Michael and Carl his face belying how he felt; he was embarrassed about Maisie being drunk and was doing his best to get her away from them and the house. After all they'd just lost their mother and had Pete betray them, and yet selfish old Maisie was off it. Just because of Linda leaving, well tough shit. She'd brought it on herself. She let Phil lead her out amid shouts of goodbye, and he sat her in the Land Rover. She crossed her arms and sat there brooding. He climbed in and started the engine. He put the heating on and sat there waiting for Maisie to say where she wanted to go. He was angry at her lately anyway and sick of her demanding ways. Unfortunately he knew he couldn't get through to her when she was like this and he struggled to keep the anger out of his voice.

'Right where do you want to go, home or the club? It's still early in our world.' Maisie looked at him in contempt and said 'where do you think? Take me to Tiffany's I want to see her tonight. She tried to tell me no! Cheeky wee bitch, but nobody turns me down do they Ginga?' Phil was furious now, 'Maisie no one has called me that since school and if memory

140

serves me correctly they were the bullies. I took them all out even though they were a lot older than me, and it pisses me off when you bring it up.' Maisie wasn't sorry in the slightest and sniggered under her breath. Phil punched the steering wheel shook his hand in pain, and drove off, ignoring Maisies over exaggerated movements as she tried to light up a joint out of her bag of goodies.

The men had all gathered upstairs now Maisie had gone. It was quiet then Billy stood up. Another of their gang who had known them since they were babies. 'We want to help that's all, you've just lost your mum TJs started a war with us, Pete the cowardly dickhead has fucked off to the devils side. Never mind that Bentley is taking the piss thinking he's invincible because most people are scared of him, but we're not are we lads? Everyone shouted no and Michael felt a surge of pride. Joey came back from the loo and said 'what the fuck is going on? I only went to the toilet and everyone's gone a bit mental.' The look on his face and the confusion made Billy start laughing and all of them joined in and laughed long and hard. Michael took the chance while emotions though running high were good, 'Okay lads, we've just got to do this on our own, we will fill you in we promise when we get back and thanks for looking out for us.' Billy satisfied for now said 'Oh stoppit you big puff we'll be going to Sadie's in town with the rest of the gays next!' 'You can talk Billy I know you've got the leather pants for when you dance to YMCA by the Village People.' the banter and the laughter continued and Michael and Carl saw their chance to leave, and walked out into the night.

Stephen had been driving round with Pete in the car, hovering round the town house, but not too close. Pete of course was nearly pissing his pants with fear. They'd gone to his place to pick up some of his stuff and the selfish bastard had taken his own kids games console and games, leaving him some crappy out of date eight bit machine. Stephen had been right about his other half; she was a young petite blonde obviously under the thumb of Pete the dickhead. What a waste she was gorgeous, Stephen stood there staring at her, imagining how it would feel to play with her. Pete noticed the way he was looking at her. Open lust on his face and yet he wouldn't say anything not to this nut job. Instead he growled at her when he thought Stephen was preoccupied with his boy Jake.

It was her fault anyhow he reasoned with himself, she'd had her hair done and was wearing makeup. Stephen told him to hurry up, and then he made Pete angry and dropped him in the shit by telling Sylvia that he had some money for her. He reluctantly got the envelope out of his pocket and Stephen snatched it off him, doing a rough count up of the money in there. He gave a wad of notes to Sylvia and threw the envelope back to him. "Don't start fucking moaning at me Pete, I gave you the money and I can just as easily take it away. The least you can do is give this delightful young mother a reward for being with you for so long.' Sylvia heard all this and was astounded by the fact that the scary man had stuck up for her. Stephen then walked over to the young lad and took a wad of money out of his back pocket. He counted out three hundred pounds, and handed it to him. 'There you go mate, tomorrow you go with your mum into town and buy a decent console, and some games. Make sure they're better than the one your dads borrowed eh?' Jakes face lit up like a Christmas tree, he also blushed down to his toes, as he was very fair and blond like his mum. Sylvia looked at him with a new found respect and thanked him, she was enjoying every minute of this watching Pete the coward who liked to use her as a punch bag, getting a taste of his own medicine.

Pete pulled Sylvia to one side, and told her that if anyone came to the door asking for him, not to say she'd seen him. He then told her what he would do to her if she let him down. Stephen heard this too. For some reason he wanted this woman Sylvia to trust him. Was it because he may pay a visit to her soon? For the first time he didn't feel comfortable thinking this. The little boy had done something to him, he realised he was very like him when he was small. He couldn't take the mother as it would leave him with this piece of shite Pete. He shook his head, and inwardly laughed at himself. He had feelings about this? It must be the coke he'd been hitting it hard lately. He realised then that it was silent and everyone was looking at him. 'Are you okay Mr. Bentley? Do you want a cup of tea or a glass of water or some pop?' Sylvia said. Pete went over and grabbed her arm, 'stop creeping round him' he said through gritted teeth. Stephen had had enough by now of being within twenty feet of this bullying dickhead. He walked over and whispered in his ear. Whatever he said Sylvia noted with joy he let go of her and went white.

Walking to the door he left without a word. Stephen enjoying his power went over to Jake and shook his hand. Then he went to Sylvia and did an awkward squeeze of her hand and told her not to worry anymore. Perhaps he may call soon if that was okay? So he could see the little boy and play some video games with him. She just nodded, thrilled at this turn in her fortune, as he left and shut the door. She grabbed Jake and said 'At last my love, we can go and have some fun tomorrow. I've got plenty of money too so we can go and have lunch in Lewis's. Then go up Bold Street or to St. Johns market and buy your console. Won't it be fun?'She gave him a final hug and told him to go and wash his hands and face and brush his teeth and they would have an early night and be up with the lark to go shopping. When she found out in the months to come who Stephen was she nearly fainted and had a panic attack, never understanding how Pete could have brought someone so dangerous to their home with Jake there. She would discuss it with her new partner in the future. He was somebody good, who made her and Jake feel safer than they ever had before.

Pete was angry and scared he stood by the car and waited for Stephen to come out. He was angry at Sylvia, he was angry that his son was going to have a better console than him, such was his selfishness. As he looked at the bags in the back of the car he realised that this was all he had in the world, and it was somehow Sylvia's fault. Stephen came out and as he approached him he didn't see the punch coming. He fell over and got up quickly, absolutely furious and held his nose which was bleeding profusely. All of a sudden his anger left him like air from a burst balloon. Stephen had a knife in his hand, the street light glinted off it making it really noticeable. Pete knew that he would have no trouble whatsoever using it. Stephen gritted his teeth and ranted. 'Aren't you fucking nice eh? Picking on a woman like that and your poor kid, I know you're a vile bastard the way you've given up your so called best mate Michael. You even hit Jacko from behind, which was a cowardly thing to do. So you will do as you are told from now on or I'll fucking tie you up outside the Moffats front door. Do you get it you dumb bastard?' If it wasn't for TJ telling me I had to look after you, I'd have slit your throat by now and thrown you in the Mersey just like I did Shelagh Moffat.'

Pete holding his throbbing nose nodded and looked at the floor, he couldn't believe what Stephen had just said; he knew now that Stephen was as mad as a hatter and a lot more dangerous. Stephen opened the car and told him to get in. When they were both seated he said 'right we're going to meet Gez now and see what information he has for us, so you keep your mouth shut and we'll see what the night brings.' Pete was shaking from head to toe, knowing he was sitting with the person who'd murdered Shelagh Moffat. 'What's wrong with you now, you are a fucking jelly shaking like that after a little slap.' Stephen sneered. The irony of this situation was lost on him, the fact that he murdered and maimed women didn't matter to him in the slightest. He didn't like the way Pete who was a snivelling coward could treat a girl in front of her son like that. She was beautiful and deserved to be treated so much better. Then one day when they were complete he could love her with his knife and she would understand. He could take Jake and treat him like his son, and train him in his ways, how good it felt to kill. He had finally lost his grip on reality, what little sanity he had hung onto was fast disappearing. His evil deeds were catching up with him, he just didn't know it yet.

Gez was happily walking down by the Pier Head, he looked up at the Liver buildings, and thought of all the people that must have passed through this port. The way they'd done the Albert Dock up in the 1980s,

143

and now they had Richard and Judy. One day they'd seen Richard without Judy so took the piss. When they were going past in a car. It was meant in good humour, but Richard must have been sick of it all and shook his fist at them. They all thought it was funny anyway. They backed the car up and he legged it much to their hilarity. Oh and he remembered the Slavery Museum being opened in 1994 was it? Yes the first half of the 1990s had been a lot kinder to Liverpool than the 1980s that was for sure. He felt good, lots of reasons to feel this way. He fumbled with his phone, the latest Nokia but he had to keep it hidden half the bagheads by him would take it off him without a second thought, especially since some of them still worked for TJ selling smack. It had been so cut you were lucky if it stopped you turkeying never mind give you a hit, that's why everyone was getting into skunk the new weed. The Moffats wouldn't have anything to do with smack, after all it was heroin that had killed their sister in a way. Also she was his cousin Sara, so if you were on the gear you were a big fat no to them, so the dregs still ran around for TJ selling little bits of smack making a decent profit. However the way Michael and Carl were taking over the other drugs, it's all he'd have left soon. He reached the part of the Pier head where the Ferry terminal was. It was dark here and no one was around. He was early and now he felt a little nervous, it was so isolated here that's why Bentley probably picked it. He made his way to the benches and could hear the Mersey roaring as the tide come in. He sat on the bench and tested his phones microphone, he pressed record and said out loud 'testing testing one two three.' He then played it back and giggled to himself. It was primed and ready for when Bentley got here, and waited where he'd been told to, third bench on the left. His cousins would be so proud of him.

Chapter 32

Maisie was angry at Phil he'd practically thrown her out the car at Tiffany's flats and didn't even ask if she was okay. Never mind saying he'd come back for her when she wanted a lift. She felt in her pockets and pulled out the baggie of drugs and the two fifties and three twenties she always had on her. She could get a taxi. Christ she could get a limo for the night for that round here, probably two nights, so she felt okay. She looked up at Tiffany's flat and the lights were off, but she wasn't fooled she knew she'd be in there. She was probably fast asleep, boy was she going to get a fright soon. She was Maisie Malone, expert lover of women, a dyke to die for, she laughed out loud at her weird thoughts.

She'd necked loads of E's, smoked a spliff now she needed a little coke to sort her out. She'd heard this was good stuff, really strong so she looked forward to a line or two. Where to do it though, she'd have liked to have done it before she got to Tiffany's flat, so she could think straight. God she didn't know if she was horny or hungry as the cannabis and E's fought in her bloodstream. She knew one thing though she was getting in the flats. She waited in the shadows, and within ten minutes someone was walking up to the door. She ran behind them, and it was the girl with the baby, only today on her own, dressed in a green uniform. The girl turned round her face white, and put her arms up in a defensive gesture. 'Keep your hair on love, it's only me from the other night I keep forgetting the key to this big door but I have a key to the flat where my girlfriend lives.' She said and shook her keys in front of her. 'Here if you let me in you can have another 20 quid to buy the little one something.' Maisie dug the money out of her pocket and gave her one of the fifties by mistake. The girl snatched the money and let her in, making sure it shut behind them. She thought it best to keep completely quiet as this woman was scary, big and off her head. All Angela wanted was to get back in after working a twelve hour shift at the new 24 hour garage where she had just started, and hug her baby. She practically run to the lift, then realised they would have to share as only one was working. 'Here we go let's get the lift' she said to Maisie, hoping that she wasn't making a big mistake. Maisie grinned and enjoyed Angela's skittish behaviour knowing that she was making her really nervous. 'Okay then, I'm ready are you? Maisie leered at her drunkenly but Angela knew pissed and this woman wasn't drunk. She was off her head, but not on alcohol that was for sure. She pressed the buttons for floor one, so she could get off and walk up the rest of the stairs, and then the right one for Maisie. They got in and as they went up Maisie forgot all about the girl in the lift with her and concentrated on what she was going to say to Tiffany to get her into bed.

Michael had tried Gez's phone and found it going straight to voice mail. Worried that he'd be with Bentley already he didn't want to keep ringing, so he sent a text. He jumped as his phone vibrated and fell off the dashboard, as Carl was turning round. He read it quickly and told Carl 'he's heading for or is at the Pier head, the benches past the Ferry terminal where it's dark and lonely of course.' Carl thought for a moment and then said 'which is the quickest way there Mikey lad? Hey hang on how do we know it's not a trap?' Michael said 'Never thought of that, I suppose it could be but I don't think it is. I'll try ringing him again.' This time Gez picked up, and shouted 'Hiya how you doing? I am on my own the nutters aren't here yet, so I'll see you soon. Give my regards to Carl.' As Gez was about to end the call Michael heard a noise in the back ground, a thud and a sort of groan, Michael shouted him but he heard nothing else and then the connection went dead. 'Carl we have to get there as soon as we can. I heard something weird then the phone was cut off. You don't think Bentley and Pete are already there do you?' Carl mulled it over and said 'Nah you know Gez he's a dick when it comes to technology, he's got a new phone he probably can't figure it out yet, come on we'll be there soon it'll be alright.' He felt better for reassuring Michael but what about him? He thought with a grim smile. For the first time worrying for his cousin who had had a crappy life too. Perhaps they should have brought him over sooner, and then they wouldn't be in this situation. It was tough at the top of their game, and if they'd have helped Gez sooner it could have been seen as a sign of weakness, but it still didn't make him feel any better. 'This is it Mikey lad, finally get to confront the tit Bentley and Pete at the same time. I just hope they don't do anything to hurt Gez.'

Unfortunately for Gez as he was finishing off his phone call, Stephen and Pete crept up on him, and with the noise from the river and his phone pressed to his ear, he hadn't heard them coming. Stephen walked straight up behind and hit him hard as he could. He heard a voice shouting from the phone so he looked at it and there was fucking Michael on the other end. The stupid bastard had even put his cousins' names on his new phone with a smiley face. He picked it up wiped it off as it had a little blood on it. He noticed that it was on record. He laughed and said into it "hello twats still think you can mess around with me. Another one bites the dust. Three Moffats gone. You two next eh Pete?" Pete was too far away to hear or see what he was doing. He put the phone back in Gez's pocket and spat at him with contempt. It served the Scouse dickhead right, he was thick that was for sure, one of the sneaky little bagheads on his payroll had told him he had good information for him. Stephen had offered him twenty quid for the information and he'd taken it fast. It was worth much more than that. He'd have paid at least a hundred for it. When the oily bastard had told him that Gez was now working for the Moffats according to Gez's mother. She was telling everyone that since Shelagh had gone they'd been looked after by Michael and Carl. She boasted that this was the start of a new era and Gez was going to be up there with his famous cousins. It always amazed Stephen just how two faced everyone was, especially from that fucking Estate. One day they hated each other, then the next minute they were best friends. It made no sense to him and he couldn't hide his contempt for these lowlifes who were so below him it was tiring just to talk to them.

So Stephen had already known that when he met Gez that he'd lie through his horrible teeth. He was going to pretend not to know anything and see if he could get some information off the little weasel by fair means or foul. The urge to hit him had taken over. He was going to wake him up and if he wouldn't tell him anything well then he'd have to administer some tough love with the great big bowie knife in his hand. He looked at Gez on the floor , he couldn't wait for the fun part. Pete being a coward just blindly obeyed everything Stephen asked him to do, fretting, wondering how long it would be before the police would catch him for Jacko's murder. Right then he felt grateful he had Stephen looking out for him. It never occurred to him that Stephen had singled him out and groomed him, knowing he'd be the easiest to manipulate. It had been almost too easy to get him to join TJ. Stephen knew that his hatred and jealousy for Carl would do all the work for him, he was that predictable.

Gez was lying on the floor, out cold by the looks of things, so Stephen stood over him and said out loud 'I need to wake this boy up, I'll have to think of something as we have no water not even rain.' Much to Pete's amazement he pulled out his penis and started pissing all over Gez's face and top. 'Fucking hell Stephen I didn't expect that!' Pete almost shouted. Gez started to groan and come awake, and as Stephen zipped himself up he told Pete that he could hold him in a minute while he questioned him. Pete didn't say anything else just nodded still stunned, not wanting to get involved with hurting Gez at all, not after Jacko. Plus he had no urge to get piss all over his hands either especially Stephen Bentleys as he felt it would somehow infect him with something dark and evil. He had that look on his face again, and Pete knew there was no way of getting out of this, the ecstasy apparent in his expression he took out the knife and went to work on Gez. Pete hid his eyes, he'd never seen that much blood from one person. He had to put his hands over his ears; the noise was too much. The phone was still recording as Gez died in agony and fear, just like his cousin Sara.

Maisie had arrived at Tiffs floor highly amused by the panic in the young woman's eyes she must have been shitting a brick. She had got off at the first floor after all and Maisie was sure she lived on the second last time she was here. She chuckled to herself when she kept imagining Rodney and herself sitting in court, a solicitor asking Tiff who do you prefer the leech or the lesbian? She laughed out loud at herself, then in a drunken parody slapped her hand over her mouth and then whispered to herself 'shut up you stupid woman.' She was at Tiff's door and she had keys, she'd paid for the new door so it was hers in a way. She put the keys in and entered a lot more quietly now, she wanted to surprise her, she might even catch the little cow with a man in bed. This made her really angry and she thought of Linda and her anger grew. It was dark in the hall and she could see a small amount of light from under Tiffs bedroom door. She opened the door and she could just see Tiffs shape in the bed, she looked like she was on her own. She waited until her eyes adjusted to the dark, and then she went over to the bed and lay beside Tiffany. Tiffany had been fast asleep but she started to come to as she felt someone by her on the bed and she felt sick with fear. What if it was Rodney? But then the bed wasn't dipping like it did with him so it must be fucking Maisie. She must have had three sets of keys made. She stayed as still as she could, willing her heartbeat to slow down. She heard her sniggering on the bed and felt genuine fear. She was off her head, it was obvious and she thought about the gun the other night, Maisie kept that didn't she? She pretended to wake up, and then sat up and screamed at the top of her voice. Maisie looked so shocked that Tiffany wanted to laugh then, hysteria bubbling up in her chest. She managed to swallow it and got a foot on the floor ready to get away, but her legs were cramped and wouldn't move properly. Fuck oh God, oh shit she was saying in her head what do I do? Then she felt a horrible pain in her head and realised that Maisie had grabbed her hair. 'SSSSHHH!' Maisie hissed loudly in her ear then whispered 'Fucking shut up Tiffany.' Tiffany decided to play it stupid and said 'Oh my God is that you Maisie?' which immediately threw her off her stride and she let go of her hair.

Tiffany sat up properly and turned around on the bed, she was really angry with Maisie but also scared. Her trembling voice gave her away. 'Maisie what the frigging hell are you doing? You know I've been attacked and hurt and then you go and do this to me. How come you got in, have you got my keys?' Maisie sat deadly still across from her on the bed, and Tiff put the lamp on, and then was sorry that she had. She could see Maisie clearly now, and she would never forget the look as she knew it well. It was the same naked lust she saw in a few of her more violent clients, ones that she'd refused to ever see again. The fact that Maisie was a woman had nothing to do with it. It was the same expression of lust and hate, and her eyes were full of violence. Tiffany laughed nervously then, she was a woman surely she wouldn't do anything to her and thought about getting out the bedroom. It was getting more and more oppressive and suffocating, but she didn't expect what happened next.

Michael and Carl drove to the Pier head and parked by the brick wall, grabbed a baseball bat each from the back seat, and ran across to the benches. Carl flicked on the torch he'd brought and swept it across. There was a figure on the bench and he was sitting up. 'That must be Gez, maybe they've not come yet. Stick the torch off Carl we'll be able to see soon once we get used to it.' Michael said, then he shouted 'Gez lad you coming or what?' There was no movement at all from the bench so unless he was playing a game with them he was either unconscious or it wasn't him. Both men automatically checked around to make sure no one was waiting in the shadows, but they knew something was wrong and they ran over to the bench. It was Gez that was for sure or what was left of him. His face was a mass of blood, his nose smashed, he was almost sitting up, his poor hands broken and twisted. He was also still warm, you could feel the heat coming off his body without touching him. Michael went to touch him, and Carl grabbed his hand. 'Don't touch him unless you have to, it's a crime scene, come on we have got to get out of here, quickly Michael.' He said urgently, pulling him backwards towards the car. Michael was still looking at Gez's body not sure what to think. He stopped suddenly panic and fear taking over, and Carl felt his brother slump. He shook him hard. 'Now listen to me Michael, who are we? We're the Moffats and we can cope with anything okay? Just get to the car and we can sort it out COME ON!' He shouted down his ear. Michael looked at him confused and then shook his head, this was happening more and more where he felt like he was leaving his body and couldn't return. He looked at Carl as if he was someone he'd never seen before, as Carl dragged him by his arm to the car. He couldn't take it in. Another dead body, all to do with them and their reputation, what the fuck was going on, how come this keeps happening, he didn't realise he was muttering this out loud and the next thing he knew he was in the car with Carl fastening his seat belt.

'What the fuck is going on Mikey, are you okay?' Carl asked as he started the car, he had to control his urges to screw away as fast as they could from the Pier head where poor Gez sat, and then it occurred to him, if Gez had his phone on him it would implicate them in all this. 'SHIT shit SHIT!' Carl screamed and Michael looked startled. Michael was okay now he was starting to be himself again. 'What's up Carl, what's up?' Carl was struggling not to shout at his older brother, to slap him and his calmness out of him. 'Gez's phone Mick we have to go back and get it now if it's there. Before anyone else comes or sees us, there may be some cameras round here too, but they are so crap they don't work in the dark. We only have an hour or so before it goes light so we have to move quick.' Michael was out of the door before he'd barely finished what he was saying, and Carl was about to object when he realised he had to keep his voice down too. It was very rare anyone came round here at night but soon the City would be waking up. The few night workers knocking off, the morning staff coming in, the ferry workers, so he had to move. He kept the engine idling and said a prayer for the first time in ages, praying if they got away now that he would show Stephen Bentley and TJ mercy. Then he burst out laughing, a strange maniacal laugh that he didn't recognise at all, as if they deserved any mercy. He flinched as the door opened, and Michael got in, holding the phone like a trophy. Carl breathed a sigh of relief, 'was there anything else on him?' he asked. Michael said 'just his wallet and I took that too, but left his keys. I didn't want to touch anything else; you know fingerprints and so on.' Carl nodded, and drove off still controlling his urge to drive like a bat out of hell.

Maisie was still staring at Tiffany and she looked insane, she was grinning and Tiffany almost smiled back. Then out of nowhere Maisie got up and lurched at her, taking her by surprise, she landed on top of her causing her to bang her head, and created a terrible pain in her chest. She thought she was having some type of heart attack, and then she passed out. Maisie had cracked two of her ribs by jumping on her, that's what had caused her to faint.

When she woke up she couldn't move she tried to pull herself up but her legs and arms were tethered somehow. She looked up and could see her arms were tied with what looked like her stockings. She rested for a moment then she looked down, and saw her ankles were bound with the same thing, and noticed with horror that she was spread eagled, her legs way too far apart for her to be comfortable, and she felt completely and utterly vulnerable, and very scared. She heard a noise over to her left and she heard the chopping noise of what sounded like someone cutting up cocaine. What the hell was wrong with Maisie she hoped to God this nightmare would end soon. She almost giggled with hysterics when she thought about how ridiculous this was. She'd had punters who liked this type of thing, but she had insisted they never tie her so she couldn't get out, and she always had a safety word, but this was a woman doing it to another woman, without her consent. It didn't make sense to her, she was so mixed up what to do, and should she try and talk to her or just ignore her. She heard her snorting the coke with a huge sniff, and then again with relish. She decided to try her luck, and said quietly 'Maisie, is that you? What are you doing to me honey I don't understand I've done nothing wrong so why have you hurt me and tied me up?' It went quiet then she felt the bed bounce as Maisie sat on it and the movement made her ribs hurt, and it hurt even more to breathe deeply. She sensed Maisie was looking at her although she couldn't see her properly. 'Linda why did you leave me I loved you more than anything? So now you're staying with me, and I'm going to teach you so you never leave me again.' Tiffany started to panic, she knew Maisie had lost it and as she struggled against the tights holding her arms and legs it made them go tighter burning and cutting into her skin. She felt a hard slap on her thigh, and immediately froze. 'Stop struggling you BITCH! I'm going to make love to you Linda so you realise what you've lost.' Tiffany felt sick, and did everything she could to quell her rising panic, the last thing she needed was to be sick and choke to death on her own vomit. She went to her safe place in her head, and as she felt Maisies kisses on her and her hand between her legs, she imagined it was Carl and they were playing love games. She felt pain as Maisie shoved her fingers hard inside her, and she imagined telling Carl that he'd hurt her and he gently kissed her better, and said he was sorry. She tried to ignore the pain spreading all over her body, bites bruising and fingers scraping and scratching off skin, but when Maisie lay on top of her she felt herself passing out again from the pain from her ribs, and not being able to breathe properly. She no longer cared she was beaten and welcomed the blackness.

Stephen was so wound up Pete didn't know what to do, he felt sick to his stomach, after watching him work over Gez. Poor harmless sod only wanted to be liked at the end of it all, his mum had lost her sister and her son over a few weeks. Even he knew that Stephen was off it and had gone too far. He kept stopping to have a sniff of coke, he had offered Pete a line but he was super paranoid anyway. He'd just found out that Jacko wasn't dead but at the hospital, so he felt a bit better. At least he wasn't going to get done for murder, and now this, killing the Moffats cousin and knew that he'd killed Shelagh too. If only he hadn't fell for his and TJs crap and he could go home, to the townhouse. He knew the Moffats would be after him now, they'd want blood for blood but he'd let them know as a parting gift that Stephen killed their mother. He'd looked in his glove box before too, and there was the silver pen and black cards used to put a message on Sara's memorial site. The Moffats weren't stupid they'd always known TJ was somehow responsible for Sarah's death but finding out he was sitting next to the mad fucker who'd killed all three was making him sick. He just wanted to get out the car and away from him. Stephen was humming and grinding his teeth. 'You're coming back to mine Peter the beater, so I can keep an eye on you and you don't' get any funny ideas about running to the Moffats or to the police to cut yourself a deal. Think on this, when we get to mine you be careful not to upset anything or make things out of place. That stupid bitch used one of my Clarisse Cliff bowls as an ashtray that's how stupid she was. Messing up my house, smelling so bad, she had to go. If she hadn't threatened me with her stupid sons it may have been different. So listen good Peter the beater, you keep your mouth shut as TJ doesn't even know yet, it's my surprise to him.' Stephen was calming down a bit if he'd just leave that crazy coke alone, he may be okay. Everyone who'd taken it had gone mental, it was really strong stuff, and some of the big dealers had made crack rocks out of it. It wasn't worth thinking about that, the amount of crazies already taking coke and now mixing it with a new drug methamphetamine as if they didn't have enough mad people around here. Stephen drove past the hotel where Pete had his stuff, and he objected weakly that he needed things. He just ignored him and drove them both to his house, where Pete would be surprised if he got out at all from here alive or not hurt. Stephen was so twitchy he just hoped that he could get out at some point and get as far away from Merseyside as he could. He promised himself and God that he'd do his best to change his ways. They were all empty promises but it made him feel a little better just for the time being. Pete missed the irony, that the debilitating fear he felt was just how he made his son and Sylvia feel every he went to see them.

Phil was knackered, he was tired and fed up and sick of being alone. He didn't want the spiteful evil little slag Natasha and he knew his son would be a whining git like her. At first when they'd split he had wanted him to stay with him. Now he frightened himself by how little he felt for the boy, he loved him but didn't like him. He had gone home slept fitfully for a few hours then got up and was driving around aimlessly waiting to hear from her ladyship or from the Moffats. What to do next. As he was thinking hard and being so tired he missed his turning and ended up on a one way road. Cursing he knew he'd have to go right to the end now on the duel carriage way and turn round at the roundabout. His Land Rover was too clunky and old to do a quick U turn. He was miles away and saw the signs for Knowsley Safari Park. He saw a little road and indicated to turn at the last minute getting a loud beep off the car behind. He looked in the mirror and saw it was a woman, so ignored her. He carried on into the little cul de sac. If it had been a bloke the mood he was in he may have followed him and kicked the crap out of him. What he saw next made his jaw literally drop open and he sat there in a type of shock. There in front of him was Linda and she was kissing a man, a great big man. When he finished kissing her he picked her up and swung her round and she was laughing, really laughing. It was early morning they only had eyes for each other so Phil just stayed where he was and turned the engine off. He was like a deer trapped in the headlights he couldn't stop watching such was the disbelief he felt. No wonder they couldn't find her! They'd gone round to look for her at mainly women's houses, no one would have guessed this. Christ even if they had known how could they have known what man she was with? Maisie would have a fucking embolism if she found out, and for some reason that made him smile. He felt better than he had for ages, and to top it all off Linda looked really happy. She had been so good to him, he didn't know yet if he would tell Maisie. Even though it was him and Maisie since they were kids, Linda had cared for him deeply and he had for her. She was that type of person loveable and loving, how Maisie had kept her so long was a mystery. He watched as the man approached what must be his car, he went in the boot and took out what looked to be magnetic plates. He put them carefully on the side of the doors and Linda come over and straightened one. Again they kissed and he got into the car she shut the door and went back to the front door. He started the car went down to the bottom and turned around, she stood waving and as he passed Phil saw the plate on the car on his side and he saw it was advertising a taxi service. It had something to do with the shop by the club. He got out his phone and left a few messages for people who owed him favours and within an hour he had Linda's mans' name, address, date of birth and blood group. It's amazing what you can buy now computers are catching on. This World Wide Web thing was taking off all over the city. He'd watched Linda go in and had sat there for over an hour while he wondered what to do. Should he go in and confront her, or leave it for the time being, he wasn't going to tell Maisie yet, it felt good knowing something she didn't. He thought of how out of it she'd been and wondered how Tiffany had got on. He knew Tiff wasn't gay but once Maisie made her mind up to seduce a woman, she usually succeeded. Sadly for Tiff it seemed like she had. But he knew Tiffany from around and had heard the same gossip as others, and knew she was also a woman who got what she wanted. He wondered what it was she wanted from Maisie. He woke himself up and did an illegal move right across the duel carriage way so he could get back to town. He pulled up at a greasy spoon went in and got a bacon roll and a coffee and the Daily Mirror newspaper. Hardly anybody bought the Sun tabloid around Merseyside because of the Hillsborough disaster. Where 96 people lost their lives and the vile reporters in the Sun had filled their paper with the most terrible things about Liverpool fans. They had long memories in Merseyside, and the Sun had stabbed people in the back at their lowest. Phil knew he'd never buy it, he'd spent the day it had happened trying to find out if his mates were alive or dead, constantly ringing the helpline to find out so he could reassure their families. His mates were okay, he loved Jacko and Jonna like they were his real kin. They had all been in their early teens, and both of them had taken a long time to get over it. The nightmares and seeing people dying or dead whenever they closed their eyes. Both had gone to counsellors, and it had taken them until they were in their early twenties before they could go to a game again. Both of them hadn't told the others what had happened until a long time after such was their trauma. So to accuse them of picking pockets and so on was despicable, the Sun had done that to sell papers, they were the lowest of the low. God what was wrong with him today, all misery and memories. He finished his coffee and bacon roll, left the newspaper for someone else and decided he'd go to Tiffany's and see what Maisie wanted him to do today.

Chapter 33

Michael and Carl had gone back to the townhouse, and told their men what had happened. Everyone was so shocked and angry that there was a rare silence amongst them. 'We may need alibis lads, so we've been with you all night. We must have missed Bentley and Pete by minutes. We had to leave poor Gez otherwise we'd be in the nick straight away.' Michael explained, and then he finally burst into tears. No one was embarrassed they had all been together through Sarah's death. There for each other through all the beatings, and cruelty from the people who were supposed to love and care for them; like errant mothers, and drunken fathers. Foster homes, with some of the abusers who got away with it and the odd kind person who they didn't want to leave, and who they hung onto for dear life. Carl went over as did Jonna and hugged him and gave him a manly slap on the back. Jonna said breaking the melancholy mood 'I'm not marrying you now you dickhead, just 'cos we've been close. I mean imagine the wedding night with him you'd never get him to bend over.' Everyone burst out laughing and soon they were talking about the events of late and how everything was changing.

Jonna followed Carl to the kitchen when he went to make some tea and coffee and whispered to him 'My Uncle Freddy rang here today, they are ready to collect your mums body and make the funeral arrangements.' Carl replied 'that was quick wasn't it? Sometimes in a murder case they keep the body for months instead of weeks. 'Typical of Shelagh to inconvenience everyone' he said sadly. He was too tired to hate at the moment, he was worried about the news would do to Michael.' I'm glad you told me Jonna lad, and am made up it's your family who's taking care of it all. It's also good that you recognised our Mike about to go off at the deep end, he's just had enough, what with what happened tonight, and we were both wound up and ready to kill Pete and give Stephen a good

154

kicking, and there's our Gez, aw God you should have seen it Jonna, you could hardly tell it was him I think he had his throat cut. I feel so shit leaving him there I really do.' Carl sighed deeply he didn't want to burst into tears just yet. 'It's okay lad you couldn't help it could you? You had to get you and Michael out of there; you'd only get put in the cells and kept in for hours for questioning. Now you've got to organize your mums' funeral, and sort out the fuckers for doing that to Gez. We will do anything you want us to do mate you know that don't you? My uncles who all own the funeral parlour said they'd do anything for you. There's Freddy, Tommy and Danny remember. Their firm was one of the biggest and best until they decided to go legal and instead of making dead bodies, decided to bury them!!' Carl laughed at this and felt a bit better. Jonna carried on 'We're like broken records, going on about backing each other up. But come on after the last few weeks it's surprising any of us trust each other with the backstabbing bastard Pete doing what he did. Have you seen his missus, she's alright you know, a right good looking girl. I may call and see if she's alright, as he ain't ever coming back to her is he?' Jonna finished looking pleased with himself. 'Only you could think about pussy at a time like this you big pervert, God I'm glad some things never change.' Carl replied laughing despite himself. Jonna laughed too, and said thoughtfully. 'Nah she's too nice for a one night stand, I may go courting like the old days, and take this fine young filly out on my arm to the cinema for a snog in the back row.' Carl laughed even harder now slapping Jonna on the back. 'She has a rug rat you know not that would bother me, but what about you? Ooh got to calm down now.' He said wiping his eyes, frightened his tears of laughter would turn to tears of sorrow.

Jonna just smiled and said 'well you know what most of us went through growing up so I'd be happy to give the little fellah some time and if his ma likes me who knows eh? Maybe I could give him a little brother or sister.' Carl started chuckling again, 'you are mental you've not even asked her out yet ya daft git.' He started to hiccough and that set them both off again. Jonna heard someone approaching the kitchen 'do you think it will be okay to go and see her and see how she is? Anyway don't tell anyone you know they'll all take the piss out of me and I'm not in the mood.' He said quickly. Carl was just about to say something when he realised the big man really liked Sylvia or he wouldn't have said about keeping quiet, so he just nodded and they both waited in comfortable silence. Phil drove to Tiffany's flats and as he pulled up he noticed the big front door was lodged open with a brick, probably someone nipping out for a smoke or a paper, and not having their keys. Taking advantage of this he rushed up to front door just in case it closed. Then ran straight into the lift to Tiffany's. As he got out he was so preoccupied with whether or not to tell Maisie about Linda that he nearly walked past the flat, but his attention was caught by the door being slightly open. When he walked in he shouted 'Hiya girls, it's Phil, are you okay or are you playing hide and seek.'

There was no answer so he carefully went in each room, then took his gun out, thoughts of Rodney hurting them. He looked in the front room, which was empty, and then he heard noise from the bedroom. He didn't know whether to go in or not but thought sod it they'll just have to get angry. He walked over and opened the door, and then for the second time that day his jaw dropped and he rubbed his eyes as he saw Tiffany tied to her bed. As he grew accustomed to the gloom, he saw her poor body which was all cuts and bruises, a stark contrast to the white sheets, then he saw the blood that had spilt from between her legs. He rushed over and made sure she was still breathing. She opened her eyes when he tried to find her pulse and for a moment Tiffany felt horror thinking he'd come to finish her off. She started to cry and begged him through swollen lips 'Oh God please Phil don't hurt me because Maisie told you to. I won't tell a soul I promise.'

Phil wasn't thinking anything like that not even for a minute. He was tired to the bone of all the violence he'd seen. All that misery and seeing people hurt each other, and Tiffany lying there made something change within him instantly.   He took in the pathetic sight in front of him, and he felt pity and compassion, tears forming in his eyes. Then out of nowhere, he thought of his oldest friend and felt nothing but hate.

Phil cut her free using his Russian knife, he used to be proud of it, but even that disgusted him now, as she trembled so badly. He had to concentrate in case he nicked her skin by accident, and made her bleed. Then she went limp and he thought how exhausted and frightened she must be. Tiffany felt odd, she had been in and out of consciousness all night and now Phil, Maisies best friend was helping her. She was amazed as he spoke so gently to her, telling her not to worry, because it was all okay now. He carried on speaking quietly as he rubbed her ankles after he had covered her up. He made her sweet tea and offered to run a bath for her, and asked did she want to call the ambulance or the police. Tiffany was still in shock but didn't want to be called a grass, so shook her head no about getting the emergency services. He really didn't want to hear anything about Maisie and her cruelty. The proof was right in front of him, but he listened to her tell him the awful truth, as he saw to her wounds.

She only told him a little finding it hard to talk for a number of reasons. He told her to tell him when she was ready and only then.

He put the TV on low and looked through her videos to put a comforting one on for her. He could tell what her favourites were by the well worn sleeves. Robin Hood prince of thieves was nearly worn out completely. He smiled, as he saw Hocus Pocus, which he was quite partial to himself. Then as with any tragedy all too quickly the smile was gone and his face contorted in anger as he thought of Tiffany and the ordeal she had gone through. He put Hocus Pocus in the video recorder and went into the kitchen to think. He had to get her to tell him exactly what had set Maisie off. She'd told him bits while he had been seeing to her wounds, but he needed more so he could add to the hate he was feeling. Plus if she wanted to go to the coppers he could back her up. He felt shock at himself. Go to the coppers? They always sorted it themselves. He'd seen this before after someone has been violated, even tough little fighters like Tiff. They just froze and wouldn't be persuaded to talk about it, or to tell the police, terrified of the repercussions if they did. This wasn't the case here he'd sort it with that bitch Maisie. He couldn't get over her cruelty to the girl, he knew all about Tiffany and what she'd been. Yet she was still highly sought after, he'd fancied her himself. She was gorgeous and Phil felt a slight tug at his heart not his crotch when he thought about kissing her. He wouldn't think farther than that after he'd seen Maisies handiwork, and was still a little in shock himself. Protecting and helping Tiff right now was all he wanted to do. Somehow it felt completely right and his heart felt lighter than it had for a long time.

Chapter 34

Maisie woke up in her bedroom, sore and bruised with a nasty cut on her eye. She didn't care about that because Linda wasn't in bed with her. She was fully clothed and still had her boots on. She felt like death warmed up, and laughed bitterly at herself for being so weak and pathetic. What had she done last night, it was a bit of a blur. Oh now it was coming back thick and fast. The delightful Tiffany, she'd give her a good seeing too that was for sure, she wouldn't be going back to any man soon. Had Linda

157

been there she seemed to remember her making love to Linda too. That's a nice threesome she thought, with a smile, hanging onto the thought knowing inside it wasn't real. God had someone slipped her an acid tab? It was so real in a way, but she wasn't so positive what had gone on. She remembered taking lots of coke after she left the Moffats and going to Tiffany's on the way home so why couldn't she remember how she got home? She'd have some coffee and then go and see Tiffany maybe she'd want more, that would be good.

She was sore all over and her pussy was aching so it must have been really, really good. The flashbacks gave her plenty to work with, and as far as she was concerned it was all okay. Tiffany must be a little hellcat perhaps Linda not being around wasn't a bad thing after all, she was enjoying herself in a way. Her arrogance refused to let in any guilt or remorse for what she'd done. It was just fun and she always took what she wanted didn't she? She remembered more and more but still not clearly enough, so shrugged her shoulders thinking so it got a little kinky but she didn't remember her complaining. Sure she made some noise but that was part of the role play. She may have been a bit rough but so what, that was the coke of course. She went to the bathroom stripped off and got in the shower after checking herself and then admiring her body in the mirror. She liked the bruises and the scratches they were her war wounds from great sex. She had no idea right then that they were entirely self inflicted.

Pete had been in Stephen's house for a while, Pete a bag of nerves because he'd decided to show him some of the handy work that he was so proud of. He now knew that when Stephen returned to planet earth after doing so much coke and whiskey that he was bound to hurt him or worse. He had never been in a state of panic for so long, it was awful and he felt himself wanting to cry and go back to the Moffats. That would be mostly Michael of course, but even stupid Carl would be welcomed right now. Stephen was singing along to some weird music from Thailand or somewhere making a terrible racket. A thought occurred to him, and the tiny bit of hope that he'd been hanging on to had just shrivelled up and died when he realised that no one could hear for miles. What would he do when Stephen went for him? He didn't know if he would try and fight back or not, because he was full of fear and bitter regrets, not the anger he needed to help him survive. Stephen had locked them both in the house, but Pete thought he was a survivor and would get out eventually if he could just survive this muttering lunacy. Hopefully that meant he'd soon pass out and he'd be free. He was jittery and flummoxed because of all that had gone on. He was really sick over the way he'd butchered Gez, and full of remorse for what part he'd played. Not because he cared about the victims but he cared about his own fate. Realising too late he'd picked the wrong side, he wanted desperately to be back with the lads in the town house playing games, drinking, smoking and just having a laugh. He was full of false hope as he thought that maybe they were missing seeing him too. Little did he know they were in a way, but only to watch him get shot or beaten to death. Fate had a delicious sense of irony and a twisted sense of humour. Especially for those like Pete, who dedicated their lives to the torment of others.

Everyone had had a nap at the house, they'd taken it in shifts, and Michael was so exhausted he'd had a little snort of coke. He didn't like the way it had made him feel, he felt angry and paranoid, and then it occurred to him, it was the coke making everyone go mental. It was well stronger than the stuff they were used to. It was usually cut with flour, anything that looked the part, even rat poison once by some dickhead. His head was aching and his eyes felt scratchy but he went into the bathroom and washed his face and brushed his teeth. Too late he realised he was using someone else's toothbrush. He and Carl were clean freaks, so he stopped when he realised what he was doing, stopped and then rinsed his mouth out with strong mouthwash and went back into the fray. He took a deep breath and shouted 'Wakey wakey!'
Groans erupted all over the room, and one by one the men woke up tired and dehydrated, but excited by the violence they knew was going to happen today.

Maisie left an almighty mess all over her flat, and rang down to the club to get one of the lads to get her some food from the café. She went through her dirty clothes and found a card amongst a few bits of change and a crumpled tenner. It was from a taxi firm so that would explain it. When John came up from the bar she was surprised he was alone. 'No Phil today? Maisie said to him, 'Nope not seen him and his mobiles off too. He sent me a text saying he wouldn't be in today as well, which isn't like him.' John replied yawning. Maisie felt anger and a tiny bit of fear which wasn't like her at all. She snarled at John and threw the crumpled tenner at him 'Get me something to eat, either a nice bacon butty or something, keep the change. What the fuck does the ginger bastard think he's doing? He'd better be frigging' dying or something.' John smiled at her feeling annoyed but refused to let her see, and said just to rub her up the wrong way. 'Maybe he's gone back to Natasha or he could have been with a new bird or something.' Maisie was so angry she slammed the door in Johns face as she went back into the flat. John let it ride over him, he knew what Maisie was like and most of them tolerated her moods and nastiness because she was always sorry later on. She nearly always gave them money or an expensive present so they just grinned their way through it. It helped that she paid well over anything they could earn in town, on the doors, and because they'd known each other a long time they got away with murder sometimes. It was all good John thought as he went down the stairs.

Maisie put the TV on loud and waited for her food. IN a few minutes she heard John knock and went to the door. As she opened it he pushed past her and told her to put the kettle on. Maisie was so stunned she did as she was told as John went to the toilet. 'Boy this better be amazing you cheeky git John, tea or coffee? She asked, without missing a beat, as she knew this had to be good gossip. John shouted he wanted tea and she heard the toilet flush, the water running as he washed his hands and after what seemed like hours he walked into the kitchen. He grabbed his drink and smiled and then told her 'guess what Maisie, I've just found where Linda probably is, and who she's with.'

Pete had waited patiently while Stephen had showed him yet more of his disgusting snuff films, and his private photos on the computer for the third time. It made him feel horrible and his fear reached new levels of terror when he realised this lunatic was responsible for so much death plus he must have supernatural powers not to have been caught. When finally he'd fallen asleep upstairs on his immaculate bed, Pete had taken a chance and walked in. He would pretend he was covering him up as he was naked, but Stephen was out for the count and didn't stir. Pete reached out to throw the duvet over him anyway and he saw his pants , keys and money on the floor. He didn't quite believe it but he grabbed them and the money and had to struggle not to run down the stairs. All he had to do was get out the front door and away from here. After fiddling with the alarm he finally got it right and was out in a flash. Getting in the little Volkswagen he was shaking so badly he couldn't get the keys in the ignition at first. When he eventually got it going he went out onto the main road away from hell as fast as he could manage, until he realised where he was, so he slowed down so he didn't get pulled over. The police would probably be after him for Jacko, the relief he felt when Stephen had let him know he hadn't killed him had almost disappeared when he realised he was so badly injured. He had some previous for G.B.H which he was quite proud of, and told people often. In reality he'd just been with the lads at football matches when it had kicked off, and he had made sure he was pulled in with them, so they thought he'd been fighting. In reality most of the time he'd been hiding behind a car. He felt his mobile phone in his pocket so took it out one handed and switched it on. It buzzed constantly loads of texts and missed calls coming in. He saw he had twenty two missed calls, and 9 unanswered texts. God he wondered who they were from? He saw straight away that two of the messages were off Michael telling him he was a fucking Judas, and how he would kill him. Then he scrolled through them and saw one off Jacko, it said *I'm okay mate, I 4give u, if you come and C me I will talk 2 Mick and Carl about sorting this out we have known each other 2 long 4 it 2 end this way.* He then spotted another one off him sent a few hours later which read *Pete lad, come and C me at the hosi, we can have a chat and sort this.* Then he read the one off Jonna saying that he'd be okay with him if Jacko was.

Pete felt real joy for one of the first times in his life, they maybe wouldn't kill him now. It only mattered if Jacko was okay about it and Jonna and so on, the others would have to accept him back. He didn't even care if he got a beating he just wanted to leave TJ and Stephen behind him and go back to the safety of the Moffats. He could tell them about Stephen saying he'd killed Shelagh and best of all he could confirm that TJ ordered Stephen to kill Sara. God they may even thank him for finding it all out, he could say that's why he did it even. That he didn't hit Jacko Bentley did, no one saw him after all. It never once occurred to him that maybe the texts weren't off Jacko at all, but off Carl and Michael and he was about to walk into a trap.

Michael and Carl and the lads sat round drinking tea and coffee quietly discussing different aspects of the plan they were putting into place. 'Right Jonna I know you are sorting out Shelagh's funeral for us, with your uncles, are you sure you don't mind mate?' Jonna sat up paying immediate attention and replied. 'Not a problem do you want me to ask them how much for any other disposals?' Michael nodded his consent and with an almighty yawn Jonna disappeared into the back. Everyone sat around pretending to watch the TV and made small talk about nothing in particular, but they were waiting to see what Jonna came back with. He came back in and went straight to Michael and Carl, and said quietly 'It's two grand for your Ma's funeral with everything including cars, food and printing as you're as good as family. Then it's another two thousand for any extra services meaning disposal of anyone else. He said do what you want within reason he will turn a blind eye if you need to use anything except the crematorium as it has to have someone who knows what they're doing. It would be an extra grand to pay the lad to do it and keep his gob shut and a grand to cover costs. Do you want me to go and confirm it's a yes? He finished and looked expectantly at the brothers. Michael just nodded after he made eye contact with Carl who had held his gaze, and without speaking confirmed his thoughts. 'Hang on Jonna I don't' think we'll need the crematorium, we're burying her so tell him for us will you?' Jonna got up again, and Michael laughed and said 'oh for God's sake you big div use one of our mobile phones.' As he finished speaking five phones flew through the air and hit Jonna all over his body. Everyone burst out laughing at his expression as he stood there with his mouth in a tight line an expression of anger on his handsome face which also turned ruby red. 'That fucking hurt you dickheads!' He shouted which just made it all the funnier. He turned around nearly crunching the mobiles under foot on purpose and stormed into the other room slamming the door so he could use the phone without being overheard. They waited for about ten minutes until Jonna popped his head round the door and said 'The uncles are fine about it all, and guess who's going to meet me in the car park to go and see Jacko?' Everyone punched the air and cheered, except for Michael who just grinned and slowly nodded his head to show his approval. Jonna grinned back his anger forgotten as quickly as it had appeared. Pete reckoned he'd be okay now, he felt so much better he even had the balls to pull into his hotel and collect his stuff, he reckoned Stephen would be out of it for hours yet if not days. He would go and see Jacko with Jonna then lay low for a while, and it didn't matter anyhow now he was going to go back to everything he knew. He'd be pissed on for a while and get the odd beating but so what? He could even go back to Sylv's she was his all said and done and so was the kid, he may even be nice to them for a bit. At some point he was going to take the brat Jakes console off him if he'd bought one with the money off Bentley like he was supposed to. The one he'd taken from him was boring now compared to the latest ones, but he wouldn't do it straight away. Just as soon as he'd got his feet under the table and everything was back to normal then he'd take it. He started to drive towards the tunnel, all was well with the world, he'd go and beg for forgiveness from Jacko, for not stopping Stephen hitting him over the head. Jonna was a good lad easy going, he'd understand. Maybe he could also fool him into thinking he'd done it all on purpose so he could find out who'd killed Sarah and Shelagh. Now he knew wasn't that good enough for them to let him off? He looked at the time; he had better get going now, so he could go and get something to eat and prepare himself to act out how sorry he was.

Tiffany had been feeling better all morning, she had something to eat, her scratches, cuts, burns and bruises were very colourful and pretty painful, but healing well. She had a lovely light kimono on that Phil had bought for her, but best of all she was falling in love with him and he felt the same way. Genuine love and kindness, and although she'd been hard and bitter and prepared to do what she had to do to get Carl, he was now nearly forgotten. The love and tenderness that Phil had shown her over the previous days were glorious compared to how she had always been treated. Even the men who'd had lots of money and were young and sometimes really handsome had just treated her like a prize on their arms, or wanted her for all the wrong reasons. All her life she'd wanted to find real love but when it hadn't come she had replaced it with wanting wealth and the power that comes with it. Especially after being hurt and used so many times. She was still sore all over but tonight she was going to try and seduce Phil even for a snog and a gentle grope. After what Maisie had done to her she felt weird and dirty and would only feel normal when a man had made love to her, she could fuck her away tonight if she wasn't so sore. God she hated the bitch but was still frightened of her, she couldn't get over how strong Maisie was, and she was just as bad as the male psychos who'd hurt her and raped her when she was on the game. Only once had another woman hurt her like this but that was because of her man, and she was punishing her for daring to sleep with him. No it wasn't the same she'd tied her up and beat her but not actually raped her. She threatened to with a bottle but never quite done it thank God. Christ almighty Maisie had even thought that she Tiffany had somehow morphed into Linda as well. God that poor cow, what had she put up with over the years she wondered muttering to herself, and then decided if she ever met Linda she'd ask her outright?

She was snuggled in bed in new sheets that were cool on her skin and a new duvet in a gorgeous cover, that Phil had insisted she needed, it was his suggestion. He predicted correctly that she didn't want to see her old dressing gown or the bedding from her ordeal again, but what touched her most was she knew Phil couldn't cope with them either. He'd gone straight out to T.J Hughes on London Road in town, and even with the traffic and queues he was back in record time. He'd bandaged her ribs and she'd felt better after that and some painkillers. She could hear him now in the kitchen washing the dishes, and pottering about. She'd been worried about Maisie coming back and as his boss she was frightened that she would try and shut her up for good or get someone to do it for her. Phil was adamant that nothing would happen while he was here and she just hoped he would stay true to his word and look after her, as he really knew how. Just as she was getting up he put his head around the door making her jump, he smiled and came in. 'Hiya my love sorry if I startled you.' He sat on the bed and she moved automatically to him. He held her in his arms and they stayed like that for a while. He then kissed the top of her head and told her he needed to go out and sort a few things out and to trust him, he'd be back in a few hours. Tiffany told him it would be okay but he noticed she was shaking, and then he didn't want to go. He wanted to see Maisie face to face, no needed to. He was torn at leaving Tiff but the sooner he did the better. He was going to tell her to stick her job and friendship and demand the money she owed him which was thousands, last time he checked.

So he had no choice but to go himself, as he didn't want anyone to let Maisie know what he was up to. She needed to pay him anyhow or he was going to tell the police all about a lot of things. He hated the thought of grassing but Maisie had lost all her privileges when she raped and abused Tiffany. No wonder some of the girls she had used behind Linda's back had come to the club in a right state, he thought. He thought of Linda with her all these years. Had she had tied her up and kept her prisoner all night, torturing her? Maisie was far from stupid she'd known what she was doing on some level even if she was off her head. He still didn't want to believe it in a way and if he hadn't seen the state of Tiffany's beautiful body for himself after the attack he probably would have doubted it.

Anyway he'd been sitting there too long and time was moving on, and he wanted to get it over with because he knew Maisie would try everything she could to keep him her loyal servant. He'd put his phone on charge in the kitchen and he saw all the messages from the Moffats and of course loads off Maisie. He didn't even read them just deleted them. He then read the ones off the Moffats and he replied straight away. 'Hello lads just saw your message count me in if you need help I'm there but let me know early if you can so I can sort something out, as I'm in a bit of a situation.' They were going to see Pete apparently and they were offering him as one of Maisie's crew the chance to join in, it was a mark of respect. He wondered if they'd contacted Maisie or just him, the way she had been behaving the other night he doubted if they still respected her as much anymore. He certainly didn't. He couldn't get over the fact that the woman he once loved and adored, and who he thought was basically good despite her faults and her cheating, stealing ways, just wasn't. He went and got his phone and decided to grab a bacon butty and a paper to give him a bit of thinking time alone. Fuck her, he would answer it when he felt like talking to her, and not a minute before.

Jonna was on his way to meet Pete, his stomach doing flips now as he knew his old mate had had it, he deserved everything he was going to get but it didn't make it any easier it really didn't. He was meeting him inside the hospital car park where he was in a little Volkswagen, he'd nicked off Bentley apparently. Michael and Carl were in the back under a blanket, and the others in a car following, but a few minutes behind. He turned in as he approached the hospital and straight away saw Pete he was reading a paper, smoking and leaning on the car. Jonna knew then that he was always going to be the same lying little shit. You could tell he wasn't even arsed because he hadn't spotted him yet as he was a little early. Jonna said quietly to Michael and Carl

'he's here the cocky little shit, standing by this Volkswagen he was going on about. It belongs to Bentley he said. What do you want to do shall I go and talk to him and get him to wait here until the others get here or what?' Michael pulled the blanket up slightly and said 'you do that Jonna lad, we'll get out the other door if you park beside him but not too close. Just remember do not lock it when you get out!' Jonna smiled then and said 'right I'm ready to do this come on.' He beeped the horn and Pete saw him and immediately threw his ciggie away and dropped the paper as if it was on fire. He knew it would make him look like he didn't give a shit. He thought he'd got away with it as he waved and gestured for Jonna to pull in besides him. Jonna did but made sure he didn't park too close and give the game away. Pete was so happy to see Jonna he walked up to him virtually with his arms out to hug, so Jonna pretended to be pleased to see him, and put his arm around him, leading him away until the lads were out of the car.

Jonna spoke first and looked down at Pete, 'So soft arse what on earth have you got yourself into this time? What the hell were you thinking going over to TJs side?' Pete saw his chance to snivel and get Jonna's sympathy. 'I knew this would happen I couldn't tell anyone in case they grassed me up, so I went along with it and met Stephen. Oh mate you should hear the things I've found out, by being undercover like. The worst part was when Bentley hit Jacko and I couldn't stop him or I'd have blown months of work like.' Jonna smiled at this, as they all knew it was Pete who had hit Jacko nearly killed him, and put him in a coma. 'That's awful mate isn't it you must have felt like calling it off then, I mean where have you been? What is the score with Gez too, the boys are mighty pissed off at that.' Pete realised that with all that had gone on, he had completely forgotten about Gez and what Stephen had done to him. He swallowed uncomfortably trying to buy some time, he changed the subject. 'What ward is Jacko on, come on I'm itching to see him and tell him I'm sorry.' Jonna just grinned at him and said this way leading him into the dark corner of the car park where there was no CCTV. Pete started to panic now, he knew this wasn't right and then like something out of a nightmare Michael and Carl appeared in front of him, and he felt his bowels loosen. Then he stopped and asked stupidly 'Jonna what's going on mate why are they here?' Jonna walked away from him and didn't even turn around, he just walked to a car that had just pulled in and Pete realised it was some of the lads from the house. He looked frantically round looking for an escape route, and then felt an almighty pain in his ear and head, and then it all went black.

165

Maisie stood there holding her breath, taking in what John had said, and she looked at him before asking rather stupidly 'What my Linda?' John laughed and said 'well D'oh! Maisie where did you leave your brain this morning? Of course Linda unless you think I go round and find out about all women called Linda then come along and tell you.' John didn't see it coming but he felt it as Maisie slapped him hard across the face. For the first time in all the years they'd been friends he'd never felt quite this angry. Most of the time he just felt bemused but the anger from Maisie and the shock and pain he felt in that moment made him nearly hit her back, it was a natural reaction. He stopped himself just in time, but he had a clear image of himself knocking her out, so he went to walk away. Maisie ran in front of him and physically stopped him, she grabbed him and screamed in his face 'don't you walk away from me after telling me that, just fucking tell me who's she with, tell me the bitch's name!' She kept screaming. John grabbed her hands and restrained her with difficulty but wouldn't let go until she stopped struggling, she broke down then and went limp and let John hold her. He guided her gently onto the couch and went and got her tea putting lots of sugar in it. She grimaced as she took as swig and John noticed something he'd not seen as clearly before with Maisie. Not just desperation there was a glint of madness in her eyes. He waited until she'd calmed down properly and passed her a cigarette which he had lit and she sucked on it greedily, her hands shaking. John then told her how he'd found out about Linda. He'd gone to the café and one of the new girls there was boasting about how she was getting to know Linda, through Joe who she'd known for ages and how he'd helped her get this job. Then she told everyone that she didn't quite believe it but Linda had fallen for him. He was one of the drivers who was doing well in his little business and what a lovely couple they made. John had pretended to know Joe well, and had asked about him. Then turning on the charm had asked her if she knew where his place was as he'd not seen him for years, and couldn't wait to catch up. That it was so easy was amazing, he'd been told the road where he was living with Linda. She was apologetic as she didn't know the exact number, but John could barely hide his glee and feeling so like the cat that'd got the cream he'd virtually leapt through the air and run around to tell Maisie.

She took it all in, she went into the bedroom and into one of her secret drawers in the wardrobe and took out a handful of fifties and twenties, counting out three thousand pounds. She put the rest back and came into the front room, where she held the money out to John who just froze looking at it. 'There you go two thousand pounds reward money for finding her, and the rest is to cover you today so you can go and find exactly where they're living. You can go and bribe a few with that extra money and use it for expenses if you need it. Half of them would sell their babies for a twenty so you come back with the right number, I don't want Linda to see me coming, and I'm counting on you John.' He nodded and put the money as quick as he could into his pants in case the new mad Maisie changed her mind. He had just the person to go to, he would get their number off one of the cabbies. There was one creep called Smithy who would tell him for a few bob, if he was working the day shift. They all covered for each other if one was sick, and had to go to each other's houses to pick up the cars. Plus if that failed he could just go and get his mate in the council to get it for him. Linda wasn't registered there of course but Joe was, as he had to be to have his taxi license, he thought with glee. He'd treat his mate to a night out if he had to ask him, it would take a bit longer because he couldn't ring him in work, but he could meet him when he went to the bookies at lunch time.

Maisie was trembling now, a bit of everything making her feel dizzy and disorientated wondering what she was going to do and where the fuck was Phil? She needed him more than ever and he was probably with a tart right now. Hah whoever she was she wouldn't last as she knew Phil's track record with nearly all his women. She was excited though because she was going to get Linda back, she was going to see her while Phil took care of this man Joe. God she was doing this to punish me she thought, a man eh? She thought briefly about Tiffany, and last night and why did she keep thinking Linda had been there? Crazy stuff that coke, did she have any left, she must have some stashed she'd bought enough. She got up, and then Tiffany was forgotten as her only thoughts were about a line of coke and finally seeing Linda when John came back with the number.

Chapter 35

Pete felt himself waking up he felt dizzy and sick, the smell of petrol and another chemical smell really strong in his nostrils. At first he stubbornly refused to open his eyes because if he did the terrible nightmare he was in might be actually happening. It was too awful to be real. Of course he couldn't resist so he half opened one after another but there was nothing to see as it was pitch black. His head was thumping and it felt wet behind his ears and knew that's how he'd been knocked out so he probably had a head injury that felt like it was still bleeding. He felt panic and went to sit up, but couldn't and hit his forehead as he realised he was in a very small space and it was freezing. He felt metal all around him, and his fuddled brain was trying to work out where he was and why he was here.

He couldn't even bring his hand up to his head to feel his wound. It was then he realised where he was, he was in a morgue in one of their cabinets, he'd seen them on TV, and he knew instinctively that the smell was formaldehyde. He started to shout and wriggle, and the door opened almost immediately and he felt himself slide out, but was still blind as the bright light hit. He squinted and still couldn't see who or what was happening, so he asked who was there. He was greeted by silence, and then felt hands pull him up and lift him roughly off the steel slab. It all came back then in a rush, the Moffats had him, of course, and he felt his bowels loosen again. He managed not to cry and stayed silent dreading with every cell in his freezing cold body what was to come next. The next thing he knew was Jojo coming in to tie him up with hands behind his back. Then he was pushed roughly forwards stumbling and trying to keep his balance on wobbly legs. As he adjusted to the light, he saw the steel tables where they prepared the bodies, and he started to retch uncontrollably the acid from his stomach stinging his throat and making it feel like red hot lava singeing his insides.

Michael and Carl had set up a room in the back of the Davenports funeral parlour, they and some of the lads discussed who would play what roles in their kangaroo court. They were going to put Pete on trial before they decided how much to make him suffer before the inevitable. There wasn't an ounce of pity for him all of them had seemed to accept that's how it went when you betrayed your best mates like Pete had. The only one who still felt uncomfortable with it was Jonna. The list against Pete was long and there was no way on earth he could worm his way out of this one. Jojo and Brandon brought him in, pushing him to the front of the room, where he was forced to sit in a chair, where they bound his ankles to the legs. He could see everything now, and he realised what they were doing, and he started to cry and mutter and beg for his life. He had sat in a few of these kangaroo courts in his life and he'd enjoyed the cruelty shown to the guilty. He had sneered in contempt as they'd begged to be spared, thriving on the power it made him feel. Jonna, Brandon, Barry, Little Joey and Billy all sat on the chairs that had been set out for them the jury, and stared at him, almost embarrassed by his sobbing but appearing indifferent to him. He had dropped them all like a ton of shit the minute TJ got in touch.

They'd all had to pick their names out of a hat the others who hadn't been chosen were either a little bit relieved or a tad disappointed and had plenty of other things to do. The one thing they all agreed on was it didn't matter how much money you were offered you didn't let your mates down, and what put the icing on the cake is they'd found out he'd been hurting his woman and son for a long time, Sylvia finally telling the truth to Michael when he'd gone to see her to find out where he was. He hadn't even had to threaten her, she had told him every bit of information she could and Michael had give her some money to tide her over, she'd never had so much and was like a little girl, her joy obvious. Whether or not they killed him Michael let her know she had nothing more to worry about. So after he shared what Pete had been doing to his girl and his kid they were looking forward to giving him his just desserts, their outrage and anger taking away any compassion they might have felt, except for Jonna. Michael and Carl came in cups of tea in hand, and Michael sat at the table on a big oak antique chair of one of the uncles as he thought it looked the part for a Judge. Carl stood at the side of his brother, arms folded and he looked right at Pete and smiled an insane grin, and Pete knew for sure he was fucked. Michael banged his now empty cup on the table 'sorry haven't got a gavel, only a big hammer and as this isn't our place we can't really use it so that will have to do.' It had gone quiet and he enjoyed playing the judge saying 'Court is in session could you now be quiet and make sure you are all seated.' Carl went and pulled up a chair and sat next to him, he winked and Michael carried on. 'We are here today as the judge jury and executioner to try one of our oldest friends Peter Jones who has betrayed us all in some way. We will read out a list of charges and if Pete wants to try and explain himself and the circumstances which have led us all here, then he will have his chance to speak.' Everyone turned and looked at Pete who was still snivelling and he looked down at the floor unable to meet their eyes.

Maisie was going mad trying to contact Phil, she couldn't understand why he was ignoring her, she'd left messages, pleading, then angry, threatening, then sweet, then angry again. She needed him to go and get Linda with her, say this Joe was a big lad and although Maisie fancied her chances with any bloke, he could be huge, and strong. All because she didn't want to lose face in front of Linda. Well she could always take the gun, then she wouldn't need Phil she could get any of the lads to drive her there, but she wanted Phil, he knew her so well, he'd have her back, plus Linda would react better if he was there. For the thirty fourth time she rang him and to her surprise he actually picked up. 'Thank God Phil, what the shit are you playing at mate? Are you injured or just fucking some unimportant little slut? I don't care where you have been or where you are, I need you now!' Her voice was getting higher and louder, Phil just sat still with the phone away from his ear letting her go on until she screamed. 'I've fucking found Linda or John did, and I want to go and get her and bring her home, so I need you there with me.' There was still silence on the phone and Maisie felt a little bit uncomfortable, there was no comforting words or noises, just an eerie silence. Phil thought about her and felt repulsion stronger than he ever had for a woman even Natasha, he couldn't see her now without seeing Tiffany's total humiliation and bleeding body tied up on the bed. Say she had done things like that to Linda, and some of the other girls she'd had flings with, it was time to let her know it wasn't okay to treat anyone like that. He kept calm and answered her 'okay I've got the message I'll come and pick you up soon, but scream at me again and I won't be there. Is that alright then Maisie, can you cope with that?'

Maisie was a little taken aback by his attitude and thought he was just angry because he had to leave whoever he'd been in bed with. Her jaw was grinding hard because of the coke, and she agreed through gritted teeth. Phil knew she was off it on coke he could always tell, but that made no difference to what he was going to do. He had to go and warn Linda and Joe, when he'd seen them they'd looked so happy. He wasn't going to let that bitch take that away from them or even try. He knew she'd get the men to get Joe on his own one night once she knew what he looked like, they'd hold him while she stabbed him or cut his face or something equally horrible. He'd seen her do it before, and he'd been one of the ones who had held the poor bastards even though sometimes they'd deserved it. No use dwelling on the past he had to make amends for his sins anyway, and it felt good getting one up on her just by doing the right thing.

TJ was annoyed as usual, but also really unsettled, he couldn't get hold of Stephen and he didn't know what the hell was going on. He'd heard about the body by the Mersey, and he knew it had something to do with Stephen and Pete, but he didn't know what. Christ what was he thinking, first Shelagh Moffat had been found dead, now one of the Moffats cousins. For all his money and his men he didn't feel right about it all. He wanted to get information on the Moffats, find out what they were doing, hijack some of their jobs, and get people to remember who was in charge. He had hired some more young bucks, and they were full of bravado. Braying like donkeys how they weren't scared of the Moffats. It was their main point of conversation when he called them in to do some jobs. TJ knew they'd drop him like a ton of shit should they take over. Only one stood out as being perfectly capable and he wanted him to take Stephen's place. His name was David something, and he was huge and muscular and he'd shown him respect so he wanted him in his firm. To be honest with himself TJ now needed him. He knew people were taking the piss out of him lately that's why he had needed Bentley but there was no sign of him. Perhaps it wasn't such a bad thing, maybe the psycho had killed himself racked with guilt. Yeah and blue pigs fly out of my arse. Rodney was skulking around as usual, and he called him in. He'd give him a job to get him away from the office. He was really unsettled, he could imagine what the Moffats would do to him if they ever knew it was him who had ordered Sara's death. He felt naked without his pet psycho. He was sure Shelagh and Gez were down to the same killer, that would be Stephen. He could tell by the M.O. He hadn't ordered those deaths but no one would believe him, they'd think he'd done it anyway. He thought about Pete, and he couldn't get in touch with him either, he'd been wondering what had become of his money, had he been stitched up and had he crawled back to the Moffats after all?, he doubted it. They had specifically homed in on Pete he was a wife beating piece of scum, ready to sell his soul for a few grand and some nice clothes, and to spite Michael his ex best mate. That was another thing he needed Pete to tell him all their secrets, their stashes what drugs they were doing, and where from, that's why he really wanted him. Anyway he was worried now, his tame coppers couldn't stop or help Bentley if he'd murdered half the fucking Moffats family. It was shit without Stephen despite his other men, he just didn't feel as safe as he should, and was David his newest main man able to protect him the same?

He lit up a cigar and decided to call Rodney, who lumbered in and asked 'what's up boss?' 'I've got a little job for you Rodney me old pal, I want you to go to Stephen Moffats house, and see if you can find out where the hell he is. If you can't find him there, try and find out where he was seen last, you know the score.' Rodney wasn't happy about it, but was resigned to being sent on TJs weird little quests. He hated that crazy bastard Bentley, everyone did except for the boss. He cheered up a little as TJ gave him a wad of money, and he liked the thought of seeing where the nutter lived too. He turned to TJ and thanked him, and picked up the piece of paper with his address on, and saw it was over the water in Wirral. 'Hey boss I might go on the ferry not been on it for years. What do you reckon?' TJ looked at him and went to shake his head in disbelief, but stopped himself in time. Rodney may be old and a bit knackered but he was loyal and still would shoot or stab anyone for him. He thought better of it as he needed everyone around him now if Bentley had gone and the

Moffats were going to come after him. He puffed on his cigar and spoke up. 'Listen Rodney, he doesn't think anyone knows where he lives apart from me, so he might not be overjoyed to see you mate. Just a warning and the minute you know what's going on give me a ring straight away. I'll see you later and good luck.' Rodney knew he was being dismissed but he didn't mind, he was going to make a day out of it, get away from everyone, and go and visit Birkenhead Market. He had money in his pocket and he'd even forgotten about Tiffany for a while, and his broken nose. As he left TJ was pretending to read something on the desk, and with a mumbled goodbye, he left happier than he'd been for ages.

Linda woke up and rolled over in bliss, Joe had gone early to work, and he'd made tea and toast for them both. They'd watched some early morning TV in bed, and as they'd started to make love slowly she'd felt truly wonderful, in awe that someone especially a great big man like Joe could be so considerate, gentle and so sexy all at the same time. He made her feel beautiful and as he kissed the scars on her breasts, she felt herself get so hot and wet that she ached to have him inside her, and impatiently pulled him on top of her and grabbed his hard cock and slid him inside her. After gently pushing into her and moving slowly, she came biting his shoulder to stop from screaming out loud, only then did he allow himself to come too. After he left she'd had lay there reliving it all, then sleep came full of good dreams. He was much gentler than Maisie, and often she'd gone a bit too far, enjoying Linda's pain. She thought back, amazed how you live with someone and think you love them for years. It's only when you break up with them, you can see them for what they really are. She shuddered remembering how she'd felt when Maisie had been aggressive and possessive after she had bedded someone else. She'd got out of hand a few times really hurting her. Then the cheeky cow blamed her for not wanting to make love to her every day. She heard her intercom buzz by their door, and she froze. Her stomach started to flip and she cursed herself for even imagining Maisie, maybe she'd brought her here just by thinking of her. She mentally slapped herself for thinking such a stupid thought and crept over to the window and peered through the net curtains.

Oh God it was Phil, she didn't know what to do. Should she answer it and face up to them. Was Maisie with him hiding out of sight? Surely she'd be close behind as usual. She felt like she was having a panic attack, but she couldn't move and just kept watching Phil. She saw him put something through the letterbox and then walk up the path. No sign of Maisie unless it was a trick. She stood there for a good ten minutes until she felt she could move, and ran down the stairs to see what had been put through. There was a white envelope with her name on, and she picked it up. Inside was a letter and she nearly tore it up but she saw that it wasn't Maisies writing it was Phil's, now she was intrigued.

Chapter 36

The kangaroo court was in full swing, Pete sat there terrified and miserable knowing full well that Michael would never forgive him. Even if he wanted to, he couldn't. He would lose face all over town if he did, as well as Carl who although he didn't give a shit about him, would still be seen as soft. He was so scared he'd almost gone beyond fear and felt like he was hovering outside his body; it must have something to do with adrenalin. He knew one thing for sure he was as good as dead and he hoped it was quick. He kept zoning out to what they were talking about and now sitting there he heard what Michael was saying. 'So I will now read out the charges against Peter Jones one time friend and basically lazy, rude, selfish and backstabbing traitor who decided to go over to the enemy. Is everyone ready to say yes to what the court decides is a fitting punishment? There were murmurs of yes and too right from the room and Michael said 'speak up can't hear you lot.' Everyone started shouting yes at the same time, it was almost deafening and Michael said 'that's better now shut up!' Which got a laugh and momentarily broke the tension. He made a show of preparing his list, shuffling his papers and took a while to review his paper work. He then started to read the list out and nobody said a word.

'One for the crime of betraying us all, and meeting Stephen Bentley who is known as TJ Murphy's right hand man. Two for hitting and nearly killing Jacko, who isn't out of the woods yet. Three for being present at our cousins murder, standing by and doing sweet F.A while our Gez was beaten to death by the prick Stephen Bentley. So that is three strikes. We have also found out that Peter Jones has been living a lie for years and that he enjoys beating and torturing his wife, and his son. What do you think members of the jury?' Everyone looked at each other and in unison shouted 'Guilty. Pete let out a loud sob and everyone just ignored him, waiting for Michael to tell them what was going to happen next. 'Right' he said 'Does the prisoner Peter Jones have anything at all to say to his peers to try and make us understand why he would do such heinous things?

Everyone again looked at Pete who was looking down at the floor. 'Well have you got anything to say for yourself or not? Carl asked. Pete put his head up and said 'I am really sorry that I did the things I did, especially to my Sylvia and Jake, and if I had a chance to make it right I would. I went to work with Stephen to try and find out things about TJ and I know none of you believe me but that's the truth.' There were sniggers and whispered exclamations from them all. Carl shook his head in disbelief 'well that's about it then, anything else to say?' Pete nodded his head and looked at the floor his trying to survive making him extra whiny and inwardly he was desperately thinking how do I play this? So he decided just to tell the truth a first for him, 'Well I know who killed your Sara if that's any good, if I tell you for sure will you let me go or go easier on me? Please, please I'll tell you it all if you just let me go. Carls face was like thunder and Michael went white. 'Come on then tell us, there are no secrets between us all here.' Carl said and Pete felt a little bit of hope he seemed to swell a little with self importance, and said 'Well Stephen Bentley took me over to his and he started to go mental taking that nasty coke everyone's been on. While he was off it he showed me some horrible pictures of women who had been sliced up and hurt, Asian women Chinese or something like that.'

Michael and Carl were getting really impatient and without realising it both had moved closer to Pete, and were both holding their breaths as they listened. 'For fucks sake will you get on with it or I swear to God I'll put you one of those steel tables and will embalm you while you're still alive myself!' Carl shouted and Pete even though he was fighting for his life, still managed to piss off Carl even more. He looked at him with a smug even pitying smile, because Pete thought he was showing empathy. He took a deep breath and said again 'Are you going to let me go then if I tell you what he said?' Michael took over and replied to him, 'wait and see Pete I give you my word you will be shown some mercy for telling us the truth.' Pete felt more hope, because he knew Michael would stick to his word. He carried on 'yeah well while he was off it he told me that nothing was as sweet as his first kill, how he'd stabbed your sister to death on TJs orders and how wonderful it had felt, almost like making love to her. Then he told me about your Ma, and how she was all over him and how he'd felt when he left her bleeding on the floor. He thought it was funny that he'd taken out three of your family and you were so fucking stupid you couldn't figure it out it was him after all this time.' Michael seemed to float the couple of feet to where Pete was and he punched him hard in the face, instantly loosening some teeth and shutting him up. He hit him again and again, then stood back and pulled out a gun he'd had tucked in the back of his jeans. He lifted it to shoot him in the head so Carl grabbed him fast. Although Michael struggled at first crying with rage at Pete's words, he eventually slumped against his brother all anger leaving him almost like he was a burst balloon. Carl sat Michael down, and took the gun off him. He gestured silently to the others awkwardly standing around some with tears in their eyes. Jonna stepped forward and silently took the gun. Even though Pete was unconscious from his beating Carl walked over and pushed him over with his foot, and he felt sideways on the floor. He got Michael up and walked away supporting him. He jerked his head back and Jojo nodded his head understanding that they were to move Pete for the time being.

Jojo and Jonna picked him up, even after all he'd done Jonna still felt a little bit sorry for him, he couldn't help it. Even though he'd always known Pete was a sneaky little turd, but was still a human being and nobody was perfect. He said a prayer to a God he didn't believe in anymore for Pete that if they had to kill him to make it quick and painless. when he thought about it he didn't want him to die, just punished and away from Sylvia and Jake. He felt angry then at Pete and at himself for being a soft bastard, and for Pete putting them in this situation. So they carried him through to the embalming room, and left him there for a while. As they went back into the main room, Michael came back in and had roughly wiped his eyes. Carl followed with a mugs of tea for everyone. Then he asked everyone for their thoughts on punishments. After a short discussion they decided to drug him and put him in a coffin and then bury him. Jonna blanched when he imagined himself in that position, it was one of his worst fears. No he thought, scrap that it was his worst fear, he spoke up even though his brain told him not to. 'God Michael, Carl come on that's terrible way to die, if he has to die just put a bullet in his brain, and then bury him. We can't do that other thing it's too awful.' Everyone went quiet and looked at Jonna, and Carl's face was like thunder. Michael went to say something but Carl put his hand on his arm to say he wanted to say something so Michael kept quiet. Carl said through gritted teeth 'does anyone else feel the same as Jonna? I need to know now, after all we have always said we decide together.' There was again complete silence in the room now, only Jonna's laboured breathing was heard.

'Well come on then anyone else?' Carl shouted 'guess not, are you forgetting Jonna apart from all the things he's done over the last few weeks, he has abused his family for years, and then he planned for months how he was going to go over to the fucking bastard who ordered our Sara's murder. Let's not forget that eh? As we all now know that Stephen Bentley was the fucker who was boasting he did it, and he took out our Ma as well as Gez, and you want to show Pete fucking mercy. If Bentley hadn't gone nuts, Pete wouldn't have met you Jonna at the car park, he would be with them now telling them all our secrets. Where we get our money from, who does our DVDs need I go on? Do you think that fucking TJ would show us any mercy if he got one of us?' Carl was livid his face was purple and flecks of spittle flew out of his mouth. He went up to Jonna and although he was huge Carl somehow seemed bigger such was his rage. Jonna visibly shrank away from him and just nodded at him, his head was telling him Carl was right of course but his heart still didn't agree, so he thought it best just to keep quiet. Carl kept glaring and then turned around `and said to the rest of the room. 'Right lads when we've sorted everything you can go and cut him free from the chair and put him in the drawer again if he's still unconscious, and if he's awake just make sure he's not going anywhere. Get some sleepers crush them up and put them in a bottle of vodka, get the stuff from our place, so there's no record of anything around here. Who wants to go back to the house and get everything? Oh and pick up some electricians tape from ours as well. Who wants to go and sort that out? Someone else can pick us up some burgers and coffee from Maccy D's too.' He took five twenties from his wallet and put it on the table before asking 'so come on who's going I'm starving and Freddy and Danny said we've got to sort this out by tonight as they need the rooms tomorrow. Good job our mother is at the other site otherwise I'd be tempted to stick the little shit in there with her, two for the price of one eh?' There were a few shocked laughs and Michael just looked at him, his face gave nothing away. He would never put his brother down even if he thought he was totally wrong in front of anyone else. Barry and Jake both offered to go and get the supplies and the burgers, and Carl threw his keys to Jake, and told them to take their car. He gestured towards the table where the money was, and Barry went and picked it up. This left Jonna and Jojo to go and sort out Pete and Jonna knew it was a test.

Linda had the letter burning in the palm of her hands and had a cup of tea and a cigarette ready. She didn't smoke much now, but she liked the feeling of control she had by keeping twenty Benson and Hedges in her bag. So she opened it with shaking fingers and began to read.

Dear Linda,

I hope you're doing well. I have a secret or two to share. Recently Maisie did something to another human being that I find unacceptable beyond words. I saw you and your new man Joe a while ago, I was turning around in my car and I saw you kissing him goodbye on the step. I didn't tell Maisie because for some reason I didn't want to, I wasn't sure why at the time, but I knew that you deserved a chance at happiness. I've been really close you both over the years and I've seen her hurt you again and again, and fooled myself into thinking that you were okay with that. But when you looked at your new man and you smiled I knew that you were genuinely happy and I won't let Maisie and her poison take that away from you. She knows where you are now and the reason I'm telling you this is she'll be here soon. John found you for her, one of the new girls at the café was boasting about knowing you and Joe, she didn't know she was doing any harm so don't go hard on her. Maisie is waiting for me to bring her here thinking that I'll be prepared to hurt you and Joe for her. I don't know what went on between you two when you were lovers but if she treated you even a quarter as bad as she has someone close to me, then you were either brave or loved her so much you didn't object.

She has been one horrible cow since you've left but that's just her and her spoilt ways. She seduced and got a beautiful girl called Tiffany who was feeling low to go to bed with her. Tiffany was uncomfortable but felt grateful as Maisie had stopped her ex Rodney beating her up. Well Maisie and I gave him a good beating and took his gun off him. Then the other night when Maisie wanted someone to play with and Tiffany had enough of her games, Maisie drugged her, tied her up and then did terrible things to her all night, it resulted in Tiffany being left tied up, beaten, bitten, raped and bleeding. Maisie left her in her bed like that and her flat door open, so anyone could have come in and raped her, again. Luckily it was me that found her like that and I helped her and now we're in love. I know it's fast but I think you and Joe will understand as love picks us. So Linda when I come with Maisie I'm going to confront her about what she has done to Tiffany and demand the money she owes me. I've been her lackey for so many reasons, loyalty, love, the glamour of the clubs, but some of the things I've done for her have been very wrong so I am trying to make amends and do good. So now get the hell away from the flat as soon as you can get Joe to come home and move you both away for the night. Don't worry I'll convince her you've gone. She will get the message I'm going to make damned sure of that. When she takes a screaming fit and thinks she can get me to break in, well that's when the fun begins. Just hope she hasn't got the gun we took of Rodney who is one of TJs dickheads. We got the better of him, Tiff broke his nose, I'll tell you more if we meet up. Anyway I've not got the time now to go into it all, my hands hurting I've written this so fast, it probably doesn't make much sense now but it will. When you're ready to get in touch text me, you take care and if we don't see each other for a while, take care and keep your eyes open at all times.

Love from

Phil

Linda was really touched, she felt herself get tearful when she realised how much he'd risked for her, and also for this Tiffany. God Maisie was going to go apeshit, she'd lost her, she'd lost Phil and now her bit on the side had gone off with her closest male friend. She was shocked at all this but she needed to think fast. She wondered if she'd been on the coke again, it sounded like it, she could sometimes go really violent on it. She'd hidden a good few bruises over the years, but she could give as good as she got, and although Maisie had the height and strength, Linda could hold her own. Of course once she'd done it Maisie was full of remorse. Anyway thank God all that was over now, she had to ring Joe and tell him what had happened. She tried ringing him straight away but no answer he must be driving, but then paranoia reared its ugly head. Was he okay or had she got to him already? John or one of the others, surely they'd have some love for her, but then it wasn't her they were kicking half to death was it? Her phone rang and she jumped then felt relief flood through her as she saw Joe's name. Taking a deep breath she answered and told Joe what had happened. He told her to hold on a moment and she heard him telling one of the other drivers to pick up his latest fare and to let the others know he had an emergency, and he'd be in touch. He then said to her that he'd be there soon and Linda got up and started to pack yet again.

Michael and Carl sat on their own in the Undertakers office, the uncles inner sanctum. With a decent shot of whiskey in each crystal tumbler that they'd located in the filing cabinet, they sipped in silence, both keen not to break this little bit of peace. It wasn't going to last long though as they heard doors slamming and shouts from outside. Carl sighed and put his head up, 'Oh well my brother, I thought it was too good to last, so what's next?' Michael smiled and told him 'well I have a plan and we can get rid of Pete perhaps without doing too much.' He carried on and filled Carl in on the rest of his brainwave, he laughed out loud at this, threw his head back and let go. It helped them both. When he'd finished he said 'you are mental Mickey.' To which Michael replied 'hey I like that Mental Mickey it's like that stupid robot we loved as kids do you remember him Metal

Micky wasn't it? It was so shit it was good.' This sent Carl off again, his laughing subsided when they heard a tap at the door. Michael put his finger to his lips to tell him to be quiet and said 'come in' Jonna pushed the door open gently and walked in looking really sheepish. 'Well big fellah what can we do for you? Take a seat and you can fill us in on all the exciting developments, and how much do we owe the uncles for all their help?' Jonna looked at the floor and said 'Freddy said that they're okay with the couple of grand you've given them, and if there's anything else I'll cover it. To make up for before, I feel ashamed lads but I just can't get me head round doing it to Pete. He deserves no mercy but the coffin thing is making me feel sick.' Carl started to feel annoyed again but now he'd calmed down he understood why but it didn't make it any better. Then what Michael said made more sense. 'Alright Jonna' Michael looked at the big man and carried on. 'You're okay about the money don't worry about that, we've always got it covered you should know that by now, and yeah it's too much for Pete but you know what happens when you betray your firm, gang whatever you want to call us. I call us best mates making money as much as we can, and looking out for each other. We have decided and you can go and tell the lads this, we're not going to kill him at the moment?' Jonna slumped in relief even though they were going to probably beat him half to death it was still better than the alternative. He went to go out again, and Michael stood up, 'hang on Jonna I've had a good idea about Pete, if you help us we won't have to worry about doing him in mate, someone might just do it for us.

Phil was back in the Land Rover, he'd popped in to see Tiffany to check she was okay, but she'd looked so small and vulnerable. The hard light he'd seen behind her eyes gone, the need for her past life and all it entailed gone too she said. She'd been asleep so he'd kissed her awake and they'd enjoyed each other just cuddling and kissing in bed for a little bit. He wanted to make love desperately but he wouldn't spoil it or try it on., He had no idea Tiffany wanted to go further as well, as she desperately wanted to get rid of Maisie and all she represented. She felt sick at how she'd plotted to get a man and how stupid she'd been to play games with the likes of the crazy cow. She had dozed off while Phil made them both some tea, and woke up whimpering Maisie's name.

Phil came over to the bed and held her and smoothed her hair and as she calmed down she felt her body come to life. She felt herself start to ache for him, she wanted him inside her even though she was sore all over. Pressing up against him, he was so shocked at her pushing herself against him, that he muttered to her that they should wait as he was scared of hurting her. Tiff who had had enough of talking, hugged him to her breast and he couldn't resist kissing her there, then he pushed up her top and licked and sucked very gently on her nipple. His hand caressed her and she pulled him up to kiss her and reached down and rubbed his erection through his pants. When she felt the size of him she gasped as his fingers slipped under her pants, she unzipped his jeans and as he sprang free she was overwhelmed by his size. A little frightened but so sexually excited she could think only of them making love. Phil had never felt like this, although he'd been selfish sometimes in the past he had no intention of doing that with Tiffany, he knew she wanted him. He was reluctant because he didn't want to hurt her, and the worry of facing Maisie hung over him so he tried to resist. He wanted to make love to her for hours, so that her pain would leave her. As he hesitated Tiffany surprised him and pushed him on his back, then straddled him gasping as she took him all into her and cried out with pain and pleasure. All thoughts of Maisie and the memories of her gone, all she could feel was Phil, she ground her hips into him and clawed at his chest. Both of them came quickly and violently, both crying out with the intensity of the feelings running through their bodies. Tiffany lay on top of him wanting to keep connected as long as was possible, she reached up and kissed him deeply, making sure he didn't slide out of her just yet. He felt himself start to soften as the anxiety returned. He gently lifted her off him and laid her down, looking into her eyes, he explained that he had to do something to protect them both, that he loved her and she was amazing and he couldn't wait to get back and feel more of the same. Tiffany hugged him as hard as she could stand and started to cry, 'please Phil be careful with that psycho bitch. God alone knows what she will do to you when she finds out about us and now she knows where Linda is, she'll come looking for me to warn me off or something. That's what happened last time, and' she tailed off, quietly sobbing and sniffling through her tears. She then explained how much she loved him, how after the person she'd been on the game she'd never enjoyed sex until now and it was glorious with the right person. He told her how he felt to reassure her, and then got up and had a quick shower. He looked at his phone which had been on silent and there were five missed calls surprisingly. He remembered he'd threatened not to take Maisie unless she calmed down. It had been a good few hours since he saw her, so he knew that he'd given Linda enough time to get away with Joe. He didn't want to go when he looked at Tiffany her bright new kimono draped over her as she laid on the bed. She had no makeup on and was a thousand times more beautiful than the ugly Tasha his ex. Even their son didn't like him anymore turned against him by diabetic Dan as he called Joe the idiot Natasha's sad and ugly lackey from work. He'd make sure his son had the money he was due and then he'd wash his hands of them all. He checked the calls log and there were two from the Moffats and three from Maisie. Not too bad then, taking a deep breath he went to Tiffany had a drag of the joint she'd just lit up, and told her to get some munchies for them both for later. She laughed at this and he threw a handful of twenties down. 'Order us a nice meal from the local Indian or Chinese, if they don't deliver text me and I'll pick it up on the way back you sexy beautiful girl'

Tiffany smiled at him, and said 'fine I'll do your bidding oh master, as long as you come back and we get back to where we left off, oh and some chocolate shall be the ultimate price to unlock my chastity belt further.' They both laughed and for a moment the fear disappeared, and Phil grabbed his chance to make it go further away. 'Tiffany you have survived so much, me too not in the same way but I've looked after myself for a long time. Right now we have each other and nothing is going to stop us feeling this way, or being together for as long as you want. Love you angel see you soon.' He smiled at her and threw her a kiss, and left to go and meet Maisie.

It was time and Pete knew it, his life was going to end and even now he still thought he wasn't to blame, he knew that it was everyone's fault but his. He looked at the embalming tables and wondered if they were going to cut him up on one of them. A funny thing happened to him then, he went beyond being scared. He thought to himself so what, if I die then so be it. He heard the door open but the way they'd left him he couldn't see who it was. He took a deep breath he was determined he wasn't going to grovel for his life, but he felt tears welling up in his eyes. He bit his tongue trying hard not to whine and beg for mercy. 'Come on bollocks it's time' he heard Michael say, and he started to cry properly. 'God Pete stop it man you're embarrassing me, you're off the hook for a while, we have a job for you to do instead, so stop snivelling you little runt.' Pete stopped crying immediately, had he heard right he was going to live, he was getting another chance. 'What did you say Michael? Is it true you're letting me go? Oh thank you, thank you it's amazing thanks.' Michael bent down and pulled out a huge knife, and Pete flinched but he just cut the rest of the ties off him, and then stood back. Pete rotated his wrist then rubbed the feeling back into his ankles. 'We have a job for you Pete we want you to lure Stephen Bentley out of hiding for us.' Pete went white, 'Michael I will do anything for you anything but that mad bastard is a monster, will you back me up then if I do.' Michael smiled reassuringly and said 'of course we will we only want you to meet him and talk to him for a bit, you know get him to admit all he's done so we can record him for the police. Then if he is in any way violent we will get him and sort him out so don't worry about that. It's better than getting cut up or a bullet in the head isn't it mate? I've got to be honest you won't ever get back with us, you're dead to me for what you've done. I thought you were my best mate you know and you've shit on me from a great height, however you do this for us and you won't die. You have to move out of Liverpool then, down South. I think you'll do well in London you have the right attitude to belong to one of the firms there, they are backstabbing bastards some of the ones we've done business with, just like you.'

As he was free Pete allowed himself to feel a little anger at the comment, then he realised for the first time, he should actually be grateful and happy. He didn't want to go near Stephen for a start. All he wanted to do was get drunk and go and pick a fight with Sylvia, or if that failed off to see a prostitute pay for some sex then shout at the stupid bitch. No he couldn't even do that they'd watch him and fat Fi was always about when he went to get laid. He would do that the minute he had done this job for them, and then he would leave in a few days. Michael gave him a bottle of water told him to wait there and disappeared into the big main room as Pete drank the water thirstily and relaxed thinking he was very nearly in the clear.

Phil pulled up to Maisie's and got out, she ran down the stairs concealing something in a handbag. Since he'd been looking out for her, driving her round he had never seen her with a hand bag she usually preferred her pockets or sometimes a bum bag. He took it as read that she had the gun with her, and he wondered if she had any bullets for it. As he watched her approach she ran up to him and slapped him hard. Phil let out a surprised grunt and pushed her away. Maisie stared at him, and shouted 'what the fuck do you think you're playing at keeping me waiting so long you arsehole Phil! I can't believe you must have gone back to your little whore for more sex, how could you do that to me?' Phil looked at her and decided he wouldn't retaliate and give her the satisfaction. He grabbed her wrists and held her solidly there, and said 'please don't ever do that again or you will be slapped back because Maisie I've had enough of your crappy behaviour. Not just to me but to everyone. However let's go and see Linda, and if you want me to take you, you can go and get rid of that piece of shit gun.' Maisie was shocked, what the hell was wrong with him she thought, cheeky twat talking to her like that, but she knew Phil and she knew if she opened her mouth now he might not take her. She turned around and ran back up to the flat, opening the door and threw the gun on the floor. Locking up quickly she ran back down the stairs hoping that he'd change his attitude soon otherwise she was going to put him in his place. She had no idea that Phil had something planned for her. He sat in the car waiting, he didn't get out and open the door like he always had. Maisie felt a genuine moment of fear, what on earth was going on now she thought, he really must like this woman I've taken him away from. She pushed it all to the back of her mind the excitement of finding and getting Linda back the only thing she cared about right now. Phil pulled out and he was silent all the way, Maisie gabbing on and on what she and Linda were going to do when they sorted everything out. She was going to take her on holiday fuck the club it could look after itself for a bit, and so on and it just sounded like one continuous droning noise to him so he switched off. Then one word brought him out of his boredom, Tiffany. He woke up then and asked Maisie 'what did you say about Tiffany?' Maisie sniggered, 'Oh you are listening I said thank God I don't have to see that little whore again.'

Phil thought he was going to have a heart attack he felt the blood rush to his face, as he slammed on the brakes. Maisie flew forward and banged her head on the windscreen, as she had no seat belt on as usual. He started to pant and genuinely thought he was going to pass out, until he took some deep breaths and realised it was rage that was overtaking his body as well as his mind. Maisie groaned as she reached up to her forehead and saw the blood on her fingers. 'God Phil what happened did we nearly run over someone or an animal or something?
Phil looked at her in disgust and grabbed a tissue out of his pocket, and passed it to her. He wanted to put his hands around her throat and squeeze but he thought with disgust then I'd be as bad as you, as he looked at her. He reluctantly asked 'are you okay, do you want to go to the hospital?' Maisie although dizzy and disorientated was still focused only on Linda. She snorted in derision and replied 'nah Phil you know me, nothing's going to stop me seeing the love of my life, just do us a favour and pull over and get me a can of coke or something.' Phil smiled grimly and had dig at her by turning it into a joke 'haven't you had enough coke for now?'
Maisie looked at him a sour expression on her face. 'Well we are nearly there now so stop giving me daggers Maisie, you'd better change your attitude and stick a smile on your gob. If not Linda will run a mile.' Maisie thought about it and just nodded and pressed the tissue to her head, the bleeding had stopped. Phil pulled up at a garage and went in to grab some soft drinks after he'd filled the tank. Maisie went into the toilets and when she come out she was swinging her jaw, so he knew she'd been snorting coke in there. He could do without it, it just made her twice as dangerous. He decided to have a snort himself just to keep himself totally alert, so asked her for some. She smiled smugly and handed over a small purse to

him. He went into the gents and pulled out the glass phial of coke, a blade, a mirror and a tube for snorting it. He helped himself to a line and put some of the coke in a bit of tissue for later if he needed it. It went straight to his head and he felt the familiar buzz followed by a quick kick of anxiety. Good stuff he thought as he went back out to the car, where Maisie was guzzling one of the cans. He felt like just going back to Tiffany but he wouldn't until he'd confronted her on his own and said what he needed to say. He got back in the car and Maisie smiled knowingly as he'd had some of her coke. It made her feel good because Phil didn't often take it. He handed the purse back to her and they drove out of the garage and on to Linda and Joes.

Joe had picked up Linda and their stuff, and they were driving to Blackpool. They had decided to go on a short holiday, they both had plenty of money so they could afford to stay in a good hotel. Linda was excited she hadn't been to Blackpool for ages, but noticed Joe wasn't he usual cheery self. She knew it had something to do with Maisie but she wasn't sure what, so she asked him straight out. Proud of the fact that they didn't play games. 'What's up Joe come on it's not like you to be this quiet I thought you'd be over the moon us spending a week in Blackpool? Instead of a dirty weekend we can have a dirty week what do you think?' She smiled gently at him to let him know she was teasing but also asking a serious question too. Joe thought for a while trying to explain as best he could, and told her 'It's just happened so fast, and to tell you the truth I'm pissed off running away, I'd like to confront the vile bitch and tell her to piss right off. She might think I'm frightened of her and her cronies now.' Linda burst out laughing and Joe looked at her quickly and smiled uncertainly. 'What are you laughing at? He said through his smile and Linda giggling shouted 'YOU! You used the word cronies how old are you? A hundred and two? And then she broke down laughing even harder. Joe had to pull over as her laughter was infectious and the pair of them were semi hysterical .When they'd calmed down they had a kiss and cuddle and discussed what had happened. Linda said thought about it then said seriously to Joe 'listen if you really care about this thing with Maisie we can go back, but Phil asked me to return the favour of him not telling her about us ages ago. All he asked was to keep away and could we let him use our flat for a while. I've left a key for him, and he was saying that he wants to sort something out and leave Maisie and all the club stuff behind. I've no idea what exactly but he really wants to be alone when he does this. So do you want to go back and confront her anyway or should we just enjoy a bit more peace, stay away a week or two and see if the dust settles? I could really use some time away and can't wait to spend it with you.' Joe leant over and hugged her gently, thinking for the nine hundredth time what a lovely woman she was, he felt himself coming round to her way of thinking. He told her 'I love you, you daft mare, let's go and have fun and play on the fruit machines and eat hotdogs. Then throw them up after going on the fair. When we feel better we can buy a massive bag of rock and some candy floss and watch crappy TV in bed in the hotel.' Linda smiled relieved that he didn't want to go and face Maisie anymore, after all she wouldn't hurt him or her or even retaliate in public. It would be the men she'd almost certainly pay to get rid of Joe that worried her the most.

Chapter 38

Rodney finally found Stephens house in Neston on the Wirral, he'd been there so long it was going to go dark in a few hours. He smirked to himself as one of the reasons it had taken this amount of time was he'd bought loads of things in Birkenhead Market. Well tough shit he thought, it was ages since he'd enjoyed having a shop. He just liked spending money and since the crap with Tiffany it was the first time he'd genuinely had a bit of fun, some nice bacon butties and a cuppa in the café there. Then and only then had he felt ready to face the day. He got a taxi to Stephens place and it worked out quite a bit more than he'd allowed because it was miles off the beaten track. Right, he thought, all I have to do now is get in without being seen. After searching the perimeter for what seemed like forever, he noticed a way in, a path through a little wood and a space where the fence was missing. He stumbled at least four times trying to walk through the little space, and then he felt smooth even ground under feet. He got all his stuff and put it under a hedgerow, and threw a few leaves and twigs over it. No one was going to see it there anyhow, who on earth would walk here? He crossed the lawn playing a little game in his head, pretending he was on manoeuvres in the army. Then a horrible thought hit him, what was he supposed to do when he found Bentley? He hadn't thought of that, he'd been too busy imagining what he'd buy in Birkenhead Market. He'd just nodded at TJ when he'd told him what to do. Was it just talk to him and get him to ring TJ or did he have to knock him out, or ring TJ and let him know so he could get some troops over here? He felt uneasy now, how could he knock him out, the bastard was crazy. Even in his worst days, when he'd actually murdered for money, he was still saner than this nutter. God, he wished he was still like that in a way, then he'd show Stephen fucking Bentley. He realised he was standing right by the windows now they were taller than him, and the light was casting shadows where he stood. He looked around and spotted a garden chair so he picked it up moved it where he wanted it, stood on it and looked through the window. To his amazement there was Bentley stripped to the waist with what looked like writing all over his chest and arms. They weren't tattoos as far as he knew and the soft bastard was practicing some type of martial art and watching himself in the big mirror that ran along one wall.

Rodney ducked down, checked his phone was on silent and rang TJ. He didn't answer so he tried a few more times then he left his message on voicemail, telling TJ he'd found Stephen he was home, and he was acting really crazily even for him. As he closed his phone he felt the sharp prick of a knife or blade as it nicked his ear, and then felt it go to his neck. He closed his eyes furious at himself for not watching out and then he felt Bentley whisper in his ear, 'what you doing here fat boy has the old dickhead sent you to murder me?' Rodney felt his bowels loosen as he knew that what he said wouldn't make any difference. He recognised this type of crazy all too well, he knew then that Bentley had finally lost it, and that just made him want to go to the toilet even more. He'd met these types in prison and they either got murdered or battered and put in segregation or sent off to a secure hospital never to be seen again. The paranoia was par for the course, and even worse most of the time they were right. Stephen pushed the knife harder into his throat and he felt a little trickle of blood, he couldn't let him see how scared he really was. He had to try and get out of this somehow. 'Right chubs me and you are going inside where you can tell me what the hell is going on. Then you can tell me why did TJ send his old number two after his newest and best number one? If you do as you're told I may even let you go, so remember that if you try any funny stuff I'll slit your throat and piss in it, okay?' Stephen told him to get moving and on wobbly legs Rodney walked forward trying his best not to soil himself, vomit or cry. When they got to the room that just minutes before he'd been looking in at, Stephen pushed him hard and he landed on the couch, hurting his knees. Still trying desperately to cling on to what little pride he had left.

Stephen eyed him warily and sat there staring at him, and then said 'tell you what Rodney you tell me honestly what's going on with TJ and why you're here and I'll show you some of my special films. I showed them to that prick Pete but he didn't like them.' Rodney nodded and then jumped as Stephen shouted 'girls will you leave me alone, I know you didn't like it but I was only showing you love so stop fucking nagging.' He

186

started to slap himself hard on the head and pinch himself and then grabbed the pen he'd been drawing on his body with and drew a strange symbol. 'There now they've gone again, these are runes Rodney, things to stop the ghosts of the bitches I've loved with my knife from driving me mad. Sara is the worst as she was my first proper kill, and she just goes on and on in her annoying nasally voice. Rodney just nodded not knowing what to say, he may be trying to catch him out, but he suspected he'd flipped completely and was totally delusional. God almighty, he just hoped TJ would get his message and help him out. He stuttered trying to tell Stephen what TJ had said that he was worried about him, and he wasn't there to hurt him just to see why he'd not been in touch. His brain was almost hurting he was being so careful what he said. He hadn't even noticed that Stephen the psycho had gone off somewhere.

He heard a lot of noise behind him, and looked around cautiously and saw Bentley messing around with a load of videos and what looked like CDs. He could tell he was lining them up to play. He put the first one from his assortment in and a fuzzy image appeared on the huge TV in the room. His eyes adjusted and he could see it was a girl who looked dead lying on a pavement. With a shock he realised it was Sara Moffat dead on the floor, the camera panned around and then focused on her open lifeless eyes. Then it moved down to where the stab wound was, and where a huge pool of blood had gathered. It was on there for quite some time, then went back to her face. Rodney had always known it was Bentley who'd killed her but seeing it like that and knowing he'd done the same thing made him feel sick, really sick. He realised with a shock that the footage of Sara was from police files, and he wondered where on earth he'd got that from. The next one was a beautiful young Asian girl, Chinese or Thai, he couldn't tell and this one had sound, and a horrible mewling noise assaulted his ears. Then he shuddered as a cry of pain that made every hair on his body stand on end rang out. He looked at the screen and before he could stop himself he retched and threw up all over the floor. When he saw what was on the screen Rodney actually fainted, and Stephen looked over at him annoyed he wasn't watching it. He grabbed a cup of water and threw it over Rodney who started to come round. Stephen then saw some of his girls looking in through the window shouting something, and he screamed at them to go away. Rodney opened his eyes, and just stayed mute almost fascinated by the fear on Bentleys face as he looked and screamed at the empty window.

He then started to mutter 'tell them to go away please while I show you the rest of their films. They keep interrupting me, and all I want to do is go through them and show how beautiful they look. Can you see it too, see how beautiful it is? I loved them so much with my knives.' Rodney didn't know what to say, he was struggling not to vomit so for the first time in his life he did something smart, and replied. 'Yes Stephen' he said. 'I know but how about if you get us something to drink and we can watch them together and you can show me what you mean.'

Rodney held his breath as he waited for the slap or the retort but Stephen just nodded and disappeared and came back holding two cans of lemonade. He had lots of white powder around his nostrils, too far gone to wipe it off. He opened one of the cans and passed it to Rodney who guzzled greedily from it, as it helped his frazzled throat. Stephen opened and sipped his, and smiled his awful smile. He said 'I'm looking forward to this maybe you're not so bad after all fat man. It will be great I can tell you all their names and how special they all were.' Grinning Stephen walked over to an expensive DVD player and put another disc in. Rodney watched in horror as he showed him tortured girls, some screaming and begging for their lives, others drugged and quiet. It occurred to Rodney then that maybe it was part of his punishment for the things he'd done. Stephen was transfixed looking at the screen and so when Rodney's phone rang he took it out and saw it was TJ, he took a chance and answered it. Stephen took no notice so he told him quickly what had happened and TJ agreed to come over and bring some men to take care of the situation as it stood. Rodney closed his phone, and cautiously put it back in his pocket. Stephen hadn't moved an inch much to his relief. He crossed his fingers said a few prayers and sat there hoping that TJ and the men would come soon. Half an hour later he thought he heard someone approaching and thought how quick his boss had got there, not realising that it wasn't TJ and his men at all.

Chapter 39

Phil pulled into the little cul de sac where Linda had been living. Maisie was delirious with joy, anticipating seeing her. Not for one moment thinking that she may even be out or not answer. Phil grinned grimly to himself still amazed at her arrogance after all this time. 'Come 'ed lad let's go and see her come on, come on' she said impatiently. Phil got out and Maisie followed him. He told her to stay by the gate and check no one was about. He retrieved the keys quickly from the hiding place under a stone. He opened the door and shouted her, and she thought that Linda had opened it. She then ran up the path, her arms out. When she got to the door her instincts that had served her so well for so long were telling her something wasn't right. Powerless to stop she stepped into the hallway and went to look for her. Phil shut the door behind her and double locked it and put the keys in his pocket. She started to scream Linda's name, and then she had checked every room. She was furious now that she wasn't there so she turned on Phil who was putting the kettle on and checking the fridge. She snarled 'what the fuck are you playing at Phil? I mean where the fuck is she I don't understand you dickhead what are you doing?' Phil just looked at her and smiled 'do you want a cuppa? Then I'll explain what is happening and what is going to happen in the near future; hey you never know it may be in the tealeaves?' Smiling at his own joke he carried on making the tea while Maisie was so angry she ran at him screaming ready to bite, scratch and kick. In fact anything to make him feel some pain.

She hit him hard across the ear and he felt his vision wobble. He didn't hold back when he hit her back just as viciously and she fell on the floor. 'Don't ever do that again you crazy bitch or I will do it back twice as hard every time, do you understand?' Phil said through gritted teeth juggling feelings of anger with disgust that he'd hit a woman. Maisie's survival instincts kicked in quickly. She knew she had to wait this out, then she would stab the bastard no matter how many fucking years they'd been mates. Phil went back to the tea and then told her to get up and go into the front room. Maisie struggled to her feet and remembered the coke; maybe she could distract him with that while she got a knife or weapon. 'Listen Phil I need a snort now, I haven't a bastard clue what's going on, but I'm going to have a line do you want one?' Phil smiled and said to her 'nice try Maisie honey but I know you inside and out, so I will have a bit of coke when I'm ready but not while you're loose. I know I'll end up with a knife in my back as I'm leaning down for a line.' Maisie just snarled at him and he watched while she walked into the front room. 'My God does my Linda really live here? It's so boring and bland, nice and shiny and new but no character, I mean has she had a brain transplant or what?'

Phil kept his eye on her and ignored her jabbering, and told her to sit down. He retrieved his supplies from the bag he'd brought and told Maisie to behave while he tied her up, or he'd hit her again. Then he'd put a nice big piece of tape over her mouth if she tried anything. Maisie rolled her eyes pretending to be totally bored by the whole situation but inside she was genuinely frightened. How could Phil do this to her? He was her Phil, he was supposed to love her. Nothing made sense, maybe they'd all been taken over by aliens because nothing added up. Her whole world had turned upside down in a day.

She was in shock as she'd had no idea that all this had been building up for a long time. She still believed she was untouchable. She'd heard all about how life often pays you back. Maybe all the things Linda used to say about Karma being a real force, and ninety nine percent of the time you got back what you gave was true. She also said that sometimes shit happened to good people for no reason except for the chaos of life. That would be her then she arrogantly thought. She should have realised that Linda must have been talking about her and her women on the side. The love of her life it seemed had really left her. Even now she still didn't think any of it was really her fault, clinging on to the now battered excuse that if Linda had made love more she wouldn't have had to go looking elsewhere. Maisie's mind was racing trying to work out what could have sent Phil over the edge like this. She was about to find out soon it seemed one way or another.

Pete had been cautious approaching Bentley's house, the Moffats had dropped him off and told him they wanted him to see if he was in. If he was on his own to go and talk to him and tempt him outside. He wasn't as frightened as he had been before on his own, as he had two very pissed off Moffats in tow, he thought with a grin. Yes Stephen Bentley was a known psycho and everyone was scared of him, but he still didn't feel bothered because the Moffats were tooled up and ready to go. He even had the arrogance to think he'd been almost forgiven not realising he was being used as bait nothing more. He approached the windows and saw a chair already there, so perhaps somebody else had been peeking, or maybe it was just there. He looked through the window and saw Rodney watching the huge TV and Stephen kneeling on the floor watching too. Why did he have his shirt off? He didn't look the type to have loads of tattoos? He cursed his eyesight he couldn't make out if it was tattoos or God knows what? What were they watching looked like some type of horror movie. They really were a pair of dickheads he thought with a grin. Well his part was done now, he could go back and tell the Moffats, he had taken them there to the house, and now he could tell them what's going on, sweet. He ran over the lawn not bothering to check if anyone was watching, going straight to where the car was, he got straight in. Carl and Michael both sat in the front and didn't move. 'So what's going on then?' said Michael and Pete feeling very self important replied 'well the psycho's there, and Rodney the plonker and as far as I can tell no one else. They're watching a film on his big TV and something weird, Bentley has his top off and is covered in either tattoos or drawings can't tell which.' Carl and Michael looked at each other, and as Carl opened his mouth to say something Michael gave a slight shake to indicate say nothing, which Carl acknowledged.

Pete sat in the back and went to light up a cigarette and Michael said 'don't do that, you are going to get us seen you Muppet. ' Pete was a bit taken aback by the new tone of voice. He still thought he was doing okay and maybe they would give him a job again. Just until he felt he'd done enough to be forgiven. 'Alright keep your hair on Mickey lad just having a fag.' Michael adjusted the rear view mirror and looked Pete in the eye, 'listen you cocky little bastard, do not think for one minute you're back in the fucking door, just because you took us up to psycho Stephens house, and looked through a window for two minutes. So don't get too comfy in the back seat because my once trusted friend or should I say Judas, we will never forget what you've done even if we have to get our Zimmer frames customized to hold a shot gun. Do you get it?' Pete was shaking half of him pissed and angry at what Michael had said. Unfortunately the other part of him was the old fear returning that they were going to kill him or seriously fuck him up. So he bit his tongue and waited it out. Michael said to him 'me and our kid are going to have a quick chat about what's happening, so make yourself scarce over in the field to have your fag. Go on and keep it down and make sure you cover it so no one can see you for Christ's sake.' Pete thinking he may have to leg it got cautiously out and did as he was told. Michael waited until he was out of ear shot and asked Carl, 'well what do we do next, I thought we were going to take Bentley on a joyride? It's a bit harder now Rodney's there as we don't want any witnesses including Pete really. That's if we do the deed. The other lads know what we're doing but they're sound as they've proved since all this shit started.' Carl was quiet, and then decided for them. 'Come on then, let's go and see what we're dealing with. I want to see what's going on. Knowing Pete he missed something important. Then we can throw a brick through the window or something and get the crazy bastard outside.'

They both left the car and got their stuff from the boot. Out of spite Michael locked it, so Pete couldn't sit in it and he'd have to go back to the field. Michael had a tazer and a double barrelled shotgun, and Carl a machete and an old pistol. They knew what they were dealing with, when it was Stephen Bentley. They approached the windows and saw the chair; Michael stepped up on it and pulled Carl up too. They both looked through the window and were speechless as they saw Bentley dancing around with a curved knife, dripping blood. and Rodney clutching his throat the blood pumping between his fingers as he tried to stop the impossible flow from his jugular vein. He collapsed back on the couch and they heard Bentley shout 'not on there you stupid bastard you'll ruin it, you betrayed me you told TJ about the girls didn't you?' He screamed in Rodney's face and then used the horrible knife to slash at his hands, but it didn't make any

191

difference to all intents and purposes Rodney had gone, and Bentleys' couch was most definitely ruined, now slick with blood.

Michael whispered to Carl 'fucking hell bro, what the shit happened there, do we get him outside and knock him out with the tazer or what? I wasn't expecting that I thought they were on the same side.' Carl whispered back 'I know I'm stunned one thing for sure is whatever madness was in his head has multiplied by about a fucking thousand. Jesus I feel sorry for the old fat bastard well almost anyway.' As Michael and Carl tried to process what had just happened they heard a car or cars approaching. 'For Christ's sake what now, I hope it's not the police they'll get Bentley and we won't get near him for months until someone can get to him inside the nick. Come on let's go and watch from over there, and then if we need to get ready to lose the weapons and leg it.' They both ran to the cover of the hedge row and hid their stuff as best they could. They both watched as two cars pulled up into Bentley's enormous drive, Michael commenting on how they had got past the gate, they both agreed it must be TJs men. Michael put his hand on something. He pulled out two bags of shopping and showed Carl? 'What the hell is going on?' They both burst out laughing as he pulled out some sexy undies size xl! 'Ssh!' They both said the same time grinning. They heard noise from the cars so both looked over. Then they both swore under their breath as TJ got out of the first car. 'Frigging hell Carl' said Michael 'it must be really important for him to get out of his coffin; he is never seen outside or within twenty miles of where the law might turn up. Just think if he didn't have fucking five of his dickheads with him we could take him out, if we'd have known we could have brought the lads.' Carl nodded his head then said 'I wouldn't' worry too much about that, if Bentleys' convinced that TJ is bad it will make our lives easier if they take each other out. He must be otherwise he wouldn't have turned on poor old Rodney the plonker would he?' Michael chuckled at this and punched his brother softly on the arm. 'I wish I had some popcorn to watch the fun.' He retorted then his good humour went swiftly away 'shit we forgot about Pete the gormless bastard who might grass us up if he gets caught.'

Carl grinned in the dark 'have you gone soft in the head or what? Pete is the biggest coward since General Custer shit his pants, he's the least of our worries he'll be legging it across the fields now.' After TJ's men had disappeared they both crept back up to the window and saw that TJ and his men were panicking and pointing at Rodney who was now sure to be dead. Two of the men it seemed were ordered to move him, but it appeared he was stuck solid to the couch. Another man joined in and they tried to pull him free. After a few minutes struggling, Rodney's body gave way and they all went flying backwards where Rodney's corpse with the sofa cushion still stuck to its bum landed on TJ. This was too much for Michael and Carl who both trying to keep their laughing quiet fell off the flimsy chair in a giggling heap on the floor. As they tried to recover they ran back into the cover of the trees and hedgerows and sat there calming down. 'God what's wrong with us?' gasped Michael as he wiped the tears from his eyes 'I mean that's a dead man they are playing pass the parcel with, and we lost it. I wonder if it would get two hundred and fifty quid on you've been framed?' He turned round to see why Carl hadn't responded and saw he was laughing so hard no sound was coming out. Michael hit him on the arm and they both started to calm down.

There had been no sign of Bentley while all this went on and Carl's sharp eyes picked up a shape running down the path. 'Psssst Michael there he goes look' and he pointed over to where Bentley was moving pretty fast. He hesitated for a little while and then decided to get into the heavies car that was parked behind TJs and then almost immediately started to reverse out. There was a dull thud as he hit something and he stopped for a minute, got out spat then got back in and reversed over what he'd hit and drove off into the night. Carl looked at Michael and asked what he had been thinking himself. 'What did he hit then? A fox or something the noise was horrible. Let's go and have a look while TJ and his apes are checking out the house. It could be in pain.' They both went around the perimeter keeping their eyes on the house just in case. As they approached the gates they saw the shape lying on the floor, it was Pete his lifeless eyes staring up into the night. What was left of his torso was a mess all blood and guts, and Michael and Carl stared at each other in disbelief. 'What on God's earth is going on with all this death? Come on we'll go and try and chase the dickhead otherwise we'll be searching for weeks or months even years. Even though Pete let us down you know Carl it's still a shit way to go isn't it? I can't get my head round it, I think I'm in shock.' Michael was trying hard not to cry and Carl knew it, so making light of it he said 'come on let's leave him for TJ to deal with he was on his payroll wasn't he? Stop looking at the body bro it's sure to make you feel worse. Anyway we'd often told Pete for years smoking can lead to an early death!' Michael felt sick and angry at his tasteless joke but knew Carl was doing his best to cheer him up so swallowed it down and smiled, 'you're right I know but I still feel shit leaving him here like this.' Carl suddenly had a brain wave, and said 'this will cheer you up bro, let's phone the lads and tell them we're going hunting. Tell them to bring guns, knives, hammers or even pointed sticks as they say in Monty Python. Just tell them to drive slowly and don't attract any trouble, and see if they can get to the tunnel now, as Bentley is bound to be on his way to Liverpool. Hey

Mikey one of your fave films is Hard Target, we can hunt him down only difference is unlike good old Jean Claude Van Damme he's the bad guy and we're the good guys!' Carl smiled and looked at Michael who was smiling; he just nodded and got out his phone and rang Jonna and the boys.

Chapter 40

Phil had sat there in silence freaking out Maisie, who was genuinely frightened now because she wasn't sure what she was guilty of. 'I'll tell you the word you should be worried about and it begins with T' he said almost in a whisper. Maisie looked puzzled and tried to think, but she couldn't she needed a snort of coke and a Jack Daniels. Anything like that would be nice right now. Christ she'd settle for a snort of speed and a bottle of Thunderbird right now. Phil knew she needed a snort of coke to keep up the bravado and would give her one if she was good enough. He laughed at giving Maisie one, and she just looked on wondering what was funny.

'So any ideas then your majesty something precious and frail and beginning with T second letter I?' he repeated. Maisie saw all too clearly at that point, and said it out loud. 'Fucking hell Phil please don't tell me this is over that stupid little whore Tiffany?' Phil froze and felt himself nearly unable to breathe such was his anger at her comment. He took a deep breath and counted to ten otherwise he would strangle the stupid bitch right now and that's all he wanted to do. He turned round and looked at her and her expectant face thinking she was back on familiar ground made him so angry he punched the wall by her head. He nearly broke his hand and made a hole, and it wasn't chipboard. The pain centred him plus he couldn't strangle her now. He turned around to look at her and took a deep breath, 'you are not fit to mention her name so don't Maisie I'm warning you. This is what it's about, I want to make you pay for what you did to her, and I want you to be sorry for it.' Maisie couldn't keep the look of amazement off her face for the second time today with Phil. She just gasped and whispered barely audible 'Jesus Phil, what is she to you, and what the fuck did I do wrong?' Phil dug his nails into the wounds on his hand and when the pain brought him home to sanity he just shook his head and said 'you are a piece of work you don't even remember what you did? You a woman have done more harm to Tiffany than years of being on the game, being with men like Rodney and her step dad. You held her down and raped her, and then left her tied up, with her flat door open? Anyone of the bastards from the flats or from TJs could have turned up. Took photos anything or worse raped her again. You raped her Maisie and you left her for dead. A woman doing that to another woman is even worse if possible than a man doing it. Because although you like to think you're a man your body tells me otherwise.' Maisie knew then she'd done wrong but still didn't care about Tiffany. She only cared about the effect it was having on her and Phil. All she wanted now was to salvage their friendship which she realised she needed or at least get out of this unscathed. 'I'm sorry Phil, it was the coke you know I'm cruel sometimes but I wouldn't do it on purpose, I sort of thought I'd dreamt it you know? If I did that to Tiffany I'm sorry I thought she wanted it too. The leaving her vulnerable was my fault I was so off it I just walked out. That's unforgivable and I'm sorry.'

She tried her best to sound earnest but it came out patronising, and Phil knew she was trying to save her sorry skin. 'Nice try queen, but nope not buying it. I'm going to do to you what you did to her, then I'm going to your house and taking my wages for the last how many years? You've owed me so much for so long. Always saying just ask me if you need anything. It's all down to your controlling people. But fuck that I'm going away from you and everything about you okay?' Maisie felt a bit hysterical then, surely Phil wasn't going to rape her, no he'd never do that would he? But as her whole world had been thrown on its head she didn't know for sure. Phil smiled at her then, it was a smile to make her stomach turn and he picked her up and took her into the bedroom where he threw her down on the bed. Maisie didn't move as she knew how deadly Phil could be with his knife. He straddled her and tied her wrists to the bed, then he cut her ties on her feet and then pulled off her pants, she was so shocked and frightened she went limp. Phil left her knickers and top garments on, on and tied her to the bed the way she'd tied Tiffany. He put on the lamp and said 'I'll be seeing you Maisie, I'm going to leave the door open, and if I hear of you doing anything to Linda and Joe then I'll be back to see you again. Do you understand?' Maisie nodded and then started to plead with him, but it fell on deaf ears and Phil left the room. She glanced to both sides and she noticed he'd left water with a straw in, just within her reach,

as long as she was careful she'd be able to get it to her mouth. He left the house and very quietly locked up, he wouldn't do to her what she had done to Tiff. He wasn't that evil anyway no way would he stoop to her level. Even more importantly he wouldn't risk anyone stealing from Linda and Joe. He had it covered as one of the lads from TJs who'd approached him about working for Maisie or the Moffats had been given a hundred quid a spare key and told what to do. He trusted him, so he would go and let her go in around 20 hours from now enough time to get what he wanted sorted, and get him and Tiff to an airport. He set off for Maisie's flat for the last time he hoped and went to get the money he was owed. He had left Tiff too long so he had to hurry, and the jeep had sustained a few injuries that needed sorting, but for the first time in years he actually felt happy, really happy and he liked it. He'd get the jeep mended then swap it, just because she had bought it for him.

Linda and Joe had checked into a nice hotel and had were enjoying their holiday. They'd made love in different ways gently, passionately, lovingly. They had experimented the way new lovers do, and fell completely and utterly in love. What they thought had been love before paled into insignificance to how they felt now, away from worry and work and Maisie. Linda was happier than she'd ever been and so was Joe. It went unspoken between them that they would do anything for each other and do anything to protect what they had. They agreed that they didn't have to return to Liverpool, but as they shared a strong and loyal love for the city they would. With Linda's money and Joes business thriving the world was their oyster. She was even prepared to sell her share of the club now, she knew she'd only wanted to hang on to it as it was her security blanket. As for Maisie she'd be happy never to see her again. It was the freedom to choose that was important to Linda not having it very often in her past relationships. Joe understood as he'd had to do things too without any choice. For example stay in a loveless relationship for his son. His ex was with someone, but he'd had a few flings but wouldn't introduce him to a woman because he had a real problem with daddy having a new wife. Well his son would have to get over it eventually and accept Linda too. With work and kindness it would be okay. He stopped thinking about it and decided to do what Linda recommended and that was live in the moment. He did and started to brighten immediately, and as the weekend approached they decided another week was on the cards. They decided on
London and a really luxurious hotel, to see the sites of the capital city and do the whole tourist thing. As they were packing Linda heard her phone chime to signal she had a text. She looked at it and smiled, 'Phil said hello, not to worry and he reckons Maisie won't come near us now. Also to relax and enjoy being in love.' Joe smiling said 'was he always such a big softie?' Linda laughed and replied 'nope he wasn't it must be being in love that's doing us all good.' She suddenly looked sad, and Joe noticed her change. 'Come on out with it why the sad face? You may as well tell me or I'll have to tickle it out of you.' He said, and she looked at him straight in the eyes, and answered 'don't hate me for this but I can't help it after all the years. I feel sad because Maisie will never know love like ours or Phil's because

she can't, she is unable to love.' Joe smiled and hugged her to him. 'I think it's amazing that you can feel that after all she's done. It's fine it really is and no she won't, but it wouldn't make her happy anyway. She's too hedonistic to ever feel joy over something as simple as a nice cup of tea and watching a daft film together, and that being enough. The best part is' and Linda said it with Joe in unison 'it's not our problem anymore.' They both laughed and finished hugging, and carried on packing looking forward more than ever to their trip to London, and their new life together.

Stephen Bentley was in a stranger's car, he had a shirt covered in blood, and had no idea where he was heading. Maybe he could go and see that dickhead who'd got him sacked now from the slaughter house, he was going to get him one day after all, but he couldn't remember his name. Just that he'd had a nice wife and a bit on the side. Shit what was happening to him? Then he remembered and he looked in the mirror dreading what he'd see. Sure enough Shelagh Moffat was there, as were two of the Tai girls he'd murdered. They were almost skeletal, bleeding, and grinning, he wanted them to go away. Their skin was stretched tight over their skulls and they weren't beautiful anymore. He'd even run over someone on his way to escape TJ who'd obviously sent Rodney to kill him. Cheeky bastard then the plastic gangster and some heavies had come to finish the job. Well he wouldn't kill him the stupid fat dick. He was going at a steady 30 miles per hour, and then Shelagh screamed in his ear, 'my boys are going to get you, you bastard cutting me up, but look at the other girls you tortured them for days you sick fuck.' He screamed at her to shut up, and kept going not sure where but just moving helped. He thought he'd aim for the Pier head where he'd seen off Gez, then he could get his head together. He was in the tunnel he realised, so it wasn't bad when he got out of it, he could do an illegal turn and get to the Liver buildings so he didn't have to try the one way system. It was quiet enough now so he could just ignore the turn off and go straight across to outside the Museum; then he could get down to the seafront to think. It was then he noticed a car behind him, they'd been with him for ages. He laughed he was in the tunnel they couldn't change lanes unless they wanted a pull off the police. He took no notice, and it was just as well because Carl and Michael were behind him and had caught him easily going at 30 miles an hour. It was almost too easy they rang Jonna who was with Little Joey and Billy. The others were getting the house ready for their Ma's funeral which was happening soon, and they were waiting for them by the tunnel. They had an idea he'd do the illegal turn across to avoid the one way system, so they were parked by the museum. They saw Bentley come out and do exactly as they'd thought. Carl and Michael followed as there were no coppers about, they dipped their lights to say hello, and Stephen realised he was being followed. He didn't spot the other car with the three men in. He didn't want to look in the mirror as he was scared who was there, but he had to see who was following him, it was bad enough the ghosts wouldn't leave him alone, but now some other trouble. It couldn't be TJ as he'd legged it from his place with them all there. He looked in the mirror and to his relief the women weren't there, but two sets of headlights were and he knew for absolute certain they were after him.

Chapter 41

TJ stood in the middle of the room, the goons he'd brought with him had wrapped up poor Rodney in bin bags, fuck the forensics they could have Bentley now, he'd give the police him as a gift. He'd gone too far and now he'd lost his sanity probably for good. Even the Moffats would back down if he got Stephen blamed for everything, he could pretend he'd sacked him. Everyone had commented on seeing him, and knew that Rodney had gone over to try and find out what was going on. A couple of the men had known Rodney for years, and all of them felt sick about what had happened. They all hated Bentley anyway and thought TJ had gone too far hiring him, all the whispers about him stabbing and murdering people like Sara Moffat now proved to be true. They went out to the cars, and come back in as TJ wiped all the handles and things anyone had touched. A big man called Colin who'd been on his payroll for a few years told TJ that they had a problem. 'What now?' asked TJ 'Is this fucking night ever going to end?' he asked him. Colin replied in a tight voice 'Well we're in a bit of a mess, as it looks like Bentley has taken our car and he's only gone and run over Pete that dickhead you hired from the Moffats.' TJ thought he was hearing things, and then it hit him. He went a funny colour and went to sit down being careful not to touch anything. 'Christ Colin I assume Pete is dead, and you're going to have to report the car stolen or torch it, in fact anything so the coppers won't be able to trace it to him.'

Colin looked put out, 'do you want us to scrape up Pete as well TJ or shall we leave him?' TJ thought about this and said 'no leave him, he's associated with the Moffats not us, let them sweat for a while with the bizzies crawling all over them. It may take the heat off us.'

Colin nodded and stood there wondering what to do next. He hated the way TJ talked about the police and saying things like take the heat off us, he was stuck in Miami Vice alright. Any respect he'd had for him disappeared when Rodney's corpse had knocked him over.

TJ was watching him closely picking up on his negative attitude towards him. 'If you want to stay on my payroll you stroppy bastard I would show me some respect and it's Mr. Murphy to you. You can go and put Rodney's body in my car boot and I will ring now for one of my other men to come and pick you up. I don't trust you to do the right thing. You can go on about Bentley all you like but at least I didn't have to explain to him every fucking detail in case he got it wrong. Now go and do as you're told or not only will I kick you off the payroll I'll pay someone to sort you out.' Colin had grown red with embarrassment and anger, because he knew what TJ said was true, so he swallowed his pride and mumbled 'okay Mr. Murphy I'm on it.' TJ just nodded at him and turned his back. Colin went out and TJ went through Stephens DVDs and took them in case there was anything incriminating on them to do with him. Then he swept up a pile of his paperwork, for the same reason. He didn't' notice the one left in the actual DVD player and shut the door using the tee towel he had and went out. He saw the men standing around waiting for him, and could tell by the belligerent attitude that Colin had told them what he'd said. He didn't care, so he walked over to where Pete's corpse was. 'God they're dropping like flies tonight aren't they?' He said it to let them know he was still boss and didn't give a toss about blood and guts and death.

In reality his stomach was churning at the expression of pain frozen on Pete's face, and he had the urge to put his jacket over it. He got out his phone and made a show of ringing for a replacement ride for the men. He went and checked that Rodney was in his boot tightly packed in bin bags. He called over David one of his newer employees who got in the passenger seat, and then without another word he got in and started the car and drove out, leaving the rest of the men to wait for their lift. They all looked at each other unsure of what to do, Colin spoke first 'the prick is leaving us here, say the police are on their way, what shall we do?' Ken who was Colin's friend and ally answered 'I don't know about you but if this lift doesn't turn up in ten I reckon we leg it, after all we've just moved a bloody corpse and now we're standing by one.' They all looked at each other and nodded their agreement. They heard a car approaching and decided to hide, as it got closer they recognised it was one of their mates Mack so they came out and flagged it down and all gratefully got in the car. 'Thank God Mack' said Colin and every one muttered their agreement. 'We have to take it easy and not get a pull now, and try not to run over the corpse by the gate. 'It's Pete ex best mate of Michael Moffat.'

199

'Wow' Mack the driver replied. 'I knew he was joining the firm who the hell did that to him?'

Colin shrugged and said 'who do you think TJ's little pet Nazi Bentley.' 'Right then' Mack said 'as they say in the movies let's get the hell out of dodge.' They drove off into the night discussing how they were going to approach the Moffats or Maisie and see if there were any jobs, TJ was finished and everyone knew it.

Maisie lay there terrified, and every little noise in the flats made her jump. This was a new feeling for her feeling vulnerable, the last time she'd felt like this was when she still lived with her parents. She had lain there for hours. She had no idea how long, she knew she had slept thankfully, even if she did keep waking up. She'd even prayed to a God she didn't believe in. She needed a piss and a drink she was so thirsty. Phil had left some water with a straw in where she could reach it but she'd drank that hours ago. She stopped then and listened as hard as she could. Someone was definitely coming up the stairs and into the flat. Oh God no she thought, please don't let it be a man who wants to do something. She felt tears form in her eyes, she felt so dehydrated she wondered how it was possible to cry.

The door opened and she screamed, and a voice said. 'Take it easy, I'm here to let you go, and see you're okay, so calm down and you can be on your way.' Maisie still felt scared when she realised the owner of the voice was untying her legs, and she kept her eyes shut in case she wasn't supposed to see him. He covered her up while she got the feeling back in her wrists and ankles, and went into the kitchen he came back a few minutes later and gave her a hot sweet cup of tea. Maisie flinched as he handed it her, and she opened her eyes and saw it was a boy more than a man. 'Thanks whoever you are' she said gratefully 'I will have to give you a few bob if you leave me your number.' She sipped her tea and the boy as she thought of him, disappeared again. She sat there for quite a while before she realised he'd gone. She got up on shaky legs, and went into the kitchen. Her pants were folded up on a chair with five twenty pound notes on top and a little post it note. She read it out loud. 'Take a cab and go home and forget Linda and we'll call it quits forever.' It was signed Phil and Tiffany.' 'Cheeky bastards' she said out loud, the tears forming again, realising that she'd lost her best and most trusted friend all over that tart Tiffany. She almost laughed then and thought go and be happy for now. Revenge is a dish best served cold and she could wait to sort Tiffany out, let them get really cosy and if they were still together in a few years she would do it then. Until then she needed to sort herself out and let Linda go. She'd do that one and maybe in a few years she'd do what she wanted to Joe and maybe even Linda. She could and would wait and for now she had to find someone to replace Phil, someone she could rely on to watch her back. There were plenty of lads she'd gone to school with who worked for her, but Phil had always kept them in order, they respected him. She got up and looked at the flat for the last time, and thought properly for the first time. She said it to the empty kitchen. 'You know what you can go Linda, you were getting on anyway, you were always too tired for sex. Plus you old cow you let me walk all over you, so fuck you. I'm over it, and out of the goodness of my heart I'll even let you sell your half of the club to me.' She felt okay, she noticed the other little present Phil had left her, her drugs, so she set herself up a line, snorted it and went out to flag a taxi, the world was sparkling again and so was she.

Phil left Maisies place with a sports bag full of cash. He'd known for years about where she hid it and that her safe was full of incriminating evidence she had on some very powerful people. He'd gone in and after checking the wardrobes and shoe boxes he'd found thousands of pounds. He'd counted out one hundred thousand which was easier than it sounded as they were in thousand pound blocks, and put it in the bag. He then went and tried the safe, she'd given him the number a few times and he couldn't remember it. Then he remembered it was Linda's and her birthdays put together. He went and tried it and the safe popped open. He was amazed at her stupidity but then she never had to worry before as she was surrounded with men like him who had her back. There were a few envelopes, some with diamonds and some paperwork and photos. He knew some of these were dirty photos that had been used to blackmail and get whatever she wanted. As well as paperwork to show some unscrupulous dealings with some local politicos. He made sure his name wasn't anywhere on any of the documents and put most of them back. He kept one off a Wirral counsellor to her about swinging vote, and one about a judge and the photos. She'd shit herself when she noticed them missing. He had no intention of doing anything with them, but he knew he held power over her. He would make sure if anything happened to him, Tiff, Linda and Joe that they would be with a solicitor who'd give it to the police.

He probably wouldn't but it would help his cause. He had no illusions about Maisie he was sure she'd wait for a few months, or longer then try something, but they'd be prepared. It would do no harm to have as much insurance as he could. He shook out the diamonds picked the clearest nicest one, and put it in his pocket wrapped in paper, and then he'd left. He was nearly at Tiffany's and he felt a pang of anxiety just in case Maisie had gone to see her, he doubted she would, but knew how vicious Maisie could be. He practically ran up the stairs as the lift was on a go slow, and reached Tiffany's door. All types of thoughts were swirling through his head, say she'd bottled out and gone, and didn't love him. He let himself in practically hyperventilating and saw her standing there. She ran to him a glorious smile on her face, and he hugged her gently to him. 'I've been so worried Phil, you forget I know Maisie too and what she's capable of, is everything okay?' Tiffany said. Phil picked her up and swung her round, being gentle still and he replied 'everything's fine honey, we're going on holiday remember so shall we get ready to go shopping in the morning, we can book the holiday in town then or if there's nothing we fancy go and get a flight somewhere.' Tiffany looked at him lovingly and then asked if he needed any of her money as she had some savings. He loved her even more then, for being honest and being the opposite of everything she had been before. 'No gorgeous' he replied 'we've got enough to be going on with, come and take a look.' Her eyes grew wide when Phil showed her what was in the bag, and then told her he had to find a jewellers as well. He took the diamond out of his pocket and held it carefully over Tiffs left hand resting on the wedding ring finger. It caught the light and you could tell it was a perfect cut, as it was sparkling beautifully.

Tiff looked shocked at first then told him straight about how she used to be, and how much of a gold digger she'd been and how ashamed she was of her past. She was also a little taken aback by how little it all mattered now, as long as her and Phil were a couple doing okay that was all she needed or indeed now wanted. She couldn't believe so little time had passed since she'd wanted to get with Carl Moffat, and now the thought repulsed her. Not because Carl was ugly or bad, but because she couldn't imagine kissing anyone but Phil. She told Phil she would love a ring off him, but she'd love a smaller stone and maybe not even a diamond. She noticed he was looking at her with a puzzled expression on his face so she smiled and told him she loved him then kissed him hard on the mouth. Tiffany took his hand to lead him into the bedroom, both of them safe for now, and although both damaged by life many times they didn't care about any of it anymore, like Linda and Joe they were just happy to be together.

Chapter 42

Stephen was still watching the two cars behind him, the women had been a bit too loud a couple of times, but he was concentrating on his driving. They were silent for the time being, just staring at him, so he kept trying to avoid looking in his mirrors. He would go to the woods where he used to practice his hunting skills and where he'd learnt how to make himself invisible. So yes he knew it quite well, he could lose all of them in there. He could survive anything if he had his favourite knife with him. He headed towards the Priory Wood in Aigburth, it had been ignored for decades. Then in 1984 the Garden Festival a well run but a little too expensive gala of flowers, trees, games and people, had brought some much needed tourism in. This part had been done up and used as the main entrance to it. It was quite spooky in parts as there were lots of ruins there, from the big houses that the rich had built centuries ago. He remembered it clearly now, as he used to spy on couples thinking of killing the man for fun and taking the woman for pleasure. He didn't as he was saving himself at the time.

He approached the entrance and had a good head start on whoever was chasing him. He pulled in and switched off the engine, got out and legged it the adrenaline pumping through him, making his paranoia grow. He just hoped he'd managed to shake the ghosts, he could deal with whoever was following him, he thought it was TJs men. He didn't take them too seriously. Michael and Carl following were surprised at where he was going. 'He's turned into Priory woods hasn't he?' said Michael and Carl nodded his agreement. 'I'll just let the others know, I'm surprised a Southern boy like him knows this place, usually only us Scousers go there.' He rang Jonna and told him, laughing at his exclamation of surprise.

They reached the gates and spotted the car, and the fact he wasn't in it. Jonna pulled up just behind and they all got out. 'It looks like we're going to have a little go of one of our fave films Hard Target, like you said before Carl' said Michael, 'he's out of the car and is hiding in there somewhere, so be careful lads he's a grade A nutter. He's killed Rodney the plonker and taken out Pete in the last few hours, plus remember what he'd done to our family. Our Sarah alone is enough to make him pay but as we all know he's taken out our Ma and our Gez and although they weren't the best of folk at the end of the day they were still family.' Jonna, Billy and Joey looked at each other, 'how did he kill Pete Mickey? I didn't want him to die you all know that.' Jonna said.

Michael said sadly 'he ran him over got out spat for some reason, and ran over him again we think. I know Pete was finished with us, but even he deserved better than that. Don't think we had anything to do with it Jonna will you?' Jonna shook his head and knew that he was telling the truth, but it made him even angrier with Bentley the prick, if that was at all possible. He looked at them both and said 'I know Mickey, Carl I know you would have done it properly and you would have told us. That is one horrible way to die, he's made it a joke, so I really want to be the one to take out that little shit now.' Michael looked at Carl who took over and said 'we all feel like that. Us more than anyone remember, but we want him alive, it's important as part of what we have planned for the scummy little dick is part of his punishment. I'm sorry lads but death is too easy. I've got a tazer for each of us in the boot, so all take one each, and use your own weapons if you want. Listen up though lads, I can't say it enough, don't kill him. Okay let's go.' They all got their various weapons out, crossbows and machetes were enough, no use using the sawn offs as they could kill him plus they'd create too much noise. Each of them had a tazer now thanks to Michael, so he gave them a quick lesson how to use them. Then they all ran into the park. Stephen was hiding behind some of the ruins, thinking he was invisible, and within minutes Michael had spotted him, so signalled Carl who was not far behind.

Carl saw it and ran over to him. Michael whispered. 'He's sitting behind the ruins over there, he seems to think he can't be seen, the nutter. Where's the others in case he gets a bit feisty and runs off.' Carl said 'they should be over there' and pointed. They could just make them out in the dark. He took a chance and whistled and the others ran over to them. 'Right lads we are going to get him and we'll shout our heads off if he makes a run for it you stop him, and Jonna try not to tazer any of us' They both crept up to where Stephen was now lying down and without any fuss Carl took out his tazer and shot him in the back. The prongs were barbed so they lodged there, Michael following did exactly the same only lower so they were just in his bum cheek. Stephen looked up at the brothers, puzzled, and then they pressed the buttons in perfect synch until he resembled a fish out of water. He jerked around on the ground, unconscious. Carl grinned at Michael 'fun isn't it?' They stopped and approached the now prone Bentley carefully, Carl kicked him to see if he'd react but he was out cold.

Jonna and the others came running up, when they saw what had happened Billy and Joey were excited and relieved it was over so quickly. Only Jonna pulled a face. 'Oh what now Jonna, frigs sake why the daft expression on your ugly mug?' Joey asked, taking the piss out of him, and Jonna replied 'it was over too quick I wanted to use me crossbow and have a bit of fun.' There was a silence for a second when everyone started to laugh, and Joey replied 'well tell you what, we'll wake him up and let him go and then we can hunt him down again what do you think?' Jonna's face lit up until he realised they were still taking the piss. He turned his back to them and stormed off, while they tried to keep straight faces and look suitably sorry. They all grinned and Joey got out some plastic tags, and trussed the unconscious man up quickly, after checking him for weapons and taking away his knife. Carl rang Jonna then and asked how he was, then said 'get over your strop and make sure no one's around by the cars and warn us if anyone is. We've tied his lordship up so he won't be going anywhere, so you can give him a slap or two when we get him home. You know to make up for not being able to shoot him.' The others listened and all chuckled Billy exclaiming 'stop it now Carl or we'll drop him. The four of them were carrying him, whispering with joy at finally getting Bentley and how he was the final nail in the coffin for TJ. They were going to make them pay for all they'd done wrong. Michael said then not to worry that TJ was getting sorted too and he just had to wait for the phone call to confirm that all had gone well.

Then he decided to take their minds off what he'd just said, so said loudly 'maybe I will let my new woman the very sexy PC Byrne get her first big collar. Leave him on her doorstep like a good kitty leaves a nice present. You know like a rat only I won't chew his head off.' Michael commented and Carl knew he was teasing but the others went quiet. Then Carl laughed with Michael and Billy and Joey joined in, realising they'd been had again. Michael grinned and said 'oh boys you are too easy sometimes.' They heard a stirring as Bentley groaned, and it reminded them to put tape over his mouth so he couldn't shout or scream and attract unwanted attention. They had reached the cars and they put Stephen in the BMWs boot, and checked he was securely tied. They all high fived and went straight back to the flat as the town house was too public. No one would bat an eyelid on the Estate if they got an unconscious man out of the back of a car, even if it was the boot. They entered the flat and made sure their next door neighbour Kay wasn't on the prowl. As much as they loved her and she knew them better than most they didn't want her to get involved so they could protect her and themselves. Kay was wonderful but prone to gossip so they hurried in. Her lights were off and hopefully she was at her sisters, in case it got a little noisy. They dumped Stephen on the couch in the front room, switched on their big TV and all went into the kitchen. Michael started to make a cup of tea for everyone as he enjoyed the familiar routine. It distracted him from wanting to go into the front room and cut Bentley up into little pieces, and he was sure Carl was feeling the same. So as the kettle boiled the five men stood around contemplating what to do with Stephen Bentley? TJs ex right hand man, grade A psycho and murderer of their mother, their cousin Gez, Pete and who knew how many more. Of course the most important of them all, their beloved Sara.

TJ had Rodney's body in his boot and was driving a little erratically, he'd had enough now, and kept seeing in his mind's eye what Bentley had done to his only real friend. They'd been prepared to kill Bentley, but he'd out done him and the bunch of idiots he'd taken with him. The only good one there was the new lad. He was really angry about Stephen and how it had turned out, he'd washed his hands of the little prick now. He was going to hang him out to dry for the police to get him, and pretend he sacked him months ago. He remembered the face he pulled when he was thinking about some woman or something bad not so long ago in his office and he looked really weird. It had given him the creeps and truth be told frightened him a little bit.

He looked sideways at his newest recruit a big strong lad called David. He had approached him a few months ago and asked for a job. TJ had him checked out and he seemed okay, he'd got people to ask around, nothing bad came back. It was a surprise that no one already employed him. He was known to be a hard man and the gossipers said to watch out for him in the future. He just didn't see the point in paying for another private detective after all he'd had Stephen Bentley checked and they said he was okay. Shit he should sue them or ask for his money back after all this, he was very bloody far from normal. He was testing David out to replace Bentley. He seemed to be strong and pleasant enough, he'd do for now until he disappeared abroad. Who knows if they got on he might take him with him, anyone would do anything if you gave them enough money TJ thought. He had always got what he wanted so was ill prepared when a situation like this happened. How dare Stephen Bentley do this to him, and his oldest friend.

He felt bile rise in his throat as he thought of Rodney and how he'd looked with his throat cut. It was disgusting and he couldn't get over it. He knew the psycho loved his knives and torture. That's why he'd hired him in the first place. He'd proved his worth when he killed Sara Moffat after she'd stolen off him all those years ago. He'd paid him a lot of money but nowhere near what he should have at the time. He'd been generous with Bentley ever since. Still at least he had it to spend. There was a lot in his safe, cash, gold and diamonds; if he wanted to he could see off most lottery winners, and that was without all his properties and investments. He'd had enough of it all now, it was a persistent thought that kept resurfacing. He was bored of being a Scouse godfather. He felt a spark of optimism. Life is too short I'm going to sell them or get an agency to rent all my property out for me. He muttered all of this and said the last bit out loud. 'I'm going to get out as soon as I can.' He was lost in thought. He snapped out of it when David asked 'Mr. Murphy what are we doing? Are we going to throw the body in the Mersey and are you okay? I'm a little worried as you keep muttering to yourself? Wouldn't it have been better just to leave Rodney at the psycho's house or something? We could get caught riding around with him in the boot.'

TJ felt embarrassed at him mentioning his muttering. It was a habit he hated. He growled and hit his hand hard against the steering wheel. 'Now listen to me, you are being a prick David, Rodney was my best mate, he'd been with me for years. He'd never let me down in all that time. He thought he had but he hadn't. He just wasn't up to the job anymore. He did time for me too, he was that type of bloke, if it wasn't for his women and fine dining and good wine, he'd have a lot of money now, remember that when I start paying you properly. They don't make them like that anymore.' David blushed with anger at being called a prick but he took it as he had a far more important task to do, so he swallowed it down for now, and replied. 'So Mr. Murphy have you got somewhere for Rodney in mind? It's a lucky coincidence you have a shovel in the boot? TJ looked at him slyly and nodded 'I nearly always have stuff in my car, be prepared I always say, and I've brought you with me because I need a strong young buck to dig his grave. It was to bury Bentley but it's okay, the police can have him now. I promised Rodney years ago if anything happened I'd bury him somewhere nice, he had a fear of being cremated, of fire. No wonder really after what he did. I sent him to scare a young family and set a fire, as they wouldn't move from a flat I needed. However the fire went crazy as they had lots of cheap furniture and they all got trapped and he had to watch them burn to death. He came out virtually unscathed.' They drove into the countryside, through the dark winding roads into Wales without speaking, the silence uncomfortable so TJ put the radio on, and they both relaxed a little, each of them thinking about what mattered to them.

Maisie let herself into the flat, worn out from all the walking she'd done, and angry thoughts wouldn't leave her as she wondered what to do next. She couldn't sleep so she walked miles around town to tire herself out. It had only been a short while but she'd gone right down the pan. She'd rang a couple of the girls she'd been with, one after another and when they'd come over, she'd used their bodies. After sex she just looked at them as if they were shit and thrown money at them, and told them to get out. They'd made her feel worse, and that heightened her anger at Tiffany the only other woman she'd considered having for a partner. How had the bitch had got her claws into her Phil, so much that he now hated her! How could he hate her the years they'd been together, what happened to him being in love with her? She muttered out loud 'Virgin Mary I swear to you that even if Ginger Phil comes crawling on broken glass to beg forgiveness I'd spit on him and wouldn't piss on him if he was on fire.' Her features were twisted and hateful, and people who knew her and were aware Linda had gone off with a bloke, were wondering what had happened to Phil. All the lads commented she'd aged over night, her beauty hidden beneath the anger and hatred. Her usually gorgeous dark brown skin looked purpley grey, so her teeth looked yellow, her eyes were bloodshot from lack of sleep and drinking and taking too many drugs, and her curls were knotted and tangled. She hardly went to the club after her solicitor sent Linda some money as she'd bought her out, plus she was starting to run out of ready cash for her lavish lifestyle. She'd gone through most of the thousands she'd had in the flat on gambling, drugs, taxis and booze. She contacted the Moffats who bought Linda's share and gave her a good profit. It was all legal and above board but they paid her in cash and put the deeds and paperwork in one of their safety deposit boxes in Sara's name. Maisie decided to sort herself out after the day when she went down to the club. She'd walked in after her days of bingeing, and people swerved past her trying to avoid her eyes, and didn't know what to say to her as she was so aggressive. It suddenly hit her how she looked, and how she behaved. She ran upstairs ashamed. The morning after that she woke up looked in the mirror and saw what she really was. It was painful and she threw her ashtray hard at the mirror and as it smashed she collapsed and cried her heart out. She cried about her parents, for all the abuse she'd suffered. She screamed for all the misery Linda and Phil had just put her through. Then she started to calm down and lay there quietly sobbing until she fell asleep. She had an amazing dream where she killed Linda, Phil and Tiff, and when she woke up she felt hungry for the first time in weeks. Her stomach rumbling she rang out for some food, when it arrived she ate so much her stomach still hurt but in a better way. Then she started to tidy the flat and ended with a hot bath and some conditioners to sort out her hair. She felt much better overall, and she knew why she had pulled herself out of her pit of despair. She had a purpose now; her dream had showed her the way. It came back to her then why she had felt so sparkly when she had left Linda's flat, apart from the cocaine of course. It was the thought of revenge, of course how could she forget how good thinking of getting even made her feel. She would get fit and make lots more money through the Moffats, and then she would bide her time and then she would make Linda, Joe, Tiffany and Phil pay for what they'd done to her. The club was doing okay but she knew some of the staff were stealing and letting people in for nothing and selling drugs that she or the Moffats hadn't supplied. So she got out her mobile and rang around organizing the lads to help her give them a beating and sort it out. After she told her tale most of them had sided with her to her face at least, thinking Phil had done the dirty on her, and stolen money. Every time she told someone she exaggerated. Tomorrow night they would storm the club and give the ones taking the piss a lesson, women or men. Then everyone would know she was back and no one would dare cross her again. Her other plan getting even well it didn't matter if it took ten months or ten years she was going to wait until it was the perfect time. When it was she would take everything from them, hell they might even have kids, when it happened, which would make it interesting. She smiled in satisfaction, knowing that when she put her mind to it, she would turn her dream into reality. While she waited and planned she would enjoy life anyway she saw fit. She felt alive again knowing she had something to live for and to look forward to. She went through her little pink book looking for a date to take to dinner and then back here for some fun. She was looking forward to tomorrow getting the lads organised to take out the little bastards who were stealing off her, and taking the piss. Look out everyone Maisie Malone is back.

Chapter 43

TJ was nearly at the place where he and Rodney had played as kids, it was still the same, down the road were all the hills and valleys, a caravan park, and a pebbly beach with no sand. It had been perfect to them after the boredom of school and every day Liverpool. He had driven them to Talacre in North Wales, as they had so many good memories here. He smiled to himself as they even used to bring birds up to their caravan here, him and Rodney. They would party into the night the girls trapped as it was so remote, so they always nearly got their way with the little tarts. He had never truly loved anyone but himself. Women were there to be used for entertainment, sex and a good time and that was all. He pushed all those thoughts away now, concentrating on finding the right spot in the woods, where he could bury his mate good and deep so no one would find him. It was all about respect and he'd be fooling himself if he thought anyone still respected him now, after what had happened with Bentley. It was after all the end of the nineteen nineties nearly the new millennium everything was changing. The opportunities to make money were vast. He'd heard about the Doomsday virus and things like that, and these CDs and DVDs were everywhere. If he wanted to he could invest in computers. It sounded like hard work so why bother he had enough money for three centuries of good living if he didn't work another day in his life.

They pulled up at the end of a wooded area, it was pitch black and really out of the way so he waited for his eyes to adjust and reached for his torch. They were so far from civilisation it didn't matter if they used it or not. TJ got out and gestured for David to do the same. TJ unlocked the trunk. They lifted the corpse out, and thankfully because he was in bin bags he didn't have to look at Rodney's face. TJ made David take his feet and he carefully handled his head. He'd never thought he'd have to do this. He had sat behind his desk for so long he had almost forgotten how to walk over fifty feet, and they had to keep stopping so he could get his breath. God I have to cut down the cigars he thought, breathlessly saying to himself I can't wait to go away. Barbados, South America, the world was his oyster. He could get healthy too, swimming and walking on the beach, some women, he'd soon get fit. He needed to get away before Bentleys fuck ups were associated with him. He was screwed though because he didn't trust anyone enough to look after what was left of his businesses anyway. It was only Rodney he would have left in charge and here he was carrying his body to be interred. He saw the copse in the woods which was perfect it was so dense plus in all the times they'd been here they'd never seen another soul in this part. He wasn't just doing this for Rodney he admitted to himself, he didn't want one of his main men turning up dead, especially murdered by his other main man. His tame coppers had helped over the years, but with the advances in forensics, and so on, he didn't even expect them to even try to cover all this up. People had been dropping like flies since Bentley had lost the plot. What a mess he thought, then concentrated on reaching his destination. They finally got there and his muscles were burning. He was even more out of breath and he was thankful they'd made it to where he'd wanted to bury Rodney. He told David to stop. 'This will do fine lad, we can dig a grave here for him, it's way off the beaten track, and he would be made up as he had a fear of getting cremated as I said so let's get cracking. Me and him, we had some damned good times here.' They had rested the shovel on Rodney's body as they'd carried him, and David picked it up and started to dig. He was muscular and super fit he hadn't got out of breath once, in fact he should have carried Rodney on his own thought TJ. He went off while David dug his hole and he made sure he could get his breath again before he lit up a cigar. He sat down on a comfortable old tree trunk, and dozed off then he woke himself up by snoring loudly and sat up startled. He was stiff and sore as he'd been out for at least two hours. He looked over and there was no sign of David, Rodney's body was still lying there by the looks of things. He went over to look properly at the grave, and it was really deep and wide, way too big for Rodney. He shouted David then and there wasn't any noise, so he must have gone somewhere to have a pee. He wanted to get out of there as soon as he could; being on his own made it creepy and Rodney's body was making noises too, which although normal was still making his stomach churn.

He took a deep breath so he wouldn't panic, and managed to convince himself there was nothing to be scared of. It was only Rodney after all. It was so silent that's why he could hear the body making little farts and rustles in the bin bags. He was concentrating so hard on listening to the weird noises from Rodney that he didn't hear David come up behind him. He hit him hard across the back of the head with the shovel. He collapsed and landed on the edge of the grave. 'Oh God TJ Hooker is there nothing you can do right?' David asked him nastily, 'you were supposed to fall in there to make it easy.' TJs head was reeling it was agonizingly painful where he'd been hit, and he felt fear grip him and wrap it's icy hands around his testicles. 'Come on lad why are you doing to me? Stop now and I'll make you really rich and we'll never talk of this again eh? Who are you working for come on tell me and whatever you're getting paid I'll treble it and some.' TJ was trying to keep the tremor out of his voice and not succeeding. 'Do you know what old man, that would be a tempting offer but you see I'm doing this for the Moffats. They sent you a message which I will tell you in a minute. I'm getting well paid, and am now part of their crew which is what I've always wanted. But even if I wanted more money and it meant working for you, I never would you nasty little man. You killed my mum when I was just six years old. Rodney the prick did the deed but you ordered it and that stupid fat bastard getting away with manslaughter was a joke. I knew all this but I decided to verify it with your tame coppers, the ones that have retired. Do you know it's amazing what someone will tell you when you cut off a few toes, it was almost funny.' David said sounding almost cheerful.

TJ knew he was screwed so he tried to scrabble up and fight back, lost his footing then fell into the grave. David laughed and said 'trying to help me now won't work, I've never been happier digging a hole as it is for both you and Rodney. Which is a double score wouldn't you say? Oh and the Moffats said to tell you they have taken over nearly all your businesses. Plus we are going to have fun with what's in your safe and that this is payback for Sara. They hope you are going to burn in hell. They would have loved to have done it themselves but they are far too busy with Stephen Bentley. Oh and just so you know I'd have done this for free, in fact I'd have paid them!' David laughed loudly, and then he spat on his hands, grabbed the shovel and jumped into the grave where he methodically beat TJ to death and felt nothing except repulsion at his begging and pleading. After he was dead, he went through his pockets and took his keys, phone and wallet. He and the Moffats were going to divide up what TJ had in his safe, they would keep the gold and diamonds. Then they would give the cash to some of TJs other victims and their families. He stripped off his bloody clothes and put them in too. Then he dropped Rodney's corpse in on top of TJ and then he covered the bodies, and then dragged over the log TJ had fallen asleep on, and placed it over the grave. It had two purposes, it looked much more natural and hid some of the freshly dug earth. He also needed a marker should they have to go back to the grave for any reason. As he had TJs keys the Moffats told him he may as well keep the car. He just needed to get some papers, get it to a professional cleaner, a re-spray and new Registration plates and he had a cracker of a car. He was sure the Moffats would sort that for him, after all it he'd done a good job, and he was looking forward to working for them. He put on the clean clothes he had stashed in the car, and started the drive back to Liverpool. Just like the others he was careful not to go over the speed limit or attract any attention. When he finally got some bars on his mobile phone, he pulled over and rang Michael to tell him the news.

Michael and Carl were in the flat having a cup of tea, when Michaels phone rang. He smiled grimly at the news, ended the call and told Carl that at last Murphy had been taken care of, and that was that.
They hugged quickly so no one would see, and Carl said 'Loads down, one to go, here's hoping it all goes to plan eh? Michael replied 'it will, nothing will stop us now it's nearly over. That David is a bit of a psycho but then he did see his mum murdered, and I'm glad he's on our side. He asked about the car I told him to drop it off in China Town so it could be sorted, we'll pay as an extra thank you. Anyway we have the keys to TJs domain, all his staff are gone, so we'll be sorted and can play Santa to some of the people he shit on over the years. It's something to look forward to after the funeral.' Carl nodded his agreement and went to check on Stephen who was locked in their old room. He was tied up, his mouth taped up, and he wouldn't be waking up anytime soon. They had got one of the old junkies called Stuart off the Estate to get them a kit together which comprised of a syringe, a spoon, Jif lemon juice, some cigarette filters and a candle. Some heroin and the strongest sedatives and sleeping tablets they could buy. They paid well for it so it was all new, not that mattered to Bentley but it did to them, and the last thing any of them wanted was to prick themselves with a dirty needle. They'd got Stuart to load up the hit so he wouldn't overdose just sleep. He'd obliged, and got another forty quid on top of what they'd already given him. He was over the moon, and he was sworn to secrecy so he felt important too. They were good at that making someone feel part of their inner circle. Even if they weren't. It meant loyalty and they could ask nearly anything of the person.

They had no malice to the junkies on the Estate because of growing up with them, and seeing them suffering like Sara. To them it was almost an illness, something they couldn't help. However they wouldn't tolerate any of them stealing off their own and anyone who did got sorted out. The bigger dealers who did it just for money were another matter, and one they were going to sort out in the very near future. They both knew in their hearts it was double standards and they were getting rich on the profits from every other drug but heroin, but they didn't really care and they felt like they were doing something to honour Sara. Once they knew how to do it and had injected Bentley they crushed up some sleeping tablets and put it in a drink knowing he'd be so thirsty and dehydrated when he woke up he'd swallow it down. They had asked the lads to take turns but Carl had found Jonna slapping him round, so he was forbidden even if it did mean an extra shift for them, it was important he stayed alive for the time being. They were angry at Jonna but knew it was sheer frustration that made him do it so they told him off and he went off as usual to sulk. It might have been funny but it was the days before Shelagh's funeral so they were fed up themselves. Just knowing what they had to do. They hated all the falseness, most of the Estate were coming after it had been put in the Echo, they'd asked for money to be sent to the local kids hospital Alder Hey. They sent five hundred pounds to cover people who couldn't afford it, and as it was only family flowers they ordered the usual mum bouquet in white carnations. They also bought a lot of expensive wreaths and exotic flowers as they were going to put on a good show. It was to flash their money about and also to show how important they were now. She was also getting buried in the same cemetery as Sara. They'd deliberately bought a plot a good way away from her grave, it didn't seem right putting Shelagh near her. Not after what she'd done to Sara when she was alive. Sara's grave got weekly flowers, mostly simple daisies as they'd been her favourites. If they couldn't do it they paid someone to keep it perfect and make sure the flowers were always fresh.

They kept Stephen unconscious while they prepared for the funeral. They'd had nice suits custom made a while ago and had them ready to put on. As an extra gift they'd bought all the lads one each too. They took turns around the clock to watch Bentley, Jonna had to have someone with him as Carl wasn't sure he could be trusted not to smother him or cut his throat. When he came round for a few minutes he kept shrieking and screaming about the women. While he was conscious Carl pulled out the black cards with silver writing that he'd put by Sara's flowers on the anniversary of her death. He also had the one he'd slipped into Shelagh's bag. At first Bentley looked at them and almost sneered, and said they were to upset the Moffats. Carl wanted to bite his ear off, but controlled himself. He took out Bentleys knife and threatened him. He realised he was wasting his time when he went totally hysterical looking beyond him at some unseen horror. He kept saying he was sorry to the women, and he was sorry to Sarah and Shelagh and some strange names. He was making so much noise they had to shut him up, so they pumped him with more drugs to keep him quiet. Everyone discussed the tabloids. It was all over the place about the police man hunt for him. They were full of gruesome details about his trail of devastation and murder so of course it was being taken very seriously.

Michael had fallen hard for PC Dana Byrne who was still in the police for the time being. She held no illusions about staying there as soon as they moved in together. Or someone grassed them up and reported that they were a couple, whatever came first. Carl was a little jealous at first but Dana was the type of woman who everyone eventually liked. As she had treated him with respect and kindness even before she knew them, he saw that she was good. It was pretty unusual for a copper. He had told Michael that although it had only been a short time, she seemed like she was the one, and if they both felt like that they had his blessing. Plus she'd be an asset to the business, once she crossed over to their side. They'd both laughed at that but it was true, she was smart and beautiful and they'd rather she was on their side any day. It was obvious she had the same feelings for Michael too, they'd discussed their predicament on the phone, in bed enjoying a few snatched moments, and they both agreed she should stay in for the time being. Or until she found out what was going on with the murders and if they'd been named as responsible for anything. She wasn't privy to all the information but she had really good hacking skills and found it easy to get the files she needed. The software was so outdated that the police were forced to use made it too easy. DS Frank had spoken to her at length as he had a feeling she wasn't telling him everything, but she kept up the facade. She told him she was going to the funeral as she had been asked to go and could report back anything untoward especially about TJ Murphy or Stephen Bentley as someone was bound to know where they were.

She knew the police were going to have others reporting back, but as she was going to leave pretty soon, she didn't care if they saw her hugging Michael or anything that would be considered unusual for a police officer. They had found a dead body in the drive leading up to Bentleys house and he was well known as Peter Jones once a member of the Moffats little crew. It was common knowledge he had gone over to TJs side after nearly killing his friend Jacko who still wasn't fully recovered. Michael and Carl had secretly paid for him to go private so he was being well cared for, at one of Bupa's finest hospitals. Dana arrived on the eve of the funeral and was bursting to tell Michael and Carl the rest of her information. She was hoping to put their minds at rest before they buried their mum. She explained that the Crime scene technicians had found a match to the tyres on the car that had killed Peter Jones, abandoned by where the Garden Festival used to be, and it was covered in Stephen Bentleys prints. The police had also been sent a load of CDs and tapes with homemade films and still photographs on them. After careful examination much to their horror what was thought of as cheap snuff movies proved to be real. So they had contacted the Thai police who had a missing persons database longer than Father Christmas's naughty list, and they were working on finding the identity of the girls and telling their next of kin. Stephen Bentley had been so vain he'd actually filmed himself doing some of the most awful things to these poor women. Even some of the most hardened coppers threw up after watching him and what he did to those beautiful girls. He'd also filmed some of the scenery and landmarks so they could identify where in Thailand he'd been so that would help to find the missing girls bodies.

The stab wounds on Shelagh Moffat matched one of the many knives they had taken from his house. There were some questions unanswered about inconsistencies, such as whose blood was on the couch and why were there two cushions missing, and so on but for the time being the police were waiting on other information.

They were convinced that Bentley and Murphy were together somewhere abroad, and the local police were working with Interpol. If they were found they would be deported straight away and tried and sentenced in Chester. Rodney was being sought too, but he didn't rank high on the polices most wanted. It was known he was past it now. His wife eventually reported him missing, as he'd disappeared off the face of the earth. Dana finished filling them in and Michael offered to run her home, and she told him she could stay to support him if he wanted. He said he'd like nothing more but he had things to do with Carl and he needed her after the funeral when it would hit home. She gave Carl a hug goodnight and went out to the BMW while Michael had a quick word with some of the lads. After he'd finished telling them what he wanted to, he went out to the car. He wanted it all to be over yesterday so he and his new love could get on with their life. They'd only made love a few times, but it had been mind blowing and Michael had held her close and not wanted to let her go. As much as he felt like that he wouldn't tell her about Stephen Bentley not yet. Probably never, as there were things that he and Carl, were going to do that would make him less than human. He didn't want her to know that side of him ever. She had no illusions of who he was but what they

215

were going to do would drive a wedge between them that most probably would never heal.

He couldn't risk it, as she may not understand the punishment must fit the crime. Stephen Bentley had done nothing but cause heart ache and horror and was pure evil, so that's how he would be treated. There wasn't an ounce of compassion left in Michaels or Carls hearts concerning the evil little bastard. He was going to reap a part of what he'd sowed to their family and all the other poor bastards who'd come across him and lost their lives in the process.

Chapter 44

The morning of the funeral had finally come Michael and Carl had taken Bentley somewhere and locked him up where he couldn't get out in the middle of the night. Not that he would he was so doped up he was almost in a coma. No one would find him. They didn't tell hardly anyone what they'd done just two of their clan Jonna and little Joey, who they knew would keep it to themselves. So he didn't make any noise until the funeral was over they'd given him enough dope for about twelve plus hours. It wouldn't be nice when he come to, as they knew he'd really crave heroin and would start a cold turkey off the drugs they'd been injecting him with. They hadn't had time to do make it as bad as they could but it would still be horrible, Stuart had assured them of that. Good that was part of the punishment. Karma that's why they'd picked Sara's drug of choice it all mattered for what he'd done to her. They'd put their suits on and all the lads were there. Even Jacko in a wheel chair much better after his head injury and operations, but still not quite strong enough to walk. They were all at the townhouse that's where they were leaving from, Everyone from the estate was invited to the funeral. They'd hired a hall by the cemetery, supplied it with free booze and food. It was bound to be packed to the rafters. They decided they didn't want the horse drawn glass and wooden hearse for Shelagh. They had their own reasons, apart from the stereotype of a cockney gangster's funeral Shelagh would have loved it. So they picked an extra large white and very expensive coffin and Jonna and little Joey were going to carry it with them; no one else was allowed to touch it after it had left the undertakers. It was under Jonna's watch, his Uncles letting him take charge of it all, happy with the money he'd made for them by turning a blind eye.

One of Danny's men Bozza had helped move the coffin and commented how heavy it was. Jonna laughed and replied 'it's lead lined you dick, and extra big, you know it's only the best for the Moffats.' Bozza blushed and felt stupid because everyone else joined in laughing. No more was said about it, the flowers were already arranged in the hearse so they just put the coffin in. Then they made sure the mum bouquet went centre place so everyone knew who it was at the Cemetery. The priest was early and talking to Carl and expressing his concern for them. He told him that within six months he had changed from naïve and trusting, to canny and suspicious due to falling for a few cons from the locals. He loved it where he was even more now he laughed. The Moffats had checked him out and he seemed to be a good man with a healthy appreciation of the more mature female form. He was of course celibate, and he often joked to the men of the parish how he could look but not touch, just like a nice cream cake. Everyone liked him, even if he was always relentlessly pursuing money for the church funds. He lived simply not like the old Catholic priests had. With good food, cars and expensive alcohol. He used all the money for good things not for himself. He wouldn't be swayed once he'd made his mind up over a worthwhile cause. He had been offered extra today to shorten the service, but he wouldn't be bribed, and told Carl if he just asked him nicely he would do it. Carl amused nodded his agreement and gave him another two hundred for the church fund, which he pocketed so fast Carl thought if he'd have blinked he'd have missed it. 'Well Father Jacob are you sure you're working for the right one?'Said Carl as he pointed up and grinned. Father Jacob laughed and replied 'God likes his naughty children best, so yes!' Carl laughed and said 'okay Father you've convinced me' and nodded to him as he left. Father Jacob was a little unsure what to do next, and wondered what had just happened. Was this him being accepted by the local hard men? Then he felt the reassuring wad of money in his pocket underneath his cassock and shook his head, thinking to himself that he was already in love with Liverpool and its people. In fact Merseyside people. He admired their fight and spirit after Hillsborough, then in the eighties, unemployment and drugs, and still they made jokes and created wonderful art and music. He had heard about the Moffats and talked at length with a few of the local women and their next door neighbour Kay, who wouldn't have a bad word said against them. He looked at his watch and realised he'd been lost in his own thoughts. Thank God he wasn't late, he had a feeling that it wouldn't be a very intelligent thing to do upset the Moffats. No he wanted them on his side, and for the foreseeable future. He wanted to make it his home, and be someone people came to and relied on. He had wanted to talk to some of the mourners, and get to know even more of his congregation. Then drop some very large hints about funding and fixing the roof. It was tough luck, he was due in the church so it would have to wait for now.

Michael, Carl, Jonna and little Joey carried the coffin into the church where it was put at the front, and the services began. They took their places in the first pew and stood waiting while the priest stood and said his sermon. Michael had a look around and saw that it was a full house, and he was pleased, he would find out later who had been there for the right reasons and those for the wrong. They wanted it over as soon as possible, and although they were feeling a little agitated they stood proud and calm to everyone who saw them. The church bit was over so they all walked out and they lifted up the coffin again, and balancing it on their shoulders took it to the prepared grave. At the graveside people started to queue up to throw in a piece of soil or a flower, all of it for their sake. No one had liked Shelagh Moffat. In fact she was hated for what she'd done to her kids. But it was all for show. As the coffin lowered the only person to cry out loud was their Aunty Cath who had only buried her son Gez a little while before burying her sister. She approached Michael and Carl as she threw in her rose, and told them 'I know there wasn't much between us sometimes lads, and I know she was a lousy mum, just like me. You see we didn't have a very good time growing up either, and it's nice to know you and our Gez were friends at the end. He was very proud of working for you both you know.' Carl for the first time that day felt himself welling up. Both he and Michael regretted getting Gez involved with them. They felt it was their fault that Stephen Bentley had beaten and stabbed their cousin to death. It wasn't fair for that to happen just as Gez had sorted out his life. He'd died because he had tried to make them proud and they both knew it. Carl said trying not to cry 'it's okay Aunty Cath, we are very sorry he's gone, he turned out good in the end didn't he?' Cathy mistakenly thinking that his tears were for Shelagh said 'yes he did, and I am sorry for the way my sister treated you. I'm even sorrier I didn't help you either, I hope you can forgive me.' Carl hugged her to him and said 'don't worry we've all done things we're not proud of, and we're so sorry about Gez getting involved with that psycho Bentley, don't worry he will get his.'

Cath reached up to her nephew and said into his ear 'make sure you do and kill the bastard don't let him go to some cosy mental hospital. That shit knew what he was doing when he murdered my boy.' Carl looked her straight in the eyes and promised that it had been taken care of. She nodded and joined everyone in a final prayer before they went to the wake. Carl and Michael stayed behind and watched as the grave diggers started to cover the coffin. When it was done they gave each other a smile and the men who'd just buried their mother a fifty pound tip each. Then started walking to the wake just up the road. Dana had been in the background all the time watching her man, and she was at the gates. She greeted Michael and Carl and walked between them linking arms, not caring who would see her or what they'd say. She'd leave as soon as she could and start her new life with Michael, and Carl too she mused. She had no intention of trying to get between them. She accepted they'd been together all their lives and as long as she accepted them as one package she hoped to always feel safe and loved by them both. She was happy to share Michael with Carl. She also knew that some of the women in the past who tried to get their claws into the boys were dumped quickly and completely the minute they tried to get between them.

The wake was in full swing when they got there, and they walked in and sat at the table that had been prepared for them. The booze was flowing freely and some of the old Irish neighbours off the Estate were singing Irish rebel songs. Then of course someone eventually sang Danny boy. Most of the old aged pensioners Shelagh had stolen off were there. For some reason this struck Carl as really funny so he wandered off to look at all the messages and commiserations they'd received behind the bar. There was a huge wad of twenties off Maisie for the kids' hospital, and apologies that she couldn't be there. He didn't mind that she wasn't coming he had seen how bitter and twisted she was over Linda the last time they'd spoken. He'd heard on the grapevine how she was putting her house in order. Kicking out staff literally who'd taken the piss. It hadn't taken her ten minutes to get over Linda leaving her for a bloke, and that she'd fell out with Phil. That intrigued him, as he'd seen Phil by the grave with a really good looking girl on his arm. They were about somewhere here. She was gorgeous he wished when he'd met her once before he'd have taken her number. Wasted opportunities he mused. Her name was Trinity or something, the name Tiffany popped into his head. She had smiled shyly at him, and then he noticed she hardly took her loving gaze off Phil. He asked the women off the estate about her when he was at the bar. He couldn't believe some of the gossip he heard about her. She'd been on the game as well as an escort, and a past girlfriend of Rodney the Plonker TJs bully. He didn't really believe it all. Even if it was true, he wouldn't kick her out of bed. The legacy that Sara had given Michael and Carl was they were guilty of double standards like everyone else. So that meant they wouldn't judge anyone for doing what they had to do to survive, they weren't hypocrites.

Carl wanted to talk to Phil, he knew he was a good bloke and wanted to find out if he would work for them, now he and Maisie had fell out. They were still partners with Maisie in the club, but he could keep them separate. Phil could help them out a lot as he was experienced and had hundreds of contacts. He must have had his reasons for why he left Maisie, and that was good enough for him. He went over where Phil and Tiffany were sitting and both moved so he could sit between them. Both gave him their genuine sympathy, which he accepted graciously. Virtually straight away Carl asked Phil if he wanted to work for them, and Phil grinned and accepted on the spot. Although he had a good amount put away from what he took from Maisie plus his own money it wouldn't last forever and he wanted to treat Tiff like the princess she was. Tiffany wasn't comfortable with it anymore; part of her new way of looking at life was that she didn't want lots of expensive stuff, just love and kindness.

They had booked some holidays and were looking forward to exploring new horizons It would be good to be away from England for a while. As long as they were together they were sure they'd be okay. Fat Fi was there too she had already hugged the boys at the church but was doing her best to show Shelagh some respect. She found it hard to be false and she'd drank for the first time in ages. This meant that she started confessing to whoever would listen that although she hadn't liked Shelagh, she would almost miss her. She kept saying that no one should die like that. Tiffany heard her and went over and told her to keep it down in case Carl or Michael took offence at her big gob. She did it jokingly but got the point across, and Fi looked ashamed. Carl pretended that he hadn't noticed but had and was impressed, she was calm and loyal. He had jobs that Tiff could do he would discuss it with them later. God he fancied her. Such was life. Who knew she might get bored of Phil one day. That'd be good. He pushed it out of his mind for now. He'd spotted one of the girls from the club, Rebecca. He'd been to bed with her a few times. With any luck he'd be getting laid tonight. Why should Michael be the only one getting some the thought and grinned as he waved to her. He felt his phone buzz and saw it was a text from her He read it and grinned and walked over to her. . His luck was definitely in that was for sure.

Sylvia was there with little Jake, Pete's ex partner she'd been questioned by the police and told them nothing. Michael went over to her and introduced Dana, and left them chatting. He went and had a word with Jonna who'd fancied Sylvia years ago, before Pete had snagged her. He knew her well so he told him to go for it. Jonna blushed but grinned and said 'I don't mind if I do Mikey lad what do you reckon just ask her out

220

or take her and the little one to Maccy Ds?' Michael laughed and said 'if you are going don't forget to get me a happy meal will you?' He reached into his jacket pocket and pulled out some envelopes. He found the one with Jonna's name on it and handed it to him. 'Here's a little something off me and Carl to thank you for all your hard work. The others have a few bob too, but some might have more than others so don't flash it about will you? Jonna shook his head no, thrilled at the extra bonus. He could feel through the envelope it had a tidy wad of cash in it so he sneaked off to the toilets to count it, and they'd given him five grand. He spoke to himself in the mirror of the gents and said 'fuck Maccy Ds I'll take her out and then we can do something with the little one.' He walked straight over to ask Sylvia if she'd like to go for a posh meal and then do something with Jake like Southport the next day. Michael had a rough idea what was going on, so when he saw Jonna pick up Sylvia and swing her around, he knew that something good was happening for them. He was pleased but wished Carl could have someone too. He'd never been big on relationships he'd always preferred one or two night stands.

He smiled remembering some of the women who he'd been with. Good memories and some of them liked not being tied down too. He would give them all up for Dana in a heartbeat. She had changed that and he wanted Carl to feel the same. Fingers crossed he thought I may get him to go on one of those speed dating nights, it would be a laugh if nothing else. Carl was doing okay he watched him go round the hall talking to people playing the perfect host. Well the funeral was nearly over, they'd have to go to Pete's funeral they supposed if only to show support to Sylvia. Michael was made up she seemed happier than she had for a long time. I suppose when someone bullies and hurts you like that you can't wait to see the back of them. Now Pete was gone she could be herself, and Jonna was the right bloke to look after her he thought with a smile. Pete hadn't been with Sylvia for a good while. But no one told him and he persecuted her regularly. God he hoped she'd not slept with him, Pete was fond of paying for prostitutes. Michael had known it all, but thought his warning had made him back off his ex and son. He felt regret but realised he didn't miss him. He missed being young and having fun. As for his mother, well he felt a mixture of feelings like all children do when they're abused. He snapped out of it and went to join the throng.

The wake carried on until late in the evening, and Michael and Carl went to the toilets and both had a line of coke chased down with a shot of vodka as a way of saying goodbye. 'Phew here's you in love with a copper and us doing this in the bogs, still life has been a bit manic lately to say the least' Carl said, Michael laughed he was still full of emotion and his head was spinning with the coke. 'Good stuff that bro much nicer than that one that was turning everyone mental, including us.' He said then he went serious 'listen Carl do you think we've done the right thing with Bentley?' Carl and Michael checked there was no one else in the toilets. It was empty so he carried on. 'The punishments could never be enough for what he did to us, but surely everyone will start asking what we did and where he is. I can NEVER tell Dana, it would be too weird for her to know that side of me. I want to protect her against that whether she's an ex copper or not.' Carl nodded and said 'yes mate we'll sort it. It will be fine. Michael carried on 'do you like Dana really as much as you seem to, I mean you're not just putting on a show for me are you? I know it's early days and we're still too young in a way to commit to another person for life. But you know what Carl after this short time I feel like she's the one, and so does she. She is prepared to give up her job for me, and would have already as you know but she's trying to make sure nothing too dodgy is down to us. The police suspect we're in it up to our necks, but can't prove anything.

They're are putting most of it down to TJ attacking our firm in a sort of gang war. I want her out of it as soon as possible before they start scrutinizing her even more than they are already.' Carl listened and answered slowly so he answered all of his brothers thoughts with ones of his own. 'Well Michael I am made up with your choice of partner I just wish it was me with her. I think she'll be great for you and the business, and I'm happy to have her as a sister in law. Let's persuade her to leave now if we can, the other stuff well that's simple. We cannot tell anyone about TJ or Bentley it's as easy as that. TJ is somewhere by Talacre keeping Rodney warm and the only ones who know that are you me and Davie. He's happy now he's avenged his mum, both of them caused her death so no remorse for us. Bentley killed Rodney so less blood on our hands. No Mikey do not tell Dana ever, it would be a disaster. We've worked hard on getting our tough but fair reputation. What we have arranged for Bentley and some of the other things we've done. I sometimes think it makes us like them.' Michael straightened up and bristled with resentment. 'We will never be like Bentley! He did it for pleasure, the sick fuck. TJ did it to prove what a hard man he was which was fucking sad. We did it for better reasons than any of theirs.' Carl noticed the change in his brothers demeanour and knew he'd hit a nerve. 'Hey take it easy we are full of mad emotions and that. We've just buried our mother and some nasty memories eh? So don't get upset please Mikey. We're also coked up so don't get defensive at the slightest thing. We will never be like them but we've still done some bad shit, and we have to live with it. Yeah I agree we did do it for the right reasons.' This seemed to pacify Michael so Carl carried on, 'I think it's about time we had a proper holiday. Don't you? We can pay the rest of the lads their bonuses, and as long as someone's around to take care of the house and businesses we can go for a week somewhere hot and worry free. Boy do we deserve it, oh and remember what we discussed about Phil he's now working for us too, so if we left him and Jonna when we go that would cover us. Jacko's on the mend isn't he so he'll be back soon.... The two brothers carried on and when they felt they'd sorted what they needed for now they went back out. There was a queue of lads outside. Michael raised an eyebrow and Jonna laughed. 'I told them you were in conference so to wait. Some of the daft bastards have used the women's.' Carl did a thumbs up to him and they walked back in. Michael laughing at Jonna doing the bouncer bit on the bog doors.

Kay was still there she'd had a few and was squawking with laughter at Fat Fi's tales of when she was on the game. Phil and Tiff were at their table and laughing at her stories. Their friends from school were all still there, loyal as always and each happy with their bonuses, they'd all got the same but Carl liked mixing it up and saying not to tell each other as they were different. He knew by the end of the night they'd all know they had five thousand pounds each. They hadn't even gotten together with Davie their old mate and new employee to split what was in TJs safe, that could wait until tomorrow. Luckily only they knew about the safe eh? Carl thought. He looked at them all then, and was grateful for all they had, the good friends, his brother and their new friends and what lay before them. In their twenties and already millionaires just not on paper or in their names. Sara would be so fucking proud and if they could do this now what would the new millennium hold? it was only a few years away.. He couldn't wait to find out.

Stephen felt himself coming round, it was cramped and cold, he felt rough his eyes glued together through lack of moisture. He tried to move but couldn't, was he still tied up? His consciousness was starting to return and he felt weird, and had a horrible craving for the stuff the demons had been injecting him with. That's what they were demons, the women who he'd tortured and murdered brought them and they had tortured him relentlessly. Sometimes really scaring him. They weren't here now and if he kept his eyes shut a little longer he could decide what he was going to do next. The next time the demons come he'd struggle and soon he'd start to try and get out of whatever was holding him there. If he could just move a bit I could get free he thought. It was dark though, so he opened his eyes waiting for them to adjust. He could feel something now something stiff and cold next to him, there was something shining providing an eerie green light. It was a load of luminous rosaries and some low level torch. His eyes adjusted and he could start to make out shapes. Whatever he was in had silky material right in front of his face, so he looked to his left and screamed. In the greenish light there was Shelagh Moffat looking very weird, her face was full of horrible marks, the heavy thick make up had been put over her wounds and with absolute horror something snapped.

She was dead and next to him, and he realised he was in a coffin with her, and he couldn't move. He started to scream and cry and wriggle, and beg a God he'd never believed in for mercy. 'Please please help me God please I'm so sorry I am sorry, I'll even say sorry to mummy and daddy.' He stopped and there was total silence for a while and then he heard a strange creaking noise. He made himself look at Shelagh and she had turned her head and was looking at him. Her eyes had gone so they'd put glass ones in and she smiled a terrible smile at him. She opened her mouth a smell of decay seeped out and assaulted his senses. He started to sob again and Shelagh said in a voice straight from hell. 'Don't worry Stephen I'm here with you, do you still think I'm beautiful? Shall I get the girls to talk to you too they're all here waiting for you, they can't all fit in the coffin so they will take my place one at a time. They will eventually leave us though. It's sad but they're going to heaven and me and you well we're going to be together forever in hell.' She finished in a sing song voice. His mind had gone completely but it didn't stop the horror for a second. He couldn't stop crying and asked God for one small mercy, he would rather face hell than be trapped in here. 'Please God spare me or let me die now, or soon, don't let this go on please. PLEASE!' However God wasn't listening, just as Stephen never listened to the men and women he had killed when some of them had begged for mercy too. His descent into complete madness escalated, even Gez and Steno turned up to say hello when he slept, Gez with his wounds, and Steno without his eye and his rotting skin. It took three days to die, as the coffin wasn't completely air tight, the Moffats had made sure of that, it was the lack of water that finished him off completely. In the future if anyone ever had to open Shelagh Moffats coffin for any reason they would find deep grooves in the lid, covered in blood, skin and bone and two bodies one of them a screaming corpse with an expression of terror that would stay on its face no matter how far it fell into decay. That was the final thing that Stephen Bentley shared with nearly all his victims.

The End

224

A note from the author.
This book has been re-edited and re released. I apologise for the grammatical errors that were present. Unfortunately I had trusted someone and they'd let me down. So this version is professionally edited.

I enjoyed writing this book. A little of it's real a lot of it isn't. The sort of supernatural ending can be taken in two ways. It's either Stephens madness making him see the ghosts of his victims or they really have come back to haunt him. You decide. Thank you so much for buying my book. With love always Suzy. X

OUT NOW ANOTHER TALE OF ONE CITY
LEAD AND SILK. A NEW YORK STORY. LAUNCHED ON THE 25TH OCTOBER.
A story of a dominatrix who finds love in the big city. She stumbles onto a clinic run by Dr. Donaldson who's nick name is Dr. Frankenstein. Can a woman who only wants casual sex as a hobby learn to find love in this vibrant city? Read it and find out.

Coming next year.
A tale of one city. Part 2. The noughties. The Moffats have grown up. Some of the relationships that the people involved thought were forever aren't. Carl and Michael now run most of the City and it's in this dark underworld that they realise too late that they've almost turned into TJ. Their youthful ideals have gone, and they deal with anyone who crosses them with brutality and pain. Phil, Tiffany, Joe and Linda are also faced with Maisie's revenge. She has waited nearly ten years to get it but when she does put her plan into action the consequences will be both unforgettable and deadly for all those involved.

18458693R00128

Printed in Poland
by Amazon Fulfillment
Poland Sp. z o.o., Wrocław